AUTOMATED FINGERPRINT IDENTIFICATION SYSTEMS (AFIS)

AUTOMATED FINGERPRINT IDENTIFICATION SYSTEMS (AFIS)

Peter Komarinski

With contributions by:
Peter T. Higgins and Kathleen M. Higgins
Lisa K. Fox

ELSEVIER
ACADEMIC
PRESS

Amsterdam • Boston • Heidelberg • London • New York • Oxford • Paris
San Diego • San Francisco • Singapore • Sydney • Tokyo

Acquisitions Editor	Mark Listewnik
Project Manager	Sarah M. Hajduk
Associate Acquisitions Editor	Jennifer Soucy
Developmental Editor	Pamela Chester
Marketing Manager	Christian Nolin
Cover Design	Eric DeCicco
Interior Design	Kenneth Burnley
Composition	SNP Best-set Typesetter Ltd., Hong Kong
Cover Printer	Phoenix Color
Printer	The Maple-Vail Book Manufacturing Group

Elsevier Academic Press
30 Corporate Drive, Suite 400, Burlington, MA 01803, USA
525B Street, Suite 1900, San Diego, California 92101-4495, USA
84 Theobald's Road, London WC1X 8RR, UK

This book is printed on acid-free paper. ∞

Library of Congress Cataloging-in-Publication Data
APPLICATION SUBMITTED

British Library Cataloguing in Publication Data
A catalogue record for this book is available from the British Library

ISBN: 0-12-418351-4

For all information on all Elsevier Academic Press Publications
visit our Web site at www.books.elsevier.com

Printed in the United States of America
04 05 06 07 08 09   9 8 7 6 5 4 3 2 1

To my family, especially my wife Mary Kay, who supported my endeavors, and my friends in the AFIS community who work tirelessly to make the world better. It is an honor to work with so many dedicated and talented individuals.

CONTENTS

FOREWORD

AFIS systems are amazing. With AFIS, people can be fingerprinted and have their criminal history records checked in a matter of minutes; a mug shot and palm print might be included on the rap sheet returned to the inquiring agency. The technology has moved from exclusively forensic or criminal applications into other areas, such as social services benefits and other emerging applications.

The greatest use of AFIS technology is for tenprint identifications, in which rolled fingerprint images are compared against enrolled records. The greatest potential value of AFIS systems lies in the area of latent print identifications. The ability of AFIS systems to search millions of records in minutes and present candidates to the latent print examiner borders on the incredible. As amazing as the AFIS systems are, however, they still rely on the latent print examiner to make the identification.

The New York City Police Department Latent Print Unit has made thousands of latent print identifications using the Statewide Automated Fingerprint Identification System (SAFIS), maintained by the New York State Division of Criminal Justice Services. Some of these identifications resulted in the arrest of burglars, some identified victims, and others resulted in the arrest of killers. Our latent print examiners have the background, training, and expertise to utilize AFIS.

Following the attacks of September 11, 2001, on the World Trade Center, the NYPD Latent Print Unit worked endlessly to identify the remains of the victims. Ultimately, the latent print examiners were able to identify over 300 victims, bringing closure and comfort to their families. This would not have been possible without AFIS technology.

AFIS systems have changed the way we do business. AFIS is a valuable tool, but nonetheless only a tool. It relies on the people who use it and those who maintain it. AFIS can help to protect our communities by identifying those who might do us harm, and is an invaluable resource in solving crimes and making our communities safer.

Kenneth Calvey
Commanding Officer (Ret.)
NYPD Latent Print Unit

CHAPTER 1

INTRODUCTION

1.1 WELCOME

There is a world in which every crime is solved in 60 minutes, DNA matches are made "While U Wait," and staff work on only one case at a time. But it is a fantasy land, an imaginary land; it is not the real world. This book is about the real world of biometric identification technology. It is a fascinating topic. This technology can confirm the identity of an individual in a split second; it can also reach back in time to place a suspect at the scene of a crime that occurred years ago.

With no more information than a picture or a fingerprint, it is possible to match a subject in question with a known individual. With or without the subject's cooperation, his or her DNA, fingerprint, portrait, or some other physical characteristic can be matched to a known person.

An identification can lead to a record, a description of a person's past. If the person has been previously arrested, the arrest information can be retrieved. If the person has previously applied for a job that required a fingerprint check, that information can be requested. Biometric identification does not need to rely on spoken information from the subject in question; even amnesia victims and the dead can be identified. Once the necessary information has been entered into a biometric database, future inquiries require only the successful comparison and matching of the biometric for confirmation of identity.

Biometrics has many implementations. Some are extremely complex, requiring massive arrays of computers and a dedicated staff. Others are relatively less complex, requiring only ink, paper, training, and experience. For example, access to secure areas can be allowed by the matching of a finger image or an iris scan. Telephone conversations using voice recognition technology can confirm the identity of the caller and allow transactions in the caller's financial account. The Federal Bureau of Investigation (FBI) master criminal file requires hundreds of people to support the database, communication lines, and inquiry processing. A latent print examiner can compare a print from a home burglary, eliminating known prints such as those belonging to the home occupants. Each of these examples uses biometrics.

Biometric technology is often in the news. Since the events of September 11, 2001, biometrics has become increasingly of interest as public and private officials look at various methods of making positive identifications. The need for increased and improved security has become both a national priority and an area of opportunity. Many readers have experienced this increased demand for accurate personal identification firsthand when traveling on commercial flights. All air travelers must show both a boarding pass and a photograph on a form of government-issued identification, e.g., a driver's license, to pass through the airport security checkpoint. The airport Transportation Security Administration (TSA) personnel compare the photograph on the license with the face of the license holder in this simple form of biometric identification.

In an increasing number of situations, identity is confirmed by checking a verbal statement of identity or information on a written submission against a database or credential. Names on boarding passes are compared against the name on the document; faces are compared against photographs. Baggage is checked; packages and persons are subject to search.

More secure applications seek to connect a verbal statement or written document with a biometric that will not only absolutely link the person with the application, but also retrieve any personal history information stored on a database. A person's identity may be linked to a history of activities, as the identification connects to a history associated with that person. A police officer checking a driver's license, for example, can obtain the driving record of the holder. Any outstanding driving infractions, penalties, and convictions are visible for the inquiring officer to review so he or she can then determine how to proceed. To be secure, a paper form of personal identification such as a driver's license must include a biometric that is tamperproof and that will link the information on the license, not just the photograph, to the person in possession of that license. Government and industry are examining biometric options that will make driver's licenses more secure, for example, incorporating a biometric such as the characteristics from a finger image.

The U.S. government is also focusing on biometric methods used to identify terrorists, produce new passports, and allow passage into the United States by casual and business visitors. To this end, the federal government is pouring millions of dollars into biometric applications, research, and products to create new identification methods, revamp existing procedures, and make their processes more interactive from a security standpoint. New methods may include deployment of innovative software such as that used in facial recognition and improving upon technologies such as those based on fingerprints. An example of a revamped procedure is a state identification agency moving to a

24 hours a day, 7 days a week schedule rather than a 9 a.m. to 5 p.m. schedule in order to complete criminal background checks on all arrestees before arraignment. A more interactive process might include the need for agencies to collaborate on sharing database information. Decisions are being made today as to which of these changes will produce the greatest effect.

Most people have probably heard the word biometric and have a vague notion of what it means. It can conjure up images of laboratories and white coats, scientists peering over pipettes and reading printouts. A biometric is the measurement of a physical characteristic or personal trait. Certainly some of its applications do require laboratories, but many others do not.

There are also stereotypes about identification processes. Many forms of identification technology are emerging, with varying degrees of success and application. Iris scans, voice recognition, and DNA are just a few of the biometrics that have recently caught the interest of the general public, who is becoming more and more interested in security. More than ever, citizens and their governments want to have the ability to find the identity of a person and, from that identity, the history of the person. They want to know if a person has a criminal record in their own or another locale, if a person is a wanted fugitive or is dangerous, or if a person entrusted with the care of children or the elderly has any history that would make them unfit for a job with those age groups.

There is no "magic bullet" biometric. Each biometric application has strengths and weaknesses, supporters and detractors. Limitations for extensive use of a particular biometric might include the expense of the components, the speed of the processing, or the limitations on daily volumes. If a biometric device costs $100,000 per unit, plus $20,000 in maintenance per year, it may have less appeal than a device with the same accuracy but slightly slower throughput that costs $10,000 with $2,000 in annual maintenance.

The degree of public acceptance of one biometric over another is also a factor in the type of biometric used. The process of speaking to a machine that recognizes a voice pattern does not seem invasive to most people. Staring into an eyepiece for a retinal scan, however, produces a very different, very negative, reaction. Each has advantages and disadvantages, supporters and detractors.

1.2 FINGERPRINTS

There is one biometric that has been systematically used to make identifications for over 100 years. This is a biometric that has been measured, copied, and examined extensively, a biometric that does not change and is relatively easy to capture. It is a biometric that is not invasive and does not require sophisticated hardware for analysis, making it relatively inexpensive on a per search level. This biometric, of course, is the fingerprint.

Compared to other biometrics, fingerprints are relatively inexpensive to capture. Making an identification of a print from a crime scene may not even require the use of a computerized identification system; the examiner may rely instead on the images from a tenprint card, the latent print, and the expertise of the examiner. Fingerprinting does not require a laboratory for analysis, and fingerprints remain relatively constant over time, with the exception of injury.

Each person has ten fingers, ten unique tokens tied to his or her identity. No two fingerprints have ever been found to be identical. The finger images may be scarred or cut, but can still contain enough information to link the image with the owner. The friction ridges on each person's palms also provide unique images.

Every day millions of identifications are made using fingerprint images. Each person arrested and charged with a felony, as well as many misdemeanants, are fingerprinted and have their criminal history checked. Officials want to know if people in custody have been truthful when asked for their name and background. They want to know similar information for job applicants. The huge numbers of these searches, the speed with which the identifications are completed and returned to the inquiring agency, and their accuracy verges on the unbelievable. This accomplishment would not be possible without fast computers, sophisticated software, and dedicated and talented people, and these searches would not be possible without Automated Fingerprint Identification Systems, or AFIS.

1.3 WHAT IS AFIS?

This book describes the AFIS process in summary and in detail. The following is a brief explanation of the four components of its name. The automation (A) process has eliminated the need for a print classifier to locate fingerprint cards from a file and compare two physical cards. The searchable database is composed of fingerprint (F) images collected from individuals either by using fingerprint cards or by electronic capture using a device similar to a scanner. The identification (I) aspect occurs when the person is fingerprinted, and the resulting images are searched against the database of fingerprint images on a local, state, or national database. It is considered a system (S) because it uses computers and software and can interact with subsystems and other identification systems, including other AFIS systems.

AFIS applications exist in almost every instance in which a finger image is rolled onto a fingerprint card. AFIS systems are the primary identification tool for virtually every law enforcement agency in the United States and the rest of the world. An AFIS system can be immense, such as the 46 million records held by the FBI, or it can be small, such as when it contains information about only one city or county.

AFIS systems may be linked to other databases, even to other AFIS systems, but there are also some AFIS systems that stand alone and effectively do not communicate with any other agency. As more agencies begin working together, the number of AFIS systems connected together will grow. Stand-alone AFIS systems are more likely to join related systems, creating larger networks of fingerprints to search. The technology and applications of AFIS systems are just beginning to emerge from initial development. The scope of this technology has moved from a select few uses to everyday uses. The core of AFIS technology, the computer and related software, progresses on an almost daily basis. In particular, the software that runs AFIS systems improves constantly as companies develop faster, more accurate programs. New markets have emerged in AFIS-related applications as manufacturers carve out niche products. All of these advances, however, continue to rely on a biometric that has been systematically used for over 100 years: the fingerprint.

The use of fingerprints as a biometric used for identification of large population groups can be traced back to the 1890s, when Sir Edward Henry promoted a system of classifying the curving friction ridges and the direction and flow of ridges, patterns, and other image characteristics that allowed trained examiners to translate these images into a set of equations that could be understood by any other examiner trained in the rules of classification. The resulting classifications, in turn, dictated how the records were filed for future retrieval and comparison. A new industry emerged based on the ease with which fingerprints could be captured and a uniform method for measuring these images and storing them for future comparisons.

AFIS systems search databases for candidates based on these image characteristics. The characteristics include the points where ridges end, the points where they split, the directions that ridges appear to flow, and even dots. The AFIS system translates what a human sees as a picture, selects key features, searches these features against a database, and produces the best match from that database.

These systems are amazingly fast. It takes only a few minutes to capture the ten finger images at a booking station. Within another few minutes, the booking officer can send the images and arrest information to a state identification bureau. The state can determine the identity and return the identity information and criminal history file (known as a rap sheet) in as little as 30 minutes. If it is the first time the subject has been fingerprinted, the event becomes the first entry in the subject's computerized criminal history. If the search is for a subject charged with a criminal offense, it includes a check of all 46 million records on the FBI database, yet it normally takes less than 2 hours, the same amount of time required to watch two episodes of JAG or the time it takes to read this book, to get the results. In that short time, the subject's images can be compared with millions of records at the state and federal level with surprising accuracy and speed.

It also takes about 2 hours for a latent print examiner to digitally capture the latent finger image found at a crime scene. By using photographic techniques and software, the latent print image can be made to appear more distinct as the image background is muted. AFIS coders extract the image characteristics from the print, such as location of ridge endings, bifurcations, and direction of ridge flow, and search all or any part of a criminal database. Databases containing millions of image records can be completely searched within minutes. This was not possible just a few years ago.

Not all AFIS systems are identical. Some large metropolitan areas have their own independent AFIS system that may or may not directly connect to the state identification bureau. The databases may be mutually exclusive or may overlap. The state AFIS system may come from a different vendor than a metropolitan area's AFIS, and one vendor's software may not seamlessly interact with another's. For example, some systems store images from the two index fingers, some use the two thumbs, and others use a combination.

In addition, some AFIS systems provide only identification information and are not connected to a computerized criminal history file. And not all AFIS systems operate on a round-the-clock schedule. Data entered into the database may not be immediately available if the database is updated only once a day. Yet in spite of these differences, the various AFIS systems have a great amount of commonality. They require the same maintenance that other computer systems require, and are subject to the same threats to security and database corruption that other information systems share.

Today, more image information, such as palm images and mug shots, are being captured and stored on AFIS systems. A single palm image may have as much ridge detail as that found in all ten fingers. Latent palm prints are estimated to be found at 30% of all crime scenes. Mug shots are used in photo arrays of suspects, and also help visually identify persons who are wanted. These are relatively new capacities made possible by better and less expensive data storage and transmission. In addition, more categories of people, such as health care workers, are being fingerprinted. These new information sources and fingerprintable categories lead to more extensive data-processing requirements, and to the increased responsibility of AFIS managers and technicians, who are handling increasingly larger and more complex systems. While not everyone in the United States is enrolled in a fingerprint-based identification system, images from an inquiry can be compared against perhaps over 50 million records. With the U.S. population at just less than 300 million, that means that one in every six residents of the United States has a record on an AFIS database. That is a lot of records that must be maintained to accurately and reliably produce search results.

AFIS systems were developed as a result of the government's need for prompt accurate identification and industry's response to that need. The response, however, was not uniform, because standards did not exist in the early years of AFIS. Many large identification bureaus that pioneered the development of AFIS systems found that some of their services were not interchangeable with other AFIS systems, leading to challenges that are still being addressed today.

The AFIS process might have never reached its current level of development had not the federal government initiated two important programs that advanced AFIS systems to their current level. First, the adoption of national transmission standards for communication with the FBI provided a "single sheet of music" to sing from. Second, a massive federal funding program for state identification bureaus through the National Criminal History Improvement Program (NCHIP) paid for that "sheet of music" and the band that plays it. In addition, the introduction and widespread use of computers in the 1980s found a direct application in the field of identification. The infusion of millions of federal dollars, primarily through the NCHIP, combined with a federal presence in the development of standards for transmissions and image capture produced a strong formula for success.

The largest AFIS system in the United States is the Integrated Automated Fingerprint Identification System (IAFIS), operated by the Criminal Justice Information Services (CJIS) division of the FBI. The creation of IAFIS became the impetus for new communication and identification strategies. The criminal history database of the FBI found a new home when it moved from the J. Edgar Hoover building in Washington, DC, to Clarksburg, West Virginia. IAFIS is the national linchpin to which identification bureaus are connected. IAFIS is also the conduit for states to obtain information from other state criminal history and wanted files.

The development of AFIS systems has not been restricted to the United States. Several countries in Central America, the Middle East, Asia, and Africa require that all their adult citizens be fingerprinted, and AFIS systems are used to confirm these identifications. In these countries, AFIS may play a role in determining eligibility for government benefits. It can also be used to ensure that persons do not exceed their lawful allocation of goods such as social services benefits and services such as voting.

AFIS systems are also used in military applications. Without obvious clues such as a military uniform, it can be increasingly difficult to tell friend from foe, e.g., distinguishing a civilian trying to protect a family in a war zone from a terrorist. With an AFIS system, latent prints found at bombings or other enemy actions can be compared against a database of known individuals. If there is no match, these same latent prints can be retained in the AFIS in anticipation of a match in the future.

Fingerprints have no names, no sex, and no nationality. Fingerprints do not lie about their past, or appreciably change over time. Fingerprints are relatively easy and inexpensive to capture either with ink and paper or electronically. Combined with sophisticated technology and a skilled staff, AFIS emerges as a practical identification process.

Examples given in the following chapters are considered to be representative of AFIS systems. As with automobiles, there are differences between AFIS systems. Some are small compacts, serving only a single community. Some are large trucks that contain all the fingerprint cards in the state. Some are older, less robust systems; others are state of the art. Just as not everyone drives the newest model of automobile, not every ID bureau has the latest and greatest AFIS system.

The pre-AFIS systems worked because of the dedication of the staff and the commitment of government to provide criminal history information as quickly and as accurately as possible. In an age before computers, however, the process was very compartmentalized and somewhat tedious. The advances in AFIS technology cannot be fully recognized without some understanding of the tasks that it replaced and why fingerprints are so important for identification purposes.

1.4 IDENTIFICATION PRACTICES PRIOR TO AFIS SYSTEMS

Identification systems did not originate with AFIS systems; rather, AFIS systems have automated an already existing process for identifying individuals. Many states and the federal government had an identification system in operation years before the introduction of AFIS. Fingerprint images, the essential element of this identification system, have been collected for over 100 years.

In movies from the 1930s and 1940s, detectives would "check with R and I" (records and identification), a request based on a name or fingerprint card, to see if a suspect had a criminal record. Files would be pulled, records removed, and names and fingerprints compared. Perhaps a criminal record with the same name as the suspect was found, but the fingerprints did not match, or perhaps a record with matching fingerprints was found, but not with the suspect's name. It would take hours or perhaps days for the detective to receive the response, a typed report.

These pre-AFIS identification bureaus employed hundreds or even thousands of staff, who were entrusted with the responsibility of confirming, based on fingerprint images, that a subject did or did not have a criminal record. The clerks, examiners, and supervisors at these identification bureaus had to learn many skills during their careers. Whenever a new tenprint card arrived, for example, it had to be recorded. An examiner skilled in the complex rules of fingerprint classification would look at the pattern using a reticule like the one pictured in Figure 1.1 and begin to classify each of the ten finger images based on, for example, whether the pattern contained an arch, a tented arch, or perhaps an inner central pocket loop whorl.

The number of ridges from the core to the delta had to be counted. A closer examination might reveal more detail in a smudged area of the inked impression.

While the card was being classified, other technicians would look through their records to see if the subject's name was already on the fingerprint files. If there was a name on file, the state identification (SID) number assigned to that record was noted and a search was started. If there were multiple occurrences of the same name, clerks would check to determine if any of the available biographical information would be helpful in narrowing the number of records to search. If the pattern and primary and secondary classifications of the index fingers of the records found in the name search matched those of the inquiry, the cards would be physically compared with the card on file. If the inquiry finger images matched the images on the record on file, the inquiring agency was notified by phone, fax, or mail that the subject had a criminal history.

If there was no record with both the same name and fingerprint pattern, then all the records with the same pattern and primary and secondary classifications had to be checked, as it is not uncommon for arrested subjects to be less than truthful about their names and past. Sometimes a person with a criminal record would provide just enough incorrect information to be beyond the

Figure 1.1
Fingerprint Examiner
Reticule

normal search parameters. Perhaps the subject lied about his or her age, just enough to miss on a name search or normal tenprint search before the introduction of AFIS. Perhaps when arrested previously, the individual had not only claimed another name, but another sex. The identification agency, which could be miles away from the booking site, had no way of knowing why there was a difference in the record: the subject could have given false information, or a clerical error could have introduced incorrect information. The identification agency might not be able to determine which name or sex is accurate, having only the fingerprint images and biographical information on the card to work from. If it could not make a match after several comparisons with records already existing on file, the identification agency would assign a new SID number and send a response to the inquiring agency indicating that the subject had no criminal record known to the state, or presumably anywhere else. The subject would now have more than one record on file with prints of the same fingers taken at different times. The names on the two records might be different, the ages might be different, or the sex recorded might be different. The subject might have had many records, each with a different name, or sex, or age. The number of possible matches, however, may have helped to hide the subject's identity.

In addition to criminal history checks, the records from these identification bureaus would be used for crime scene investigations. Detectives or latent print examiners would be dispatched to crime scenes to look for clues. A broken window pane might hold fingerprints of a burglar; a knife might contain fingerprints of an assailant. If a latent fingerprint was found at a crime scene, it would be lifted with dusting powder and brought back to the detective bureau. The latent print examiner would inspect the print for image characteristics such as a pattern, a delta, or the number of friction ridges between two points. If there was enough image information to effect identification, i.e., if the print was "of value," it might be compared against records in the database. Before AFIS, however, latent print searches were usually limited to suspect prints and elimination prints. It was a slow, labor-intensive process undertaken by specially trained examiners.

1.5 CURRENT IDENTIFICATION PRACTICES

AFIS not only automated identification, it forever changed how the process was performed. Computer software replaced fingerprint classifiers, and data farms replaced card files. AFIS systems allow the almost immediate identification of a subject on local, state, and national databases. AFIS replaced a mature identification process that was labor intensive, expensive to maintain, dependent on paper, and relatively slow; but system that worked.

With current AFIS technology, not only can the resident database be searched for a latent print match, but so can the federal database. There are multiple search options for these latent prints that did not exist 20 years ago, and using AFIS, a determined latent print examiner can search a latent print against millions of records in a few minutes.

Today, detectives use computers to view a subject's criminal record, or the rap sheet, which comes from the new "R and I," AFIS. The rap sheet may also contain a mug shot, information on scars, marks, tattoos, and prints of the palm areas of each hand.

AFIS today is not just used in criminal applications. In addition to searches as part of a criminal background investigation, state identification bureaus use their databases for comparing fingerprint images for job applicants and licensing. Based on statutes and following the requirements of a use and dissemination agreement, government agencies and private corporations can request a fingerprint-based background check for job applicants. Many states have created an AFIS for exclusively non-criminal, i.e., civil, applications, such as social services programs in which enrollment of a subject's single index finger or both index fingers into an AFIS database is a requirement for receiving benefits. AFIS not only provides access to funding, but also reduces the opportunities for fraud. With a statewide AFIS system, it is becoming increasingly challenging to illegally collect benefits from several jurisdictions using the same or even different names.

The equipment and software currently used in AFIS systems have also migrated into other identification areas. For example, single print readers allow access to restricted areas. These devices record the finger images of an authorized person through an enrollment process. Together with a personal identification number (PIN), the devices retain a computerized record of the finger image. To gain access, the finger is inserted into the reader and the PIN is entered. The information is compared with the stored data; if there is a match, access is granted. These readers have a variety of applications. School districts, for example, use single print readers to authenticate enrollment in subsided school lunch programs, and homeless shelters use portable singer print readers to authenticate the identity of a person entitled to spend the night at the shelter.

Single print readers are an example of a one-to-one (1:1) search. The subject is enrolled into a system by capturing a finger image using an image reader. Biographical information and access rights to functions such as entrance to secure rooms are provided by a system administrator. When the subject places a finger or thumb into the reader and enters a PIN, the image is again captured and compared with the record on file for that subject; the correct PIN and image will allow access. The system can only match a known image with a known image. Either the door is unlocked, or it remains locked, 100% success or 0% success; yes or no, black or white.

The other type of search is the one-to-many (1:N) search. When a booking officer prints an arrestee, there may be questions as to the authenticity of the information provided by the arrestee. The one-to-many search looks for commonalities of image characteristics, such as minutiae, ridge flow, and ridge endings. The search produces a candidate list based on a score derived from the matching process. The score reflects the match between the images in question with the records on file. The higher the score, the more likely the two images come from the same person. The terms 100% and 0% are not relevant in this context. There is no black or white, yes or no; there is only varying shades of gray, levels of probability.

1.6 WHY FINGERPRINT-BASED CHECKS ARE IMPORTANT

There are several methods of obtaining background information for a person, with or without their permission. A background check will often be performed on one person or a group of people for a specific reason. Perhaps that check is a condition of employment. What information is checked and by whom? Does this check provide accurate information about the person in question? Just as important, what is done with the findings and what appeal process exists if the information is wrong?

There is no single accepted definition of what constitutes a background check. There is no universal understanding as to whether it includes fingerprints, or which databases will be checked. This is becoming an important issue, for as the amount of information collected on each person increases, the chances of collecting incorrect information also increase.

One source of incorrect information, identity theft, is increasing as informational databases are used and misused. Through accident or fraud, identities are being compromised. For a fee, major credit reporting companies provide a credit report that includes the information collected about a person, such as credit accounts, public records such as bankruptcies and civil judgments, inquiries, employment data, and current and previous addresses. A periodic review of this information is encouraged to assure the accuracy of the data and the correct identity of the person. There is an appeal process for information believed to be inaccurate, with a response due within 30 days along with an updated credit history. From this example, it is apparent that some of the items that people use to confirm their identities are subject to misuse. Names can be fraudulently changed; faces can be altered, identities hidden, histories covered. Fingerprints, however, do not change. Fingerprints link a person to a history, even if the history states that there is no history.

Federal agencies that undertake background investigations begin with fingerprints, because with the fingerprint match, there is nearly absolute confirmation[1] that the person is the same as the one about whom the information is provided. The agencies will check the federal database, IAFIS, or perhaps a state database to determine if there is a criminal history for the person. Once the identity of the person can be confirmed, the "leg work" can begin in earnest with phone calls and visits to confirm or refute the information.

1.7 FROM PAPER TO PAPERLESS

1.7.1 PAPER: THE FINGERPRINT CARD

In the pre-AFIS days, the inked fingerprint card was the physical center of the identification process. These cards, made of thick paper stock, would be handled by many people throughout the identification process. It would first be touched by the booking officer, then by the person who was fingerprinted, and then sent through the mail. Classifiers would examine the cards, write the classification information, and send it to the files. Clerks would file the cards, retrieve the cards for comparison, and return the cards to their proper location. The cards could not be replaced. If a card was misfiled, it was effectively lost.

The card was printed to meet standard specifications and so was uniform in size and layout. As shown in the card pictured in Figure 1.2, there was a space at the top of the card for arrest and biographical information. The center of the card has a row of five boxes for each of the fingers of the right hand, and immediately below are five more boxes for the fingers of the left hand. At the bottom, there are four boxes for simultaneous impressions of the right hand fingers, then right thumb. This is repeated for the left hand.

In the past, the identification process was based on the inked tenprint card. The subject was fingerprinted with special ink and the images captured onto this card. The card was mailed to the state identification agency, where the images would be classified and the identification search completed. The card and any subsequent cards would be kept in file cabinets, perhaps thousands of file cabinets.

1.7.2 PAPERLESS: LIVESCAN

AFIS systems are not limited to inked fingerprint cards for identification, however. In many areas, the booking officer, instead of using ink and a

---

[1] The term "nearly absolute confirmation" is used because few things in life are absolute. There are other factors that could affect the absoluteness, such as errors introduced through human intervention, but that is a topic for another chapter.

1.. SID No.	2. Name (Last, First, Middle)		3. OBTS/Court Control No.	4. Classification (Leave Blank)

5. Street No.	6. Street Name	7. City/State Address/Zip	8.	

9. Alias or Maiden Name	10. Place of Birth (State or Country)	11.	12. Facsimile Control No.	21A. Contributor/ORI

13. Date of Birth	14. Age	15. Sex	16. Race	17. Skin	18. Hair	19. Eyes	20. Height	21. Wgt
MO DAY YR							FT IN	

22. Arrest Officer ID No.	23. Arresting Agency Name/ORI	24.	25. Arrest No.	26. Court of Arraignment/ORI

27. Arrest Date	28. Place of Arrest/CTV	29.	30. Arrest Time	30A. Weapon Type	40.
MO DAY YR					

31. Date of Crime	32. Place of Crime/CTV	33.	34. Arrest Type	35. Soc. Sec. No.	35. FBI Number
MO DAY YR					

36. CHARGE(S)	Law	Article & Section	Sub Section	Cls	Cat	Deg	Att	Name of Offense	Cts	NCIC	43. Signature of Arrestee
											X
											44. Arrest Agency Case No.

1. RT	2. RI	3. RM	4. RR	5. RL

6. LT	7. LI	8. LM	9. LR	10. LL

Left Fingers Taken Simultaneously	Left Thumb	Right Thumb	Right Fingers Taken Simultaneously

Figure 1.2
Blank Fingerprint Card

preprinted paper stock, can capture finger images on a glass platen of a device called a livescan. The livescan takes a picture of the finger in a fashion similar to rolling a finger onto the glass platen of a very compact, very well-engineered copy machine. In this process, a picture of each finger of the right hand is taken, then the left hand, then the four fingers for simultaneous impressions of the right hand fingers, then right thumb. This process would be repeated for the left hand and the palms, and a mug shot might also be taken.

These livescan images can be sent to the state identification bureau electronically, so that within minutes of receipt, the images have been electronically classified for pattern and minutiae characteristics. There may be more than 100 of these unique minutiae for each finger and over 1,000 for each palm. The database can then be searched for similar pattern and minutiae configurations for two or more fingers, usually the index fingers or thumbs. In a parallel process, the subject's name may also be checked against all the names in the Master Name Index database. When the search of each of the index fingers produces the same candidate that the name search produced, there is a very high degree of probability that it is a match. The images are considered to belong to the same person regardless of the sex, age, or other information captured in earlier fingerprintable events. It is an ident, an IAFIS term for a positive identification.

1.8 THE IMPACT OF AFIS SYSTEMS

AFIS completely changed the identification business model. Identifications are now made on finger images based on minutiae and ridge characteristics. Computers search millions of records in seconds. If the images match an existing record but the sex does not, the record is updated to indicate that both male and female genders have been reported for this person. Regardless of name given, sex reported, height, weight, age, etc., it is rare that a suspect will not be identified if his or her finger images are already on file.

While AFIS systems have migrated into a variety of uses, their primary purpose remains to determine if a person has been previously printed (enrolled) and has any history in the locale. Identification based on fingerprints is among the most accurate form of identification in existence. Identification is not affected by the name, sex, or year of birth entered in the database. What affects the search is the clarity of the finger images and the clarity of the images in the database.

Table 1.1 details how AFIS systems have changed the business model for identifications.

Table 1.1

*AFIS Changes to the
Identification Business
Model*

Before AFIS	AFIS
Finger classification	Coder identifies minutiae
Fingerprint cards	Images on RAID storage
Magnifying glass	High-resolution monitor
Manual or semi-automated search	Fully automated search
Mail, photo, laser fax	Livescan
Response in hours, days	Response in minutes
Search local files	Search local, state, and national databases

1.9 OTHER AFIS ISSUES

Everything that can be invented has been invented.[2]

From the success of AFIS systems, it might appear that there are no new challenges or opportunities to improve the identification process. However, Commissioner Duell's statement above would receive the same reaction of disbelief today if he was referring to the development of AFIS systems. There is a great deal left to do.

Many of the early AFIS systems were developed prior to the introduction of national standards. As a result, databases used by identification agencies and sold by various vendors do not necessarily directly communicate with each other. Interoperability, particularly in the area of latent print (crime scene) searches, is still in the future. In addition, the latent print search capabilities offered by these systems are not yet being fully exploited. Progress is being made, but it will be awhile before agencies can search each other's databases. Even when this becomes possible, from an operational approach there will be many administrative hurdles to overcome, such as agreements on use and dissemination of information by other agencies.

Personnel issues rank high on the list of AFIS concerns. As AFIS systems assume more of the work involved in the identification process, the number of those who are intimately familiar with the uniqueness of fingerprint images and the process is diminishing. With the diminished demand for fingerprint classifiers, and increasing retirements of the examiners, there is a smaller pool from which to draw future AFIS supervisors and managers. The expectations of other agency policy makers and managers may also be unrealistically elevated because of false or misleading information from the media.

---

[2] Attributed to Charles H. Duell, Commissioner, U.S. Office of Patents, 1899.

The inked and rolled finger images on a tenprint card are gradually being replaced by electronic images captured on livescan machines. These images, captured at 500 pixels per inch (ppi) or higher, are becoming a larger percentage of the AFIS image database. Electronic cards eliminate paper and multiple entries of the same data during the booking and identification process. However, unlike the paper tenprint card, the electronic card does not physically exist unless it is printed. Great care must be taken to ensure that the data and images on the electronic card are the true and accurate reproduction. Quality indicators must be in place to ensure that the print on the file belongs to the person whose name is associated with it. While it is increasingly unlikely that a paper record will be misfiled since there are fewer paper files, the problems created by mislabeling an electronic record are very time consuming to resolve.

AFIS systems are constantly in use. With many systems operating on a 24 hours a day, 7 days a week, 365 days a year schedule, the system must not only be accurate and reliable, but also available nearly all the time. Before system upgrades are introduced onto the operational or "live" system, the software and components must be thoroughly tested under conditions that mimic the live system. Just as computer users become mildly agitated when a new version of Windows software does not work seamlessly, so do identification staff, booking officers, the courts, district attorneys, and others who depend on accurate and prompt delivery of identification information when AFIS systems do not work properly. There is little margin for error and little tolerance for system problems.

The addition of new fingerprintable crimes and job applications that require fingerprint-based background checks has also created extra throughput demands on existing systems. Taxi drivers, health care workers, financial industry workers, teachers, and others who were not fingerprinted in the past must now undergo a background search based on fingerprints. This proliferation of fingerprint-based background checks raises important business and philosophical questions, such as who should pay the applicant fee for an applicant search of the state AFIS and FBI IAFIS. The state may charge $50 to offset their administrative cost and investment in AFIS technology, and the FBI charges $25 for an applicant search of its database. While these may be considered user fees, the outlay of $75 for a background check may not be feasible for someone making minimum wage. The cost for a school district or unit of local government that requires a fingerprint search of all employees could be huge. If the government employer pays the costs, then the costs fall on the taxpayers serviced by that government. If the employees have to pay, they may demand reimbursement as a condition of their contract. If the state chooses not to charge for these employees supported by local tax dollars, the cost gets shifted to the state taxpayers. There is no easy answer to this problem. In addition, employees may rightly be concerned about who in their business or agency has access to this information, which may not be treated with the same confidentiality as medical records.

Another AFIS issue concerns the procedures regarding record retention. Although in the past, the standard procedure was for the inquiring party to return records to the identification agency, increasingly it is to retain them. For example, if a person was fingerprinted for a job application for which the record was to be retained, the inked impressions were returned to the inquirer along with the search results. No finger images of the applicant were retained by the identification agency. Another inquiry about that person in the future might be treated as a new inquiry, since no finger image record would exist to positively identify him or her as the same person.

1.10 WHY THIS BOOK WAS WRITTEN

Remarkably, very little has been written about AFIS systems. A great deal has been written about various biometrics and the accuracy of certain biometric applications; likewise, a great body of knowledge exists on fingerprints, their history as an identification tool, and their uniqueness in the identification process. But publications describing the automated fingerprint identification process and its characteristics and opportunities are difficult to find, and the amount of published information about the advances made in the latent fingerprint identifications through the use of AFIS systems is even more miniscule.

This book attempts to fill this gap. It describes how the AFIS system works, why it works, how it came to be, and what lies in the future. There are challenges that must be addressed and issues to be resolved. There are also opportunities for better, faster, and less expensive fingerprint identifications using AFIS systems. Some suggestions in that arena are included.

This book also provides the reader with a better understanding of the complexities of biometric identification, particularly the identification process that uses fingerprints. Regardless of the biometric in use, the process involves people, technology, and processes. Each of these three elements is subject to error. The error can come in the form of a human mistake, such as entering an erroneous code, poor maintenance that causes computers to fail, or inappropriate processing procedures that miss certain types of identification. Few things in life are infallible or absolute.

Recent events have changed the attitudes of many regarding security and personal identification and, by design, who should be fingerprinted. Although once restricted to persons who were fingerprinted as part of an arrest process or job applications, identification systems, particularly automated systems, are now used in some very new applications. For example, the U.S. Department of Homeland Security has piloted a program to perform a fingerprint-based check on certain foreign visitors as part of the US-VISIT program. Many states now require that applicants for social service benefits be fingerprinted to ensure eligibility requirements. More classes of jobseekers are fingerprinted than ever before, and not only are they fingerprinted and their backgrounds checked, but also their records are retained for future comparison.

The intentions of policy makers regarding the development of identification systems may be noble, but their understanding of the issues is often less than complete and their timelines perhaps unrealistic. There may be, however, a great deal of public funding to support the development and implementation of such systems. Government has to rely on the private sector to develop and bring these technologies to market, and in this arena, are many competing companies. It is also important to realize that the performance results touted by the marketing department of a company offering an AFIS may be different from the performance targets developed by the engineers of that company. Too often policy makers embrace the hype of marketing staff without confirmation from an outside source. This can result in unrealistic or misunderstood expectations of the success of the application. And the leap from marketing to newspaper headlines can ignore even more caveats and limitations. This book removes some of those gray areas and even provide specific guidelines for improving the process.

Identification also involves probability and risk. The consequences of a missed identification or not making an identification vary based on the level of need for the identification. For example, if the hand geometry reader at a Disney theme park fails to recognize a legitimate annual pass holder, the pass holder can walk to the nearby visitor center for assistance. Requiring all pass holders to have all ten finger images captured in a database may produce a more accurate identification system, but the cost would be many times greater. Managers must determine whether the costs of having not identified a few pass holders or even misidentifying a few persons fraudulently using passes, therefore allowing them entry into the park, justify switching to a more secure and expensive identification process.

This book was written to provide information about the processes that AFIS systems replaced; it is a history not of fingerprinting but of AFIS. Before automated identification systems there were semi-automated identification systems. Beginning in the early 1970s, the introduction of mainframe computers and punch cards brought what was then state-of-the-art computing horsepower to the identification process. Before the semi-automated systems were the manual identification systems, with cards filed by fingerprint classification and transmitted by mail. To appreciate the current state of identification systems, an understanding of what was required to get here is essential. This knowledge, in turn, will help with making better decisions for the future.

1.11 WHO THIS BOOK IS INTENDED FOR

This book is intended for a large audience, including criminal justice practitioners and those who want to know more about AFIS technology. Policy makers may find this book of value for information such as the implication of adopting some policies over others, as well as varied uses of AFIS systems. There are always trade-offs in decision making; there are always opportunity costs. If there were a limitless amount of resources and an infinite amount of time in which to make an identification, virtually any process would suffice. Resources in personnel and capital, however, are not limitless. Likewise, a suspect cannot be held indefinitely awaiting the rap sheet from the state.

Decisions are being made today on who will be fingerprinted and for what purpose. Some favor fingerprinting a large number of individuals, but not capturing all ten images. Others favor fingerprinting a more select group, but capturing all ten rolled images, i.e., images of the finger that extend from one edge of the nail to the other (see Fig. 1.3). Considerations include the time involved, the resource requirements, and the purpose of collecting and searching these images. This book addresses some of these issues and provides policy makers with options for consideration.

There are major questions in any new action, including "What is the purpose?" and "Is this the best approach?" Decisions made without an under-

Figure 1.3
Nail-to-Nail Roll

standing of the scope and opportunities offered by AFIS systems may cause millions of dollars to be spent on systems that are not only misdirected, but that actually pull resources away from programs that have proven their worth as successful identification technologies. These two questions are considered below.

The purpose of fingerprinting arrestees is to perform a criminal background check on the individual to determine if there is an outstanding warrant, if the person has previously been arrested for a violent offense, or if there are other charges pending. Has the person in custody been fingerprinted in the past under the same or a different name? Government has a right to know this for the safety of its citizens, as well as personnel providing custody. Who is fingerprinted and what is done with those records are defined by law. No agency may collect or keep records to which it is not lawfully entitled.

The purpose of fingerprinting job applicants is to determine if there are past deeds, perhaps unknown or previously unreported to the prospective employer, that might have a bearing on the applicant's employment. Are there incidents, perhaps crimes, that might preclude employment or advancing the person to a position of trust within an organization? Can a company require that all of its employees be fingerprinted? (Yes, it can, if it has a policy to do so.) And if so, what databases are searched for a criminal record?

The question of "What is the purpose?" should also be considered when deciding on the level of security necessary. To gain access to a room in an already secure building might require a thumb to be placed into a reader that matches the images of an enrolled, approved individual. At the other end of the spectrum, it would not be unreasonable to require that for known and suspected terrorists, they are fingerprinted by rolling all ten fingers, palm prints are taken, a DNA sample is collected, and a mug shot is taken. This might result in a soldier in the field matching a mug shot with an enemy prisoner, or a military investigator at headquarters matching finger images for a positive identification. Each biometric has its applications.

The question of "Is this the best approach?" requires an understanding of the trade-offs when pursuing one course of action over another. The government, like individuals, does not have an endless supply of resources. Choices have to be made as to which approach will provide the greatest public good and the greatest public security. With limited resources, it may not be possible to have an identification system that can hold a database of 100 million records, with an accuracy of 99.97% and a return of results in under 10 seconds. Each element is individually possible at a reasonable cost, but the combination of all three would require tens of millions of dollars. The question to be answered is whether it is worth the cost to meet these targets.

In addition to understanding the technologies, there must be a clear understanding of the expectations of the personnel who administer and use these systems. Few government agencies have the technical staff to design, develop, test, and continually upgrade these systems, so they rely on companies that have proven themselves as leaders in this arena. However, government purchasers and managers must know more about the system than just the information in the sales brochure. They must be able to maintain the current systems and plan for future changes. And in the world of AFIS, when booking officers want to know if they are holding a wanted fugitive in their cellblock, they do not want to hear "The system is down. We'll get back to you on Monday morning."

There is a great deal of misinformation and misunderstanding about AFIS systems. They are much better than some people believe and less interactive than others might think. Some want everyone to be fingerprinted, while others believe that advances in DNA identification will make fingerprint identification unnecessary. It is possible to be fingerprinted in one state and not have the record appear on a search from another state. It is also possible for a perpetrator to leave just a tiny fraction of a fingerprint image at a crime scene and later be identified by a latent print examiner using AFIS technology.

A simple analogy is to compare AFIS databases to the information on file at a financial institution such as a credit union or a bank. To apply for a credit card from that institution, an individual must supply certain personal information that must be authenticated by the financial institution by checking it for authenticity and accuracy. Is the person who completed the application the same person whose name appears on the application? Is there any biographical or financial information that is missing or incomplete? If the applicant already has a credit card, there is a record on at least one database that can be checked for a financial history. If this is the applicant's first credit card, the process may result in a phone call to authenticate some of the information. If the criteria of the credit card issuer have been met, the credit card is issued. The applicant now has a credit card, the credit union or bank has a customer, and the credit card issuer has a file and history. Future transactions by the card owner are recorded by the issuer, and information on timeliness of payments, credit limit, and other financial data are collected and maintained. Bankruptcies and closure of accounts are noted as well.

When a person is fingerprinted, the process is similar to the credit card application process. Instead of a paper application, inked tenprint cards that contain both biographical information and finger images are completed and sent to a central database to determine if the person has ever been fingerprinted in the past, just as the financial institution checks to see if a credit card has ever been issued. If there is a record, the information is forwarded to the inquiring agency. If not, a new record is created, just as a new credit card is issued. One significant difference, of course, is that in the AFIS check, finger images are the authenticating instruments.

1.12 CHAPTER OVERVIEW

The chapters of this book are intended to appeal to a wide audience. While the topic is AFIS, the concepts and descriptions apply to other areas of identification and biometric technology. There is a chapter describing the identification process, one on the history of AFIS, and one on the uniqueness of fingerprints. Also included is a chapter on other biometric identifiers, such as hand geometry and DNA. Administrators who are considering the purchase of an AFIS or an upgrade to their existing system may find several other sections useful. The chapter on AFIS acquisition describes the legal requirements for an AFIS purchase, including contracting requirements. Another chapter describes the documentation essential for a successful implementation. While the AFIS system moves to the gradual elimination of paper, paper documents remain essential for the purchase, testing, and installation of an AFIS system.

The book also contains a chapter on contractual requirements for public officials. While written with the focus of an AFIS purchase, the concepts are valuable for any large public sector procurement. The distinctions between requests for proposal and requests for information are covered in terms that are easy to understand. Decisions made have to meet policy, regulation, and the law, as well as withstand public scrutiny.

This book contains information about fingerprints as they relate to AFIS systems. After all, fingerprints are the basis of AFIS systems. For more information on fingerprints, the reader can refer to the work by Ed German, available at http://www.onin.com, which is authoritative and masterful. Other books on the market, such as David Ashbaugh's *Quantitative-Qualitative Friction Ridge Analysis,* provide detailed information on fingerprints. As mentioned, this book briefly describes other biometrics used in identification, but a more complete review of this topic can be found in *Biometrics Identity Assurance in the Information Age* by John Woodward, Nicholas Orlans, and Peter T. Higgins (a contributor to this book), which addresses the various biometric techniques in use.

The remaining chapters in this book cover everything from an overview of how AFIS systems operate to practical information for purchasing an AFIS system, such as the documents suggested and legal responsibilities. While presented in the context of an AFIS system, these concepts have applications in virtually any area involving public monies and vendor products. The following is a brief overview of each chapter.

1.12.1 CHAPTER 2 HISTORY OF AUTOMATED FINGERPRINT IDENTIFICATION SYSTEM

Chapter 2 presents the major milestones in the development of AFIS systems. For example, an early use of fingerprints was for "signing" a contract, while the modern use of fingerprints includes both criminal and non-criminal applications, such as access to social services. This development was gradual. As with other technologies, there were competing and complementary forces at work. The ability to collect fingerprints as a form of identification was limited by a method to classify and store these images. As classification systems developed, so did the interest in collecting more fingerprint cards.

A unique perspective on the development of IAFIS is also included in this chapter. Written by the director of the IAFIS, Peter T. Higgins, the section describes how IAFIS changed the AFIS world. As will be shown, the history of AFIS is far from over.

1.12.2 CHAPTER 3 FINGERPRINTS ARE UNIQUE

Most people have ten fingers and two palms. Each of these fingers and palms has ridge endings, bifurcations, a pattern of ridge flow, and other characteristics that make that 1 finger or palm image different from every other. These images can be captured using printer's ink and rolled onto a card stock for examination and comparison with another set of images using magnifying lenses, or they can be captured electronically and displayed on a monitor side-by-side with the electronic image from a database.

Chapter 3 discusses not only the uniqueness of fingerprint images, but also their unique application in identification. They are, for example, relatively inexpensive to capture. At the most elementary level, only ink and paper are required. Unlike other biometric identification technologies, the process can continue even if required to employ manual processing. A fingerprint image can be compared against a stack of fingerprint cards in a matter of minutes. By contrast, DNA comparisons are totally dependent on laboratory processing and can take days if not weeks to complete. The chapter also gives examples of why fingerprints are both necessary and the optimum choice for certain applications. Although a person may fabricate a name, change the color of their hair and eyes, and even change their face by surgery, they cannot change their fingerprints.

1.12.3 CHAPTER 4 AFIS SUMMARY—HOW THE SYSTEM WORKS

Chapter 4 provides an overview of the forensic fingerprint identification process. There are two paths: the first is for criminal tenprint applicants and job applicants, and the second is for latent print processing. Both rely on the same database for an identification, but there are inherent differences in how this is accomplished. Another distinguishing feature is that much of the work of the tenprint identification process is automated, including some "lights out" or no-human intervention practices. By contrast, latent print processing is very labor intensive. The latent print examiner prepares the latent print for image capture, selects search parameters, and launches the search. This may be replicated numerous times.

1.12.4 CHAPTER 5 FROM PRINT TO IDENTIFICATION

Chapter 5 provides a more detailed description of identification processing. Beginning with a system overview, the various key elements of AFIS processing are reviewed, with illustrations of equipment in use. The chapter includes a process flow that provides a step-by-step description of a typical search of a forensic AFIS. The chapter describes some of the changes in processing that AFIS has created, and concludes with a description of both tenprint and latent print processing reports that should be available to managers and decision makers. The importance of reliable data cannot be overestimated. Just because data is produced by a computer does not guarantee that it is accurate or that it reports what it was intended to report.

1.12.5 CHAPTER 6 CURRENT ISSUES

Chapter 6 includes a SWOT (strengths, weaknesses, opportunities, and threats) analysis of AFIS. As with any successful enterprise, managers need to know not just how the system is performing, but what are its areas of vulnerability and growth. Among the weaknesses of AFIS described is the lack of interoperability between large federal agencies such as the Department of Homeland Security IDENT system and the FBI IAFIS system. IDENT relies on two fingers, IAFIS uses ten. They are not truly interconnected. The chapter includes a comparison of current DNA processing with latent print processing. Rather than competing technologies, these should be considered as complementary, with advantages and disadvantages for each.

This chapter also describes the advances made in the civil application of AFIS technology. More states are using AFIS technology to confirm identities of those who are qualified to receive public benefits. This has moved onward to include multinational programs such as Eurodac, in which refugees seeking political asylum and public benefits are enrolled.

1.12.6   CHAPTER 7 BUYING AN AFIS SYSTEM: THE BASIC DOCUMENTS NEEDED

If the reader is considering the purchase of an AFIS system, or an upgrade to an existing system, Chapter 7 will be useful. Written by Peter T. Higgins, who also contributed to the history of IAFIS in Chapter 2, and Kathleen M. Higgins, this chapter speaks to the process and documentation of AFSI development. For most prospective buyers, acquiring an AFIS system is a once-in–a-lifetime event, while for vendors, it is just another sale. Knowing the questions to ask and the process to follow puts the buyer in a more comfortable position with the vendor and will reduce the opportunities for misunderstanding that can easily arise in such a large and complex acquisition.

1.12.7 CHAPTER 8 STANDARDS AND INTEROPERABILITY

The standards that allow AFIS systems to communicate did not appear out of thin air. Rather, as discussed in Chapter 8, they developed as AFIS vendors developed competing but not interactive systems. Standards developed by the National Institute of Standards and Technology as well as by the FBI provide uniformity in transmission, image compression and decompression, etc. Tables in the chapter provide some of the standards currently in use.

This chapter includes a case study in which the issue of hit rate is discussed. When one AFIS manager reports a latent print identification rate of 35%, and another reports a rate of only 10%, they may be comparing apples to oranges. This chapter describes why this happens and what it will take to get all agencies to report uniformly.

1.12.8 CHAPTER 9 CONTRACTUAL ISSUES REGARDING THE PURCHASE OF AN AUTOMATED FINGERPRINT IDENTIFICATION SYSTEM

All the intentions and promises regarding the purchase of an AFIS system will ultimately be expressed in a contract. Government agencies are under particular scrutiny to ensure that their contract with the AFIS vendor meets applicable state and federal regulations while delivering the AFIS system on time and on budget. In terms easy to understand by managers and attorneys, Chapter 9, written by Senior Attorney Lisa K. Fox, outlines the steps for a request for information (RFI), a request for proposals (RFP), and the competitive procurement versus noncompetitive procurement process. Time spent developing a complete and thorough understanding of system requirements and translating those concepts into a contract will result in a document that, once signed, becomes the basis for system development.

1.12.9 CHAPTER 10 CASE STUDY—DIAMONDS IN THE ROUGH: INCREASING THE NUMBER OF LATENT PRINT IDENTIFICATIONS

Chapter 10 summarizes remarks presented by the author at the 2002 Educational Conference at the International Association for Identification. Managers are constantly striving to find techniques that will provide more and better results with a minimum amount of additional personnel commitment. This chapter describes how the New York State Division of Criminal Justice Services upgraded the existing AFIS system, resulting in the number of latent print identifications doubling over a two-year period. This increase in latent print identifications was not just due to the improvements to the system, but also to the methods that examiners used to re-search existing cases.

1.12.10 APPENDICES

Appendix A is a glossary of definitions and terms used in the field of identification and AFIS. As with any discipline, there are terms and acronyms that are either unique to the discipline or that may have a meaning different from the generally understood definition. At times, these definitions make no sense to the novice, but long-standing traditions keep them alive. For example, the tenprint file contains the images of only two fingers. The latent cognizant, or criminal, file does contain all ten images, but it may contain more than just criminal records. The tenprint technicians and latent print examiners may perform many of the same tasks. This appendix will help reduce confusion arising from these terms.

Appendix B contains the 1998 IAI AFIS Committee Report on Cross-Jurisdictional Use of AFIS Systems, which was one of the seminal documents exploring the feasibility of searching latent prints from one vendor on an AFIS developed by another vendor. While the interoperability of tenprint searches has continued to grow, the ability to search latent prints on multiple databases continues to lag far behind.

Funding through the National Criminal History Improvement Project (NCHIP) has provided the basis for many AFIS systems. Appendix C shows the NCHIP funding distribution from 1995 through 2003.

Identification systems will continue to grow and improve. It is the intent of the author and contributors that readers of this book will be in a better position to effect those changes.

CHAPTER 2

HISTORY OF AUTOMATED FINGERPRINT IDENTIFICATION SYSTEMS

AFIS systems are built on finger images and computers. Having either no fingerprint-based images or no computers would mean no AFIS. But there were well-established identification systems in place for over 100 years that relied exclusively on people rather than computers. In fact, there are references to hand prints taken for identification purposes in India, Japan, China, and the Middle East long before classification systems were developed. Table 2.1 presents a timetable of early uses of hand and fingerprints.

2.1 EARLY PRINTS

In many instances, examination of hand prints was the only method of distinguishing one illiterate person from another since they could not write their own names. Accordingly, the hand impressions of those who could not record a name but could press an inked hand onto the back of a contract became an acceptable form of identification. In 1858, Sir William Herschel, working for the Civil Service of India, recorded a hand print on the back of a contract for each worker to distinguish employees from others who might claim to be employees when payday arrived. This was the first recorded systematic capture of hand and finger images that were uniformly taken for identification purposes.

Hershel's actions introduced fingerprints into accepted British business practices. Here was a method of identifying illiterate workers to be able to pay them for their services. If there was a dispute, the back of the worker's contract could be compared with a new image of the same hand. Hershel certainly did not invent fingerprinting any more than Henry Ford invented automobiles, but he popularized the notion that individuals could be recognized and distinguished, regardless of what name they used or whether they were literate. This process worked well with a relatively small group. It is also one of the earliest examples of a one-to-one (1:1) search, in which one known item is compared to another known item. In this case, when the hand image on the contract was compared

Table 2.1

AFIS Timetable: Early Prints

Year	Event
1858	Sir William Herschel, employed by the Civil Service of India, records a hand print on the back of a contract.[a]
1880	Dr. Henry Faulds determines that fingerprints can be classified, ridge detail is unique, and fingerprints can be used to solve crimes.
1883	Alphonse Bertillon builds database of criminals using anatomical measurements.
1892	Sir Francis Galton publishes *Fingerprinting*.
1900	Sir Edward Henry publishes *Classification and Use of Fingerprints*.
1903	Captain Parke begins to fingerprint inmates using the American Classification System.
1915	International Association for Criminal Identification is formed, later to become the IAI.
1919	International Association for Identification (IAI) is incorporated.
1924	Congress requires the collection of identification and criminal records. Identification Bureau is created.
1946	FBI has 100 million fingerprint records.

[a] See Ashbaugh, *Quantitative-Qualitative Friction Ridge Analysis.*

with the hand of the worker, it would either match or not match. If they matched, the worker was authenticated as the person who signed the contract. If they did not match, there was no other method to determine who owns the image on the contract. It was a yes or no determination.

The collection of these images did not require special handling or filing so long as they were few in number. But as the acceptance of inked impression as a unique identifier grew, so did the need to be able to classify the images. A major milestone occurred in 1880, when Dr. Henry Faulds proposed that ridge detail is unique, and because of that, fingerprints can be classified and used to solve crimes. He also implied that the Chinese had used a fingerprint identification system "from early times."

This was a major breakthrough in the use of inked impressions. Faulds had suggested that there was a way to name the flow of the friction ridges, a method of distinguishing the pattern of the finger image. He implied that the friction ridge patterns for each person are unique, that no two are identical. This uniqueness would provide certainty of the identity. The proposition that finger images could be used to solve crimes moved finger images beyond purely civil applications, as in the case of contracts, into the forensic arena.

During this same time, other biometrics were becoming of interest; fingerprints were not the only identifier under consideration. While the modern term biometric may not have been widely known or understood, various methods of associating some unique physical aspect with only one person were emerging. Among these new biometrics was a system developed in France by Alphonse

Bertillon. Believing that the time and actions required to capture finger images were too cumbersome and the records too difficult to review, Bertillon devised a new method based on physical measurements of the human body. His premise was that physical measurements, once taken and recorded, would not change over time. This process is called Bertillonage or anthropometry.

The recording process, however, was both difficult and tedious. Staff trained in the process measured the head length and width, height, trunk, length of outstretched arms and fingers, etc. This information was recorded and filed. Making an identification required a significant amount of time and money. The process was very complex and labor intensive.

In 1883, Bertillon began to build a database of criminals in Paris using these anatomical measurements. The system would identify anyone who had undergone the measurement process. He began to receive public recognition for his process later that same year, when he positively identified an imposter. This identification vindicated anthropometry and assured Bertillon of continued acceptance in France as well as interest from other countries.

Meanwhile, in England, Sir Francis Galton was working on a book on the use of fingerprints for identification. Galton, a widely traveled scientist, recognized the limitations of the Bertillon method. He became familiar with fingerprints through his travels and in correspondence with luminaries of his day, such as Darwin and Henry. A milestone for the field of fingerprinting was reached when Galton published his definitive work, *Fingerprinting*, in 1892. Today, many refer to Galton as the "Father of fingerprints" for his contributions to the field. His fingerprinting work is so highly regarded that the International Association for Identification, the world's leading identification association, includes a copy of Galton's right index finger as an element of the association's official logo.

With the acceptance of fingerprints as a unique identifier, the number of uses for these images began to increase. It was not a difficult task to compare the images on an inked fingerprint card with a person who claimed the name on the card. This is another example of the one-to-one search or subject authentication referenced previously.

As the number of fingerprint records grew, so did the filing structure. Many of those fingerprinted were illiterate, so the spelling of their names was left to the interpretation of government officials, who might not always spell a name the same. A similar situation was faced by the millions of illiterate immigrants who came to the United States during this time period. A classification system to be able to file the records by the information contained in the finger images, not just by the name, was badly needed.

Meanwhile, Sir Edward Henry, who was using the Bertillon method while posted in India, added the left thumb print to each anthropometric card. Henry soon realized that the thumb impression provided a more efficient method for identification than the physical measurements of the Bertillon method. Working with Bengali officers Khan Bahadur Azizul Haque and Rai Bahaden Hem Chandra Bose, he developed a system with 1,024 primary classifications. (Unfortunately, the contributions to the field of fingerprinting by the two officers were overlooked for years.) In 1900, Henry published *Classification and Use of Fingerprints*. His classification methods began to replace the more cumbersome anthropometrical records, which gradually began to lose favor. Henry was appointed Commissioner of Metropolitan Police at New Scotland Yard, and his classification system with both primary and secondary references became the international standard for fingerprint classification.

2.2 MOVING BEYOND A SINGLE DATABASE

Becoming proficient in the Henry System required extensive training and experience. By mastering the Henry System a fingerprint classifier could examine a finger image and produce a value based on the finger location, pattern, and ridge characteristics. Before the days of fax machines and electronics, this allowed a fingerprint file to be searched by classifying a record and looking for that classification among the records filed. The Federal Bureau of Investigation (FBI), in using the Henry System in the early 1900s, was able to search against no more than 8% of its master fingerprint repository, which made searches much more efficient. This method of classification also allowed agencies to communicate with other agencies regarding a fingerprint record. Once provided the classification of all ten fingers, other agencies could quickly determine if their records contained a possible match. If a possible match was found, a copy of the card would be sent to the inquiring agency. The Henry Classification System remained the standard until the introduction of AFIS.

Although the Henry Classification System eventually gained general acceptance, it did face some challenges. Most notable is the work of Captain James Parke of the New York State prison system. Beginning in 1903, Capt. Parke fingerprinted inmates using a system he devised that became known as the American Classification System. Unlike the Henry System, which uses the finger classification numbers as the primary determinate, the American System used the hand as the primary determinate. While embraced within the state of New York, the system was not widely accepted elsewhere.

As the recognition of the value of fingerprints began to spread and the classification systems become more widely used and understood, the number of fingerprints taken began to grow. The U.S. military, for example, started to fingerprint enlistees in the early 1900s, and U.S. prisons such as Leavenworth began fingerprinting all new inmates. The International Association of Chiefs of Police (IACP) formed the National Bureau of Identification to retain copies of fingerprint cards taken by local departments. The beginning of a national fingerprint database was being developed. And as the number of fingerprint records grew, so did the need for a national repository for these fingerprint cards. In 1924, Congress issued a mandate to collect identification and criminal records and created the federal Identification Bureau. Records from Leavenworth and the National Bureau of Identification formed the nucleus of this new identification bureau. A national database of fingerprint records in a federal agency was finally underway.

2.3 FINGERPRINT (TENPRINT) CARDS

The FBI established standards early on for the ink and the paper stock used for the tenprint records. The high-quality printer's ink assured a consistency that would provide uniformity in the inked impression. The quality of the card stock ensured that the tenprint record would survive the extensive handling, such as being inserted and removed from a filing cabinet numerous times, inherent in a card search. Supervisors could not afford to misplace or damage a card. In many cases, they were the only tenprint record in the subject file and so were irreplaceable.

Most law enforcement agencies would take three sets of prints at booking. These three cards were nearly identical in format. One set of 14 images would be sent to the FBI for a search of their files. If the fingerprint had been taken for a criminal matter, the FBI retained a copy. If the search was for a civil application, such as a security check, the card was returned to the booking agency after the FBI search.

Another tenprint card would be sent to the state identification bureau for a search against state records. If the booking agency had to rely on the mail to send the card and receive the results, this process could be quite lengthy. The introduction of fax machines greatly improved response time. The third card would remain in the department for insertion into its records. Although the FBI card was distinct from the local and state cards in color and field format, the state and local cards might be identical in form. It was not unusual for the booking officer to keep the better of the two cards at the local department and send the other card to the state bureau.

The FBI maintained image quality standards for accepting records to be added to the FBI criminal record file. If a criminal tenprint record did not meet the quality criteria, it would be returned to the booking agency. This policy was also adopted at many other identification bureaus. This could cause problems for the booking agency due to the length of time needed to send and receive information by mail. By the time the agency received the FBI's notification that a tenprint record was not acceptable, the subject might no longer be in custody or available for another printing. Other identification bureaus took a somewhat different approach. These bureaus were willing to include records that did not meet the FBI quality standards in their tenprint databases. The managers of these bureaus took the position that it was better to have some finger images, even poor-quality images, than no images. Either approach may lead to missed idents, and arguments can be made for each.

The procedure of sending the FBI a tenprint card for virtually every felony booking was a contributing factor to the growth of the FBI fingerprint files. The growth of the military during World War II and the subsequent fingerprinting of new enlistees also caused a massive increase in the number of records maintained by the FBI. In addition, fingerprint records for non-criminal purposes, such as background checks and licensing, grew in number, which also contributed to the increasing number of records.

By 1946, the FBI had more than 100 million fingerprint cards on file, but since many of these cards contained prints of the same person, e.g., one person would be given a new card for each new job application requiring a fingerprint or each new arrest, the number of different individual records on file was probably less. Through the 1950s and 1960s, the FBI and local and state identification bureaus continued to increase the size of their files. In addition to the actual fingerprint cards, identification bureaus also found their files beginning to fill with disposition information.

By 1971, the FBI was reported to have over 200 million records. The standard FBI fingerprint card is 8 inches × 8 inches, or 0.56 square feet. Multiplied by 200 million records, that gives 112,500,000 square feet, or about 2.5 square miles of records. That is a large area, larger than the National Mall in Washington, DC. The accumulation of so many records offered not only challenges for storage and maintenance, but also opportunities for improving the identification process across the country. If uniformity could be introduced to the records, it would become feasible for some of the information to be exchanged with different identification bureaus. An increase in communication speed, more reliable lines, and better equipment would begin to be seen.

The National Crime Information Center (NCIC), a computerized database storing criminal justice information, began operation in 1967. The NCIC provided a mechanism for law enforcement agencies to share information, particularly information on wanted offenders. While not a fingerprint-based system, the NCIC, and its successor, NCIC 2000, offered a mechanism to query the FBI database using descriptive image data. This proved a great advancement, since this sharing of information required participating agencies to use common terms and to send messages in an agreed-upon format. By 1983, the Interstate Identification Index (III) was added to NCIC. Participating states and local agencies could not only search the FBI, but also obtain a criminal history record (rap sheet) from another state. Criminal identification information was beginning to flow more freely. As NCIC and other identification systems grew, so did the realization that standardization would be mandatory if the potential of information exchange was to be realized.

The introduction of large mainframe computers in the 1960s and 1970s marked a milestone to this end, as data could be kept in a storage system that did not depend on paper and that could be electronically sorted. While these computers started life as frail equipment subject to breakdown and high maintenance, they soon began to prove their worth, particularly in the countless ways in which data could be parsed.

By this time, many large identification bureaus, including some states, had a semi-automated identification system in place. The automated portion of the system was known as the Computerized Criminal History file, or the CCH. The CCH contained previously submitted (i.e., enrollment) information. For criminal applications, the information might include the subject's name, date of arrest, and arresting agency. The record would also include the numerical classification of each finger image, as defined by either the Henry or the American Classification System. Images were not electronically stored, but remained available on the filed tenprint card.

When the identification bureau received a criminal inquiry, the name search was generally the first search performed. That is, the name on the tenprint card sent by the inquiring agency would be entered into the mainframe computer. If a matching name was found in the CCH, the classification of the ten fingers matching that name would also be printed. (See Chapter 5 for more details on name- and image-based searches.)

While this was being done, another fingerprint classifier would enter the fingerprint patterns from the submitted tenprint card and classify the ten images using either the Henry or the American Classification Systems. A clerk would pull the filed fingerprint cards for the matching names found by the computer and compare the images on the card with the submitted tenprint record to determine if there was a match. If so, the CCH was updated and a criminal history was sent to the inquiring agency. If there was no match based on the name search, then a technical search of the database was performed. The patterns of all ten fingers were entered, and the computer would produce another list of candidates whose patterns matched those of the inquiry prints. If no match was found, a new record would be created.

These systems relied on the classification of finger patterns by classification experts. Learning the classification patterns required extensive training and guidance until successfully mastered. While an experienced examiner could

Year	Event
1967	National Crime Information Center is established.
1973	IAI adopts position eliminating minimum number of ridge characteristics.
1977	RCMP implements AFIS.
1977	IAI establishes Latent Print Certification Program.
1983	Interstate Identification Index (III) is added to NCIC.
1984	San Francisco Police Department implements AFIS.
1986	Pierce County Sheriff's Department and Tacoma police department (WA) AFIS installed.
1989	New York State implements statewide latent print searching.
1991	IAFIS funding begins.
1992	FBI has 32 million sets of fingerprint cards in the master repository.
1993	ANSI/NIST-CSL 1-1993 American National Standard for Information Systems—Data Format for the Interchange of Fingerprint Information.
1994	ANSI/NIST-CSL 1-1993 American National Standard for Information Systems—Data Format for the Interchange of Fingerprint Information, UK.
1995	IAFIS begins communications with Boston Police Department.

identify the pattern classification rather quickly, time was required to retrieve a card from the fingerprint file, compare it to the submitted images, and then return it back to the file.

See Table 2.2 for a list of events that occurred during the period of initial automation.

2.4 LATENT PRINT PROCESSING

Identification bureaus also recognized that within their files was a great untapped resource: the use of tenprint records in searches of latent prints, those finger images that remain on a surface after it has been touched. Prior to AFIS technology, latent print identification depended to a large degree on suspect and elimination prints. If a latent print was found at a crime scene, it would be lifted and compared with the prints of those who had a legitimate right to be at the crime scene, e.g., office staff at an office that had been burglarized and police officers working at the crime scene. However, there was no feasible method for searching every latent print found.

The latent print examination process became more uniform beginning in 1973, when the International Association for Identification (IAI) rejected the position that a minimum number of ridges characteristics or "points" that must be present in latent prints for an identification. Other characteristics, such as minutiae, ridge flow, and dots, can provide sufficient detail for a latent examiner to make a positive identification, not make an identification, or conclude that there is not enough information to make a decision. The IAI followed this up in 1977 with a recommendation that latent print examiners be certified by the IAI. The IAI Latent Print Certification remains one of the most widely respected standards of peer professional recognition.

A report written in 1974 by Project Search, the forerunner of SEARCH, The National Consortium for Justice Information and Statistics, described early efforts at encoding and searching latent prints. Entitled "An Analysis of Automated and Semi-Automated System for Encoding and Searching Latent Fingerprints," the report contained an appendix that described the results of testing an automated fingerprint matcher program applied to latent fingerprints. This test was designed by Richard Higgins and Frank Madrazo of the New York State Division of Criminal Justice Services to explore the feasibility of an automated fingerprint processing system. The team created an Algol program based on work by J. H. Wegstein of the National Bureau of Standards, the forerunner of the National Institute of Standards and Technology (NIST).

Higgins and Madrazo plotted minutiae location, ridge direction angles, and pattern type on 94 latent print images and searched against a base file containing 2,526 inked impressions. Following the test, they draw three conclusions:

1. It worked.
2. More memory and faster speed are required in the computers.
3. Minutiae placement has to be improved.

This was another step in the development of AFIS.

2.5 THE FIRST AFIS SYSTEM

The question of who implemented the first AFIS system is not an easy one to answer, although there are generally accepted milestones along the path of AFIS development. The Automated Fingerprint Identification System does just that—it automates the identification process through the use of computers, or more characteristically, through digital images that can be coded and searched.

There are several dates in the development of the automated fingerprint identification process that can be considered the "start" date. Some might consider it to be the first day that a meeting was held to discuss the feasibility of implementing an AFIS. Others might think the start date to be the date of the first request for proposal. The date the first contract was signed, the day the first system became operational, the date the first system was accepted as complete from the vendor: all are legitimate start dates.

In the determination of AFIS "firsts," it can be noted that not all AFIS systems are connected to a CCH file; some only match tenprint records against the AFIS database to determine if the individual is on file. If so, the records are retrieved through means not associated with the AFIS process. While not used by large identification bureaus, this has some appeal for small agencies where the criminal history records can be retrieved relatively quickly and for those users who want a database limited to specific purposes, e.g., a wanted file. Whatever criteria are selected, there is an agency and a vendor that will claim to have been the first to offer this type of AFIS system.

The size of the agency that bought the AFIS system can also be considered. One community may claim to have the first AFIS system for a city whose population is over 100,000, another, the first AFIS system for a city over 1,000,000. If the criterion considered is cost of the AFIS system, does that include the salaries and overhead of the agency that bought the system? If a single user is considered, which one agency claims the title?

Here are a few concrete AFIS firsts. In 1977, the Royal Canadian Mounted Police began operation of the first AFIS system. The system has been changed over the years, with improvements in hardware, software, management, and record keeping procedures, but it is still built on the original 1977 system. San Francisco claimed to have the first AFIS system when its AFIS became operational in 1984. Faced with a continually growing record database and recognizing the potential for latent print searches, the San Francisco Police Department, under the direction of Ken Moses, converted records and began electronic searching based on minutiae. The SFPD became a focal point for other identification agencies to look to as a means of improving throughput and accuracy.

The Pierce County (Washington) Sheriff's Department and the Tacoma (Washington) Police Departments began using the first joint AFIS system in 1986. The combination of city and county law enforcement agencies sharing resources provided a service that individually neither of them might have been able to afford. In 1989, The New York State Division of Criminal Justice Services, under the direction of Jack Meagher, implemented the first Statewide Automated Fingerprint Identification System (SAFIS). While limited to latent print searches at that time, it marked a significant departure from previous AFIS installations, since it had a statewide impact. Latent print examiners from New York to Buffalo could search the same database, use the same equipment, and share their knowledge as to how to make the system better. By 1995, SAFIS had been given a tenprint search capability that could interface with a CCH file. This was followed by the addition of livescan devices that permitted the electronic capture of tenprint records. Also in 1995, Integrated Automated Fingerprint Identification System (IAFIS) was able to connect with a large city as the Boston Police Department began direct communications with IAFIS. This was another milestone in the evolution of AFIS technology.

A serious obstacle to latent print searches remains because the existing systems cannot directly exchange information for latent print searches. The AFIS Committee of the IAI initiated a demonstration project with Cogent, Printrak, and Sagem Morpho and show the feasibility. The committee reported its findings at the 1998 Educational Conference of the IAI (see Appendix B). Many of the concepts became incorporated into the development of the FBI-sponsored Universal Latent Workstation and the companion Remote Fingerprint Editing Software, both used to search latent fingerprints.

The following year brought another major advance in identification processing, as the IAFIS and NCIC 2000 become fully operational. All AFIS systems were tested for compliance with the year 2000 (Y2K) problem and were still in operation as the world moved into a new century.

The advantages of AFIS were readily apparent, many of them due to the fact that searches could now be performed on a computer. For example, AFIS could process a record much faster because most of the information could be quickly accessed and viewed on one's own computer instead of having to search through filing cabinets located down the hall. Identifications could be made by looking at fingerprint images appearing side by side on one's monitor, rather than by laboriously moving a reticle from one image on a fingerprint card to another. The images on screen were larger than those on the cards and therefore were easier to see and compare. And if there were multiple candidates for a match, the images could be viewed in sequence without having to physically remove cards from the files.

2.6 GROWTH AND DEVELOPMENT OF AFIS SYSTEMS

The systems that developed at this time had been put into production without the benefit of national standards. With funding from the FBI, NIST began to develop standards relating to the transmission of finger images. These standards were adopted by the American National Standards Institute (ANSI) to become *ANSI/NIST-CSL 1-1993 American National Standard for Information Systems—Data Format for the Interchange of Fingerprint Information*. These standards provided a guidepost for agencies and vendors to follow in the development of their AFIS systems if they intended to interact with the FBI.

The next transmission standard, *ANSI/NIST-ITL 1-2000 American National Standard for Information Systems—Data Format for the Interchange of Fingerprint, Facial, and Scar Mark and Tattoo (SMT) Information*, includes a provision for test records.

The value of standards for transmission of finger images and related data was recognized not only in North America, but also in European countries. Interpol, an international police organization with 181 member countries, adopted the ANSI/NIST standards with only slight modifications in 1996, a process that continues with each succeeding revision of the ANSI/NIST standards. In 1997, the ANSI/NIST transmission standard was revised and updated to include scars, marks, and tattoos. At the same time, the National Automated Fingerprint Identification System (NAFIS) became operational in the United Kingdom.

With standards in place and the benefits of AFIS systems well documented, the remaining barrier was the cost of purchasing and maintaining an AFIS. The National Criminal History Improvement Project was implemented at just the right time. NCHIP provided more than $270 million between 1995 and 1999. Through 2003, more than $430 million was infused into state and local coffers to improve criminal history and identification. Large states received a massive amount of federal support. For example, California received $32 million; Florida, $16 million; New York, $27 million; and Texas, $23 million. The table in Appendix C lists the grants awarded by the NCHIP to each state by year, along with the total amount awarded to each state over the years 1995–2003.

This infusion of capital into the identification marketplace created many business opportunities. Meeting the demands of multimillion dollar contracts required a significant investment in capital for research and development. Companies such as Sagem Morpho, Printrak Motorola, NEC, Lockheed Martin, and Cogent Systems emerged as large contractors for criminal and civil applications. Companies such as AWARE, AFIX Tracker, Comnetix, and FORAY found niche market customers.

With storage and computer costs diminishing and bandwidth increasing, agencies began to consider capturing palms and mug shots as a normal part of their booking process. Following the successful introduction of AFIS systems into the criminal arena, other areas of government found an interest in the technology. The move from an exclusively forensic AFIS system (i.e., an AFIS system for criminal searches or connected to a CCH) began to move into other, civil applications.

With state social service agencies spending millions for public benefit, the opportunities for abuse became a genuine concern. The Los Angeles Automated Finger Image Report and Match (AFIRM) system was the first finger imaging system to be used for welfare applications. Following the success of AFIRM, the state of California began using SFIS, the Statewide Finger Imaging System, in 1992, which was then expanded to six other counties in the Los Angeles and San Francisco area. Following contract procurement, challenges, and another acquisition cycle, SFIS became operational for the entire state in 2001.

The New York State Office of Temporary and Disability Assistance also began to fingerprint individuals who received certain classes of temporary assistance. In addition to reducing the amount of fraud from "double dippers," who

Year	Event
1995	National Criminal History Improvement Project (NCHIP) begins[a]
1996	Interpol interpretation of ANSI/NIST standard is adopted.
1997	ANSI/NIST standard updated to include scars, marks, and tattoos.
1997	NAFIS National AFIS is installed in the United Kingdom.
1998	IAI AFIS committee conducts cross-jurisdictional use of AFIS.
1999	IAFIS is operational.
1999	NCIC 2000 is operational.
2000	ANSI/NIST-ITL 1-2000 American National Standard for Information Systems— Data Format for the Interchange of Fingerprint, Facial, and Scar Mark and Tattoo (SMT) Information includes provision for test records.
2002	Interpol Implementation (ANSI/NIST) of ITL 1–2000.
2004	National Fingerprint-Based Applicant Check Study (N-FACS) is completed.
2005	ANSI/NIST standard is up for renewal.

Table 2.3

AFIS Expansion

[a] See NCHIP state funding at http://www.ojp.usdoj.gov/bjs/stfunds.htm.

received benefits under different names or under the same name in two different counties, they became able to expand their searches to include fugitive felons and incarcerated felons. Such systems continue to demonstrate applications for both civil and criminal uses.

See Table 2.3 for a list of events that occurred during the period of AFIS expansion.

At the same time as these systems were developing, the FBI recognized the need to automate its fingerprint records and began the Integrated Automated Fingerprint Identification System (IAFIS). The following section was written by Peter T. Higgins, the former Deputy Assistant Director of the FBI in charge of IAFIS, now of the Higgins-Hermansen Group, LLC. This section provides a unique and informative glimpse of the forces at work and the application of standards in the building of IAFIS.

2.7 IAFIS: THE AFIS THAT CHANGED THE WORLD OF FINGERPRINT AUTOMATION

By 1990, many U.S. states had AFIS systems in place, and major cities were installing livescan equipment. All of these systems were using proprietary interfaces or were printing fingerprint cards to be scanned by the AFIS they were next to run on. States were starting to see same-day responses from AFIS searches, at least in the major cities, such as Chicago. The situation at the FBI, however, was not so rosy. Their investments in automation were being overwhelmed by the transaction rates, and the forecast was for more of the same.

The criminal justice community was in the process of appealing to both Congress and the FBI for federal investments to help improve turnaround time at the FBI's IDENT Division (ID). When Judge William Sessions was sworn in as Director of the FBI in late 1987, the response time was already inadequate. By the end of 1989, the backlog of user submissions had reached the unprecedented level of 750,000 fingerprint cards and several million criminal history data submissions. The number of fingerprint cards alone represented approximately 5 weeks of peak processing effort by the ID.[1] The passage of the Anti-Drug Abuse Act in 1988 and the passage of the Airports Security Act in 1989 put the FBI under even more pressure to maintain complete, accurate, and immediately available criminal history files.

In June 1989, at the Advisory Policy Board (APB) meeting in Aurora, Colorado, the FBI enlisted the support of the then NCIC APB to review the ID's strategies and plans. Director Sessions personally asked the Chairman of the APB to appoint an ad hoc subcommittee to address FBI ID matters, including services and automation.[2] The APB established an ID Revitalization Task Force, chaired by Joseph Bonino of the Los Angeles Police Department. The task force produced a conceptual road map for revitalization of the ID. They realized that this was not just an AFIS throughput problem but more of a complex system problem that called for a systems-based solution.

The only way to decrease response times even as the volume of transactions increased was to address the six basic elements of the problem in an integrated solution. The problem looked like this:

- The vast majority of incoming fingerprint images were inked on cards that had to be either mailed in or scanned and sent over the slow speed modems (28.8 kbps) of that time period.
- Responses had to be transmitted electronically, because mailed responses would never arrive in time for bail hearings, etc.
- Standards had to be developed that would permit images captured electronically or scanned to be read by any state AFIS and by IAFIS.
- The fingerprint records would have to be stored as images for on-screen verification. In the usual procedure of that time, cards were scanned, features extracted, and images deleted because disk space was so expensive, costing about $250 per megabyte (MB) in 1990.
- A high-performance network had to be implemented that would tie the criminal justice community to the IAFIS system.

---

[1] IAFIS Acquisition Plan, FBI, Version 1, January 20, 1992.
[2] FBI Memorandum from Assistant Director L. York, ID, to Deputy Director J. E. Otto, dated 10/13/89.

- An AFIS that would handle approximately ten times the daily transaction rate against a repository more than five times the largest currently in existence would have to be built. Recall that this was at a time when PCs were running at only 50 to 66 megahertz (MHz).

The plan, approved by the APB's ID Revitalization Task Force in August 1989, called for an Integrated Automated Fingerprint Identification System (IAFIS) based on back file conversion of more than 30 million fingerprint cards into digital images, an image transmission network, standards, response times under 2 hours for arrest cycles, soft copy verification of candidates, growth margins, electronic responses, semi-automated processing of dispositions, etc. The recommendations of the task force fell into three categories:

1. The electronic transmission of identification and criminal history data.
2. Substantial improvements in the ID's AFIS capabilities.
3. Major enhancements to the ID's criminal history records system.

It should be noted that the plan and the subsequent congressional direction called for building a large-scale tenprint system with a more limited latent print capability. This was due to the fact that most crime is local, and there already existed numerous local and state AFIS systems on which latent searches could be made quite productively. This fact did not calm the fears of the ID's Latent Fingerprint Section (now in the FBI Laboratory Division) that the standards being considered would impact their ability to perform their task effectively.

In December 1989, at an APB meeting, Bonino presented the task force's main objectives for the ID revitalization effort:[3]

1. To improve the timeliness, accuracy, and completeness of all ID responses.
2. To reinstitute the FBI's leadership role in criminal identification matters.
3. To ensure the ID's status as a "role model for police agencies in criminal identification matters."

At that time, the ID was housed in the J. Edgar Hoover Building in Washington, DC. One ID room, which housed the master fingerprint file, contained all 30 million fingerprint cards filed by the Henry System in over 1,000 file cabinets. At peak times, over 500 people per shift worked in this room, filing new cards, checking candidates from the existing AFIS, and so on. There was no available space to install the new system while continuing to provide service. So

---

[3] Minutes of Meeting of the National Crime Information Center Advisory Policy Board, December 6–7, 1989.

a relocation study was performed, and Clarksburg, West Virginia was selected for the new location. A purpose-built facility with an enormous data center was built in the mid-1990s.

The FBI's internal plan was to build and deploy IAFIS by 1995. IAFIS funding started to flow in fiscal year (FY) 1992 as a result of Public Law 102-140[4] of October 28, 1991. That law appropriated $48 million for the automation of fingerprint identification services, and of that amount, $1.5 million was targeted for establishing an independent program office dedicated solely to the relocation of the ID and the automation of fingerprint identification services. In the parlance of the federal budget, these dollars were fenced so that the FBI or the Department of Justice could not legally spend them on anything else. The appropriation was marked as 5-year money, meaning the money could be spent as needed rather than pushed onto contracts as the fiscal year drew to a close, as so often happens in federal contracting. Starting in FY 1993, the funding was increased to $92 million per year, based on an independent cost study performed by the MITRE Corporation.

Several key decisions were made, and the following actions were taken in 1991:

1. The FBI contracts shop was not staffed to handle the large number of acquisitions associated with IAFIS (over 15 contracts of various size were awarded). Instead, the FBI contracted with the General Services Administration's (GSA's) Federal Computer Acquisition Center (FEDCAC) in Massachusetts for pre-acquisition contract services for the three main IAFIS segments. Steve Meltzer, FEDCAC's director, and his team of experts were instrumental in shaping the procurement packages. Later, in the mid-1990s, IAFIS Program Office Section Chief Robert O. Kramer and the three segment managers (Chuck Jones, Bob Last, and Jim Shugars) spent the better part of a year working on the evaluation of three sets of proposals at the FEDCAC facility.

2. In January 1991, 986 acres were purchased in West Virginia, and by October of that year construction was under way.

3. Director Sessions asked White House Fellow Patrick Harker[5] of the University of Pennsylvania to recommend how to best organize the criminal justice services of the FBI to include the program office mandated by legislation. Harker's recommendations led to the establishment of the Criminal Justice Information Services (CJIS) Division, which eventually absorbed the ID. The

---

[4] Departments of Commerce, Justice, and State, The Judiciary, and Related Agencies Appropriations Act, 1992.
[5] Patrick T. Harker returned to the University of Pennsylvania at the end of his fellowship and is currently the Dean of the Wharton School.

first Assistant Director of the CJIS, Norm Christensen, was instrumental in implementing the vision of Director Sessions and Pat Harker.

4. ID hired, through the MITRE Corporation, then recently retired Air Force Major General Eric B. Nelson to do an audit of the FBI's Program Office skills, taking into consideration the recently enacted congressional "program office mandate."[6] Nelson found that the experience level for such an undertaking was relatively low, as the Bureau had never previously used a "program office" approach, and there were two significant, interrelated projects—revitalization of ID and the move to West Virginia. Nelson's report called the proposed 1995 IAFIS operational date into question. He worked with Pat Harker and proposed the alternative of a new, integrated FBI division. Nelson's team consisted of himself, Peter T. Higgins, two independent consultants, Robert Bowes and Frances Flett, as well as Michael Bloom of MITRE. Ed Burke, also of MITRE, while not on the team, was also instrumental in the effort.

5. An acquisition round table was held on September 12, 1991, where it was decided that IAFIS should be acquired in three major segments: FBI AFIS, to be procured through an Office of Management and Budget (OMB) Circular A-76-funded competition; the Image Transmission Network (ITN), later re-scoped and renamed as the Identification Tasking and Networking Segment; and the Interstate Identification Index (III). It also supported "performance of the integrator role by the FBI/ID, with assistance from a SETA contractor."[7] The ID accepted these recommendations. Century Planning Associates facilitated the round table session.

6. Section Chief Bruce Brotman, ID, contracted with NIST to hold a series of workshops to draft and vote on an ANSI standard for the transmission of fingerprint images.

7. In December 1991, the FBI offered the position of IAFIS Program Director to Peter T. Higgins. He started on February 2, 1992.

The January 1992 Acquisition Plan called for the AFIS request for proposal (RFP) to be developed in February 1991 and released in May 1991, with a contract awarded by December 1991. Yet none of these events occurred. The U.S. General Accounting Office (GAO) and others strongly recommended to the FBI that they readdress the 1995 target date for initial operations. By April 1992, when the RFPs were reviewed for completeness and were found to lack sufficient maturity, the FBI agreed that the 1995 target date was unachievable. A

[6] Letter from General Nelson sent to Deputy Assistant Director S. Klein of the FBI's ID, dated 11/15/91.
[7] Letter from J. T. Nocerino of Century Planning Associates, Inc. to Mr. J. Sullivan, FBI ID, dated 11/1/91.

new plan was developed with two phases: an initial capability in 1998 and a full operational capability in 1999.

With funding in place, a new organization being established, and a strong commitment from Director Sessions, the Department of Justice, OMB, Congress, and the criminal justice community, the challenge of specifying and building IAFIS began in earnest. By May 1992, the new schedule was being established and briefed. NIST started hosting workshops on the standards; Tom Hopper was engaged in discussions and studies on compression techniques for transmitting fingerprint images; and Tom Roberts and Walt Johanningsmeier were doing the systems engineering required to specify the systems. Interestingly, the three segment managers had already started developing their segment requirements without benefit of a system level specification.

The decisions made in 1992 and 1993 still form the baseline for most AFIS procurements around the world. The key decisions are discussed below.

2.7.1 TRANSMISSION STANDARD

Michael "Mike" McCabe of NIST facilitated a series of three successful workshops and produced a draft standard for the transmission of fingerprint images. Given that there were competing livescan capture rates and that some AFIS used binary images, the workshops required many compromises. The four brilliant facets of the standard developed are the following:

1. Each transmission has a header record (Type 1 record) that describes the type of transaction (for instance, a miscellaneous applicant request or a search response.) The Type 1 record also identifies the number and type of records that follow. A Type 2 record, containing information about the subject of a transaction, such as demographic and biographic data, or a response, such as identification information or an error message, always follows the Type 1 record.
2. There were four fingerprint image record types (Types 3, 4, 5, and 6) in the original standard. Communities of interest could specify which ones they would accept.
3. The fields in the records were tagged so that only mandatory and some optional fields could be used without having to explicitly show all the other optional fields as being empty.
4. Data fields could be specified as to their byte length, contents, and mandatory versus optional nature by domains of users. Among other uses, this would permit Europeans and others to use the ISO standard format for date fields while the FBI could use the American format.

The standard was approved by ballot and forwarded to ANSI for registration. The official title is *ANSI/NIST-CSL 1-1993 American National Standard for Information Systems—Data Format for the Interchange of Fingerprint Information*; it is uniformly referred to simply as the ANSI/NIST standard in the AFIS community. It has been updated twice since then, again through a series of workshops hosted by Mike McCabe and NIST. The first change was in 1997 with the addition of Type 10 records for facial images and images of scars, marks, and tattoos. Then in 2000, it was updated to add variable density records for finger, latent, and palm images as well as a test record (Type 16). The current title is *ANSI/NIST-ITL 1-2000 American National Standard for Information Systems—Data Format for the Interchange of Fingerprint, Facial, & Scar Mark & Tattoo (SMT) Information*.

2.7.2 FBI AND OTHER IMPLEMENTATIONS OF THE ANSI STANDARD

After the ANSI/NIST standard was approved, the FBI published the Electronic Fingerprint Transmission Specification (EFTS). The EFTS specified which Transaction Types (TOTs), record types, and data fields the FBI would accept and which data fields were mandatory or optional. The most significant decision made when preparing the EFTS was that the FBI would only accept Type 4 fingerprint (high-resolution, gray-scale) images. While the workshops had supported four image types, only the Type 4 has been used since the 1994 introduction of the EFTS. The other image types are still in the standard but are not used in any major AFIS system or in tenprint livescan systems.

By 18 March 1994, the UK Home Office Police Department, Police Systems Research and Development Group published their interpretation of the ANSI/NIST, entitled *ANSI/NIST-CSL 1-1993 Data Format for the Interchange of Fingerprint Information, United Kingdom Implementation*. The Royal Canadian Mounted Police published their version, *The National Police Service NIST Interface Control Document*, known as the NPS-NIST-ICD.

In May of 1995, Interpol held a conference in Lyon, France to discuss a standard for the interchange of fingerprints around the world. The different size forms and the different data fields in use included many different languages, which challenged them in finding a common solution. The U.S., Canadian, and UK representatives, including Peter Higgins, recommended moving to the exchange of virtual fingerprint records, as having digital images of the fingerprints would permit different countries to print them on different forms and in different locations on paper forms. With limited infrastructure and limited computerization of the processes, however, Interpol worked on a paper interchange standard.

By the next year, Interpol held another meeting and agreed to develop an Interpol implementation of the ANSI-NIST standard. Mr. Chris Coombs of the Metropolitan Police, London, agreed to lead the effort. He was quickly able to modify the UK implementation so that it was an Interpol Implementation. After it was approved, the UK dropped its document and adopted the Interpol Implementation. The current version is the *Interpol Implementation (ANSI/NIST ITL 1-2000) Version No. 4—19 November 2002.*

In the 2000 workshops at NIST, the issue of how to represent rich alphabets (e.g., Japanese) that required more characters than those supported by the ASCII character set had been raised. The decision made was clever—the Type 1 record would always be in ASCII, but it would have an optional data field to show if the Type 2 record was in Unicode. This permitted countries to exchange names in their native alphabet set.

2.7.3 IMAGE QUALITY SPECIFICATIONS

After the EFTS was published, the FBI issued *Appendix F: Image Quality Specifications (IQS)*. Image quality is perhaps the most significant driver of AFIS performance. By selecting ANSI/NIST Type 4 records, the FBI had already ensured that images would be captured at 500 ppi or higher, with 8 bits of grayscale and transmitted at 500 ppi (with a small tolerance for variation). But they had not provided any standards for the quality of the optics, the signal processing, the printers, or the displays. The importance of all elements of the "image chain" can be seen by envisioning a scanner connected to a PC. If a color picture is scanned in color at 2,000 ppi (24 bits per pixel or more) and is displayed on a 72 ppi black and white monitor at a 1:1 resolution, there is far more information going into the digital image than coming out. There is a need to specify all aspects of the process to minimize data loss at any point in the chain.

There were no issues with the IQS specifications for printers or monitors; all the interest was and still is focused on capture devices. The IQS standard lists six data capture attributes that specify an image chain in engineering terms (e.g., modulation transfer function), since it is very difficult and often subjective to describe image quality in any other way. Industry pushed back against the Appendix F IQS and asked for relief on two of the elements for data acquisition. The FBI responded with *Appendix G: Interim Image Quality Specifications for Scanners* for use until IAFIS went operational.

The IQS image acquisition specifications were designed for optical systems such as flat bed scanners. Using it on livescan devices and single finger solid-state devices is much more difficult. Eventually, the FBI, working with MITRE, established a self-certification process for industry. After the certification tests are run and the data analyzed, the manufacturer submits them to the FBI for evaluation. Then, if successful, they receive a letter of certification from the FBI, specifying compliance with either Appendix F or G. Almost all AFIS and livescan acquisitions have specified one of the two EFTS IQS Appendices since 1994.

It is important to note that while a vendor might have a letter of certification for their livescan and compression products, the units still need to be cleaned frequently and calibrated from time to time, and the compression rate must be set properly. Think of the EPA ratings for gas mileage—your car might not experience the same results as the tests. The same holds true for your livescan. In fact, the FBI has noted a constant creep in the compression rate of electronic submittals, from around 15:1 (the specified compression rate) all the way up to 20:1.

2.7.4 COMPRESSION STANDARD

Transmittal of the 14 fingerprint images associated with a fingerprint card (or livescan capture) at 500 ppi (in both the X and Y axis) required 10 MB per person. With 28.8 kbps modems in use, there was no way they would all make it from local police to the state identification bureau, where the FBI would provide a wideband network (the CJIS WAN). The JPEG format, being based on 8-X8 pixel tiles, was not compatible with fingerprint images, resulting in banding effects upon reconstruction. As a result of this deficiency, Tom Hopper settled on Wavelet Scalar Quantization (WSQ) compression with a compression rate of 20:1. It was specified in the *Wavelet Scalar Quantization (WSQ) Grayscale Fingerprint Image Compression Specification*; the most recent version is December 19, 1997, IAFIS-IC-0110v3. A key part of the compression scheme is that the compressed images contain not only the compressed image data but also a copy of the Transform Table, Quantization Table, and the Huffman Table to permit decompression.

In the summer of 1993, the IAI challenged the FBI's use of WSQ at 20:1 even though they had not yet seen any compressed–decompressed images. The FBI agreed to sponsor a double blind test at NIST for the IAI. The result was presented to the FBI in January 1994 by the chair of the IAI's AFIS Committee, Michael Fitzpatrick of the Illinois State Police Lab. It confirmed what the IAI had suspected. At 20:1, approximately 81% of the fingerprints had "some blurring of ridge detail with some loss of pore and ridge edge information." While there was no loss of Galton (second-level detail), the degradation of some third-level detail led the FBI to settle on a 15:1 average compression rate.

In 2000, with the advent of Type 14 variable density images and JPEG 2000 compression (also based on wavelets), for the first time since 1995 (the UK

NAFIS system) we saw any AFIS procurement that did not specify WSQ compression at an average of 15:1. Even then, these new procurements specified both JPEG 2000 and WSQ at 15:1, since they have to exchange images with existing systems.

2.7.5 CONCLUSION

IAFIS set the pace for all subsequent AFIS and livescan procurements. It brought interoperability to the AFIS market. The many men and women of the FBI's IAFIS Program Office and its industrial partners deserve a word of thanks from the buyers of today. The following by-products of IAFIS are the baseline for a very mature industry:

- The ANSI-NIST Standard, with all its flexibility
- EFTS and its all important IQS Appendices
- WSQ compression for fingerprint images

IAFIS went operational in stages, starting with the successful Electronic Fingerprint Image Print Server (EFIS) first used by the Boston Police Department in 1995. IAFIS achieved full operational capability in 1999. For more information on the IAFIS program, see *Biometrics, Identification in the Information Age*, by Woodward, Orlans, and Higgins and published by Osborne, a McGraw Hill Company in 2002.

2.7.6 CURRENT CHALLENGES

Now that IAFIS has been operational for approximately 6 years, the responsibilities and cost of ownership are starting to be addressed by the FBI. Assistant Director Michael D. Kirkpatrick, CJIS Division, has been able to fund and implement the replacement of the aging optical disk jukebox system used for fingerprint image storage and retrieval. These mechanical devices have recently been replaced with spinning disks. The now obsolete computers the FBI AFIS ran on have been replaced with newer machines with an order of magnitude increase in performance.

Kirkpatrick and the FBI are also addressing the list of major changes that are required if the FBI is to continue to be the "role model for police agencies in criminal identification matters" as was set as a goal by the 1989 report. The changes include adding the capability to do the following:

- Process variable density records.
- Accept, process, store, and search palm records.

- Store and search tenprint records for immigration violators and watch list persons.
- Maintain synchrony with IDENT and the US-VISIT program.
- Participate in "flats-only" civil searches, possibly with fewer than ten fingers being submitted.

CHAPTER 3

FINGERPRINTS ARE UNIQUE

3.1 NAMES

What's in a name? That which we call a rose by any other name would smell as sweet.

—Shakespeare

Who are you?

People can be identified by an assigned or innate form of classification. One example is the name of their family, or surname (e.g., Smith), which can indicate those persons to whom they are related. The surname may also provide information about their background or the geographic area in which their ancestors lived. Names such as Giuliani and Salamone may point to family origins on the Italian peninsula; Zahurak and Kopak may indicate eastern European ancestry. The surnames Der and Wong point to China and the Orient, Biarnes to France, and Abouelmagd to the Middle East.

A few generations ago, people claimed their ancestral home to be within a few miles of where they were born. As commerce improved, so did the opportunity to emigrate to other lands. Immigrants to the United States were welcomed with the salute "Give me your tired, your poor, your huddled masses yearning to breathe free." This migration of peoples caused the association with an ancestral homeland to become more remote. The vast majority of Americans who trace their ancestry to a foreign nation have only a distant connection to the country of origin of their surname.

The first, or given, name provides a unique identifier that distinguishes one person from other members of the same family. Rudy Giuliani is thus distinguished from Edward Giuliani, Steve Zahurak from Bill Zahurak, and Joyce Der from Jane Der. Surnames and given names may also provide information about some of the person's physical features. Names like Rudy, Edward, Steve, and Bill are male names, just as Joyce and Jane are female names. It would not be unreasonable to assume that someone named Steve is a man, and thus a mental framework or picture of that person would begin to develop. As a man, Steve would be expected to have male characteristics such as a deep voice, facial hair, and clothing common to men. Joyce and Jane, however, would be assumed to appear different than Steve and Bill. In addition to the difference in primary and secondary sex characteristics, they may be assumed to dress differently than men and be physically smaller than their male counterparts. Without knowing anything more, it is not unreasonable to assume that Juan Gonzales will look different than his wife, Juanita Gonzales. Names themselves, then, provide some information about a person that may be useful in helping to make an identification.

In addition to sex and size, there are other features that may come to mind with a particular name. It may provide an indication of someone's skin color or skin tone; height and weight might also be inferred from a name. These assumptions, however, are often incorrect. Plus, some names are ambiguous. Is Pat Francis, for example, a man or a woman? Does Pat trace an ancestry back to England, Ireland, Scotland, or Wales, or perhaps to the continent? This simply cannot be determined based on name alone; neither can someone's age be determined by their given and/or surname.

Any given name, however, is not unique to only one person. For example, an examination of any telephone directory will show a large number of entries for the surname Smith. Even with the surname Smith and the given name of John, the number of entries is still quite lengthy. A rose may be a rose, but John Smith may not be John Smith.

Names are given at birth, but can be (voluntarily) changed later in life. People change their names for a variety of reasons. For example, marriage often provides an avenue for a legal name change: Marie Pelletier becomes Mary Nimick, i.e., Mrs. William Nimick. Just as people change their style of clothing, they may change their name, to adopt a new persona, a stage name, or a *nom de plume*, the writer's name. Names also may change when used in different languages. Frederick, for example, becomes Frederic in French.

3.2 IDENTIFICATION DOCUMENTS

Names provide only a casual identifier. In many situations, a person's name is a sufficient identifier that can be recognized by another party; most will believe that the name is authentic. But when an additional degree of information is required, a form of documentation, such as a driver's license or passport, can be used. These forms of identification are improvements over one's name alone because they provide a unique identification number (i.e., the driver's license number or the passport number). They are issued by a government agency that has created specific requirements for their issuance.

Not all government-issued documents are equally reliable as forms of personal identification. A library card, for example, is issued by an agency of government (the county, city, or university) but is intended only to permit the bearer to borrow books, movies, and other media from a library for a limited period of time. Although a borrower may need to present a driver's license as identification and proof of residency in order to be issued a library card, the card is an inexpensive and insecure method for the library to account for its holdings, as the value of the item borrowed is relatively minor (the price of the book, plus administrative fees and recovery costs). The library assumes that the borrowers are members of the community served by the library (residents, university students, etc.) and thus are likely to return the borrowed items in good order; this also reduces the need for a more reliable form of identification.

As the reliability of a form of identification increases, more security is involved in generating it and authenticating the person it represents. While library cards have a low level of security and require only modest proof of residency, they are only good for borrowing books from the library. A driver's license requires stronger proof of identification (such as a birth certificate), but it has more uses than just permitting one to legally operate a motor vehicle.

Alas, not everyone is completely honest about their identity; nor is everyone completely honest about their personal history, their criminal history in particular. While a library card may be sufficient to borrow a book, other organizations, such as the airline industry, require a more authoritative form of identification. The Transportation Security Administration (TSA) requires a government-issued form of identification with a photograph, along with a boarding pass, to clear security at the airport. Simply announcing "I am John McNeil" will not convince a TSA official that John McNeil is really John McNeil, and that he is the John McNeil who has a ticket on the next flight.

3.2.1 DRIVER'S LICENSE

Most American adults have a driver's license, or wish they had a driver's license. Not only does it allow for the legal operation of a motor vehicle, but it also is becoming an increasingly important form of identification.

To obtain a driver's license, one of the most widely recognized forms of identification, the applicant has to present other supporting forms of identification. These may include a statement of identity signed by a parent for someone who is under 21, plus a Social Security card, a current U.S. passport, or a Certificate of Naturalization or Certificate of Citizenship. Some states will also accept a college or high school photo ID along with a transcript.

The driver's license includes a feature that the other documents required to obtain it may not: a biometric, in this case, a photograph. The photograph, taken at the time of issuance of the license and at each renewal, makes the license a valid form of identification for most purposes. For example, a driver's license with the proper date of birth will allow entry into a tavern restricted to those 21 and older. The photo and address on the license may be used to support a decision by the local grocer to accept a personal check. In this example, the clerk will compare the shopper's face with the photograph on the license, and may record his or her address (along with phone number) as additional information to confirm the shopper's identity.

The driver's license is, of course, also used for its intended purpose in verifying both the identification of a driver and his or her legal authority to operate a motor vehicle. When a police officer pulls over a driver for a perceived traffic violation, the officer will ask for the driver's license and will convey the information on the license to police headquarters. The information is then passed on to the state Department of Motor Vehicles and a report is delivered back to the officer. In one possible scenario, the officer may learn that the owner of the driver's license is authorized to operate a motor vehicle in that state, but the information about the owner may not match the information on the license. Closer inspection might reveal that the photo on the license does not match the driver. The license is valid, but it does not belong to the person stopped by the officer. If the person driving the car is not the person on the license, then who is the driver? Is the driver dangerous? A wanted fugitive? Is the officer's life in danger? These last three questions are the ones that promote immediate action by the officer as the arrest takes place.

Some may ask, "What's the big deal? It's only a driver's license." After the events of September 11, 2001, however, all sense of security changed. While most driver's licenses are valid, there are numerous instances of fraudulent driver's licenses, such as the example in the following AP story.[1]

> Thursday, Jul. 3, 2003—5:27 AM
>
> By MATTHEW BARAKAT, Associated Press Writer
>
> ALEXANDRIA, Va. (AP)—Two clerks at the Virginia Department of Motor Vehicles and four associates have been charged with helping more than 1,000 people obtain fraudulent Virginia driver's licenses over a five-year period, prosecutors announced Wednesday.
>
> Under the alleged scheme, people who could not obtain legitimate driver's licenses would pay $800 to $2,000 for the fraudulent licenses.

Several of the terrorists involved in the September 11, 2001 World Trade Center attacks obtained false Virginia driver's licenses, allegedly with the help of the Virginia Department of Motor Vehicles (DMV) and legal personnel.[2] There are

---

[1] See http://www.wtopnews.com/index.php?nid=25&sid=98856.
[2] See http://www.valawyersweekly.com/terrorist.htm.

many stories of individuals who obtained false driver's licenses by bribing officials or providing false documentation, combined with social engineering (i.e., gaining trust by appearing to be a known or accepted person), which resulted in the false driver's license being issued. From these examples, it is apparent that driver's licenses cannot be counted on as an irrefutable form of identification.

3.2.2 PASSPORT

A driver's license provides one level of identification, at least if the photo matches the face of its holder. But the name on the license may not be the name of the individual holding the license. Do passports provide any better identification?

A U.S. passport is considered to be a very secure document. To obtain a passport, the applicant must have proof of U.S. citizenship in the form of a birth certificate, a Consular Report of Birth Abroad, or Certification of Birth; a form of identification; two photographs meeting the application specifications; and money for the application fee.[3] The applicant must present these items, in person, to a U.S. Postal Service official or other official, such as a clerk of court, public libraries, or other state, county, township, and municipal government offices, who accepts passport applications on behalf of the U.S. State Department at designated times and locations. This must be done in person to ensure that the photographs can be compared by the official with the face of the applicant and that the documents are consistent in terms of name and other identification items.

The Passport Services Office of the U.S. State Department will accept any of the following for the required form of identification:

- Previous passport
- Naturalization Certificate
- Certificate of Citizenship
- Current and valid:
  - Driver's license
  - Government ID: City, state, or federal
  - Military ID: Military and dependents

These security checks are designed to ensure that the individual named on the passport is actually the person holding the passport. This usually is the case, but not always. A determined person can overcome several of these checks. For

---

[3] See the information on passports provided by the U.S. Department of State, at http://travel.state.gov/passport/index.html.

example, the photograph on the applicant's driver's license may not be valid, or the driver's license itself may not be valid. As the example above showed, it is relatively easy to obtain a fraudulent driver's license.

Fraudulent passports come in all shapes and sizes, sometimes even from fictional countries or authorities. These are known as phantom passports. One company recently advertised that it would, with the proper credentials and fees, provide applicants with passports from places such as the Soviet Union and Czechoslovakia. A passport from the Soviet Union? Applicants, perhaps, are making a few assumptions, such as that the Soviet Union and Czechoslovakia still exist as countries. They do not. The passport was issued "for entertainment purposes only."

Another "entertainment-only" passport is issued by the Conch Republic, located in the Florida Keys, which considers itself the world's first "Fifth World" nation. According to its Secretary General, The Honorable Sir Peter Anderson, "The Conch Republic is a sovereign state . . . of mind. We seek to bring more humor, warmth and respect into a world in need of all three." The Office of the Secretary General will provide a passport (Fig. 3.1) for the citizens of this "sovereign state" for a small fee.[4]

Figure 3.1
Conch Republic Passport

---

[4] For an application, see http://www.conchrepublic.com/passports1.htm.

Not satisfied with being just a citizen of the Conch Republic? How about becoming an Ambassador? A Good Will Ambassador passport can be obtained for just under $1000; the cost of an Ambassador's passport is many times more. A possible rationale for issuing these passports is to provide some degree of levity. Holding a passport that states the holder is a "Citizen of the Conch Republic," however, is not the same as holding a U.S. passport. As an identification document, it is worthless.

3.3 PHOTOGRAPHS

Names are not sufficient identifiers for long-term, absolute authentication. Driver's licenses and passports are more reliable, but both are subject to tampering. Photographs, as used in photographic recognition devices or facial recognition software, may appear to provide a more reliable method of determining or confirming identification.

However, photographs taken of the same individual may show changes over time. For example, Figures 3.2 and 3.3 are both photographs of the author, the first taken a few years ago (perhaps many years ago) and the second more recent.

These two figures illustrate how a subject's appearance in a photograph can change over the years. The face may not be quite as taut in one image; the hairline may have slightly receded. The subject may have different glasses, or slightly graying hair in a later photograph. It is not necessary to wait decades to note differences between two photographs of the same person. Beyond changes in appearance, such as hair color, addition or removal of glasses, facial hair, etc., there are other changes that can add to missed identifications. A

Figure 3.2
Early Photo

Figure 3.3
Later Photo

change in lighting, the direction of shadows, background color or activity, or even the size of the face in relation to the background affect the accuracy of photographic recognition devices.

The field of facial recognition has not yet matured to the level where the reality meets all the claims of its marketing staff. The hype that followed facial recognition testing in airports, for example, was less than spectacular. Still, facial recognition software is often promoted as an important method of identification. Movies and television programs, in one example, take viewers inside the secure rooms of Las Vegas casinos, where walls of monitors show live images of the players on the casino floor taken by hidden cameras. In a typical scenario, security personnel look at a screen, and then suddenly magnify the face of a gambler. "Wasn't he barred from this casino?" they ask. Did facial recognition software find this person? Not really. The first thing that drew the attention of the security personnel was the action of the player, not his or her face. Only once they noticed the unusual activity did they focus on the player's face and capture the image. Following this, the facial recognition software they were using made a comparison and presented choices; the casino personnel made the final determination of identification. This is a quantum leap from the facial identification hype that claims that any person can be found in any group purely through electronic means.

The images that are captured in photographs are subject to changes in lighting, shadows, background, "noise" from other lighting sources, etc. For an identifier to be truly unique, however, it cannot be changed either by the owner of the identifier or governmental or cultural differences; it must remain unique for perpetuity. Fingerprints remain constant. Fingerprints are unique.

3.4 DNA

Mug shots and fingerprints are not the only biometrics that can be used for identification. Due to recent improvements in laboratory analysis and reduction in costs, many agencies are relying on deoxyribonucleic acid (DNA) as a form of identification. DNA is a chemical structure that forms chromosomes. A gene is piece of a chromosome that dictates a particular trait. That chemical structure can be identified through laboratory analysis. Like fingerprints, DNA does not change over time. Unlike fingerprints, however, two people can have the same DNA. Identical twins share the same DNA, but not the same fingerprints!

Large fingerprint identification services such as state identification bureaus process hundreds, perhaps thousands, of requests each day. They respond to these requests in hours, sometimes minutes. However, accommodating even a portion of that number of DNA requests would grind the identification process to a halt, as DNA identification processes require a relatively lengthy time period.

In addition, some consider DNA collection to be much more personally invasive than taking a rolled set of finger images. A booking officer putting a subject's fingers onto a glass platen to capture finger (and perhaps palm) images creates a mind-set entirely different from the officer inserting a swab held by a gloved hand into the subject's mouth. The latter procedure assumes the aura of medical analysis, an aura that can be viewed as too invasive.

3.5 FINGERPRINTS

3.5.1 PHYSICAL CHARACTERISTICS

Fingerprints are unique. The ridges on fingers are created during embryo development in response to pressures that form patterns that can be classified by print examiners. These ridges are also referred to as friction ridges. They provide a relatively rough surface area, making it possible to grasp and hold on to objects with ease. Each ridge contains at least one pore, which is connected to a sweat gland below the skin.

The sweat gland helps to remove waste from the ridge area as well as to maintain a relatively constant temperature through evaporation. The sweat produced is also the source of deposits for latent prints, i.e., those finger images that remain on a surface after it has been touched. In addition to water, the sweat contains trace elements of oil and some minerals. These latent impressions remain on the contact surface after it is touched. The condition of the surface, e.g., if it is shiny or porous, affects how much of the sweat remains on the surface. Environmental factors such as heat and humidity also influence how long the latent print will remain.

Latent prints are left by everyone on almost every kind of surface. Virtually anytime an object is touched by the body, it retains some of the body's sweat. In the case of finger and palm images, these can form a unique combination of ridges, ridge endings, bifurcations, core and delta locations, and other image characteristics.

For a simple exhibit of a latent print, take a clear, colorless glass and wipe the exterior surface to remove any foreign material. Put some water into the glass. Next, hold the glass of water and take a drink. Put the glass down and release it from your hand. Look at the glass. The images that you see on the glass are latent prints.

Fingerprints have been compared to topographical maps. The contour lines of the maps are similar to the friction ridges of fingerprints, which consist of ridge endings, bifurcations, and dots. They generate a flow that can be identified as a pattern. They do not appreciably change over time.[5] Unlike contour lines, however, friction ridges remain relatively uniform in their spatial distances and are rarely featureless. In contrast, the contour lines on a topographical map appear more closely together to indicate a sharp change in elevation, and relatively large spaces between lines indicate that the surface has only a gradual slope.

The finger image shown in Figure 3.4 is representative of the millions of fingerprint images on file. The image contains a great amount of information that contributes to the uniqueness of the fingerprint image, particularly to someone trained to look for it. For example, the friction ridges flow around a center area. If this were a topographical map, it would be interpreted as a mountain or hill. The point at which the ridges form would be the top of that hill. The change in elevation is constant and the ridges are uniformly distant from each other. The white areas are creases or scars. The introduction of scars does not negate the value of the fingerprint image. In some instances, it might even aid in the identification, depending on the size and location of the scar.

3.5.2 PROVEN UNIQUENESS?

Can it be proved that no two finger images are the same? To do that would require that every fingerprint be collected and compared. Each of the more than six billion persons on this planet, most of whom have ten fingers, would

---

[5] The fingerprint may slightly expand or contract with age and weight, or may become scarred.

Figure 3.4
Finger Image

have to be fingerprinted. Those prints would build a database of approximately 60 billion images, which would then have to be searched by the ten fingers of each of the six billion people. In AFIS parlance, this is called a self-search, i.e., a portion of the database is searched against the rest of the database until the entire database has been searched against itself.

There are instances in which a person has been fingerprinted more than once and the identification is missed on a subsequent search, perhaps because of a poor-quality set of images on the database, poor-quality inked impressions, or inaccurate data entry. When these records are found, the images are reviewed by a print examiner. If the different records are of the same individual, the records are consolidated into one record, usually the one with the earliest state identification (SID) number. There are also instances in which an identification is made on an individual whose finger images match the inquiry card, but the name (or some other characteristic) does not match. What is the true name of the subject? The identification agency can only report on the information it has on file.

Large identification agencies may initiate a self-search of the database once the system is fully operational or when major improvements to the system have occurred, such as the installation of more accurate matchers (which house extracted image characteristics) that will match minutiae with a higher level of precision, or improvements to the coders (which extract features from finger images) that will more accurately find the minutiae in the finger image. For example, a few years ago a large state identification agency installed new coders and new matchers, and systematically began to undertake a self-search. In searching the two index fingers of these five million records, the agency uncovered hundreds of records that had to be consolidated, some with more than ten entries for the same person. In all of those searches, however, there was not one instance in which two different persons had identical finger images. Five million records may be much fewer than six billion, but it is a good representative sample and a good test. So to the question "Can it be scientifically proved?" the response is "Not in the immediate future." But there are other indicators.

AFIS systems have been around for over 20 years. Their matchers have compared millions of finger images. The FBI has 46 million records yet has not found any case where an identical image belongs to two different people. In 1999, the Latent Print Section of the FBI sent latent prints to several state identification agencies asking for a latent print search against the state database. There were no finger images identified that did not belong to the target.

3.5.3 IMAGE QUALITY

Tenprint applications require an image with detail sufficient for extracting the image feature characteristics of minutiae, direction of ridge flow, patterns, etc. Finger images may be categorized as missing, bandaged, poor quality, fair quality, or good quality. A missing finger means that the finger could not be printed, most probably because it had been amputated. Unlike missing fingers, bandaged fingers may appear on some tenprint records of the subject and not on others. If a person was printed as part of a job application and one finger was bandaged, it would be noted on the record. If the same person was fingerprinted later with the bandage removed, the record would be updated with the image from the previously bandaged finger. The newly captured image would become part of the person's image record, resulting in a complete set of ten rolled images. Because some AFIS systems search on multiple image records for the same person, this person may have a set of 19 images: nine from the first fingerprinting and ten from the second.

Following the direction of the identification agency managers, AFIS coders categorize fingerprint images as poor, fair, or good quality. These categories are generally determined by the number of minutiae extracted from a finger image. A poor-quality image may initiate a request to re-roll the subject, if possible. Any subsequent records of that person would be checked for improved quality of the images. Fair-quality images have image detail sufficient for identification but should be replaced with good-quality images in the future if possible. Good-quality images meet or exceed the standard for image quality. There is clear ridge detail and flow, and a large number of minutiae.

If an inked print is taken with careful attention to detail, using either a properly maintained livescan machine or a standard printer's ink and approved tenprint card stock, the images will be clear, assuming no dermatological problems. A great amount of detail will be captured and will be available for subsequent coding and comparison. A good capture includes three levels of ridge details:[6]

- Level 1 detail includes the general ridge flow and pattern configuration. Level 1 detail is not sufficient for individualization but can be used for exclusion. It may include information enabling orientation, core and delta location, and distinction of finger versus palm.
- Level 2 detail includes formations, defined as a ridge ending, bifurcation, dot, or combinations thereof. The information of Level 2 detail enables individualization.
- Level 3 detail includes all dimensional attributes of a ridge, such as ridge path deviation, width, shape, pores, edge contour, incipient ridges, breaks, creases, scars, and other permanent details.

The characteristics of an ideal image for an AFIS search are the same as in pre-AFIS days. It should be a clear image, rolled from one nail edge to the other, using even pressure that results in an image in which the ridge shapes, deviations, and pore locations can be distinguished. The advantage with AFIS is that features such as ridge endings, bifurcations, and ridge flows can be extracted electronically by a coder in just a few seconds. These same features can be extracted identically time after time.

AFIS systems can be used to search multiple fingers. For tenprint identification purposes, this may be accomplished by using two fingers. In most instances, the information from the patterns of all ten fingers and two finger images is sufficient for identification. In addition to the images, other biographical information, such as sex, may be used to reduce the need to search the entire database. Using two fingers does more than just double the changes of making an identification. Since each of the finger images is coded and is launched in a separate search, the results should come back with the target as the first, and perhaps, only candidate. The synergy of two fingers from the same individual supports the opportunities for identification. If all finger images on file had even clear level 2 detail this would certainly happen.

In tenprint processing, some AFIS systems use images of the two index fingers and some use the two thumbs. There are at least two arguments for using thumbs. The first is that the thumbs offer more surface area than the index finger, producing a larger print image. The second argument is that if the search on thumbs produces no identification, the record can be sent to the Integrated Automated Fingerprint Identification System (IAFIS) or another

---

[6] See Ed German's remarks on this at http://onin.com/fp/level123.html.

AFIS system where it can be searched against the database of index fingers. As a result, a search for the record would have been run on both the thumbs and the index fingers to obtain an identification.

One of the selling points of AFIS is accuracy. Its vendors claim a high degree of accuracy under certain conditions, which include good-quality inked impressions on the database and good-quality impressions on the inquiry. An accuracy rate in excess of 99% is expected for tenprint applications.

3.6 CLASSIFICATION SYSTEMS

For more than 100 years, fingerprint images were classified by the rules of the Henry System or the American System. The introduction of AFIS technology, however, virtually eliminated the need for fingerprint examiners to master either of these two principal systems. Identification agencies no longer invest enormous sums in training and certifying tenprint examiners in the most intricate rules for classifying finger images. Classes on the importance of these classification systems are still provided to staff, but their usefulness in everyday operations is on the decline.

3.6.1 THE NCIC SYSTEM

One system that does remain in active use is the classification system used by the National Crime Information Center (NCIC). Well known to officers who do not have immediate access to AFIS, the NCIC rules classify each finger of a tenprint record using a combination of patterns, ridge counts, and whorl tracing.

NCIC does not search on finger images. Instead, NCIC reports on finger image descriptors contained in its classification system. There is no requirement for a digital camera, coder, or matcher. By using this relatively simple classification system, officers without immediate access to an AFIS can query NCIC to see if their subject has a classification pattern of someone wanted in another state. NCIC is used to tentatively identify or eliminate possible wanted suspects or missing persons.

NCIC uses Fingerprint Classification (FPC) field codes to represent the fingerprint image characteristics.[7] The fingerprint class is provided on two lines, with the first line representing the right hand and the second line the left hand. See Table 3.1 for a list of these field codes. In addition to the fingerprint class, there are codes for the pattern class, which are presented in Table 3.2. These two tables are not presented for the reader to become proficient in finger-

---

[7] See http://www.leds.state.or.us/resources/ncic_2000/ncic_2000_code_manual.htm.

Pattern Type	Pattern Subgroup	FPC Class
Arch	Plain arch	AA
	Tented arch	TT
Loop	Radial loop	Two numeric characters determined by actual ridge count plus 50
	Ulnar loop	Two numeric characters less than 50
Whorl	Plain whorl	
	Inner	PI
	Meeting	PM
	Outer	PO
	Central pocket loop whorl	
	Inner	CI
	Meeting	CM
	Outer	CO
	Double loop whorl	
	Inner	DI
	Meeting	DM
	Outer	DO
	Accidental whorl	
	Inner	XI
	Meeting	XM
	Outer	XO
Complete scar		SR
Mutilated pattern		
Missing/amputated finger		XX

Table 3.1

Fingerprint Classification (FPC) Field Codes for Fingerprint Class

Pattern Type	FPC Class
Arch	AU
Loop, left slant	LS
Loop, right slant	RS
Whorl	WU
Complete scar/mutilated pattern	SR
Missing/amputated finger	XX
Unable to classify	UC
Unable to print (e.g., bandaged)	UP

Table 3.2

Fingerprint Classification (FPC) Field Codes for Pattern Class

print and pattern classification using the FPC rules. Rather, they are intended to demonstrate (1) how complex fingerprint classification can be, with descriptors such as an inner central pocket loop whorl (CI), and (2) that even when the image cannot be directly transmitted, there exists an alternative method of obtaining information from another agency based on finger image information. This method might be used by a police department that does not have an electronic link to the state identification bureau but that has access to NCIC. The subject can be inked, the images coded according to NCIC rules, and the descriptors, along with other arrest information, sent through NCIC to the Interstate Identification Index (III).

3.6.2 THE HENRY AND AMERICAN CLASSIFICATION SYSTEMS

While the Henry and American Classification Systems have a great deal in common, they are also quite different. The majority of criminal justice identification agencies used the Henry System; only the state of New York used the American System.

The Henry System was designed by Sir Edward Henry. While working for the Indian Civil Service in the late 1800s, he recorded the finger images of all criminals, including all ten fingers, a procedure unique at the time. He developed a classification system, composed of 1,024 primary classifications, that assigned each of the ten fingers a unique number, beginning with the right thumb as finger 1 to the right little finger as finger number 5. The left thumb was finger number 6, through to the left little finger, finger number 10 (see Table 3.3).

In the primary classification of the Henry System, a whorl assumed the value of the finger in which it appeared. The even-numbered fingers were designated as numerators and received a value of the whorl value plus one. The odd-numbered fingers were designated as the denominator and also received a value of the whorl value plus one. If there was no whorl in any of the ten finger impressions, the primary classification would be 1 in the numerator and 1 in the denominator, i.e., the primary classification would be 1 over 1.

In addition to this primary classification, there were secondary classifications for the index finger of each hand. Using the pattern types (radial loop, arch, tented arch, ulnar loop), a capital letter would be assigned to the index finger of each hand, e.g., T for tented arch. A secondary classification was also developed for impressions with a radial loop, arch, or tented arch for any finger except the index finder. This was known as the small letter group of the secondary classification. Finally, there was a subsecondary classification, also referred to as the grouping of loops and whorls, which coded the ridge of the loops and ridge tracings of whorls in the index, middle, and ring fingers.

Table 3.3

Primary Values for the Henry Classification System

Finger number	1	2	3	4	5
Primary value	16	16	8	8	4
Finger number	6	7	8	9	10
Primary value	4	2	2	1	1

The American System was developed by Captain James Parke and was used primarily within the state of New York. It was a departure from the traditional Henry System (and, interestingly, was not named after its chief proponent) by providing a different score for each finger that was repeated on each hand. While the Henry System of classification used values derived from the odd/even finger numbers, the American Classification System was based on the hand. For example, in the American System, the right thumb (an odd-numbered finger) was assigned an initial value of 16, as was the left thumb, finger number 6. (See Table 3.4.) In comparison, under the Henry System, finger number 1 (the right thumb) has a primary value of 16, while the left thumb, finger number 6, has a value of 4.

Finger number	1	2	3	4	5
American value	16	8	4	2	1
Finger number	6	7	8	9	10
American value	16	8	4	2	1

Table 3.4

Primary Values for the American Classification System

Why were there two different classification systems? An excerpt from a presentation prepared by the New York State Division of Criminal Justice Services to mark the 100th anniversary of fingerprints reports the following:

> The first and most obvious problem was storage. The Henry System called for fingerprints to be recorded on large paper sheets called "slips." These slips were filed flat on shelves or in pigeon holes, which consumed a great deal of space. . . . This prompted Parke to propose developing a fingerprint form of stiff cardboard and of a less awkward size which could be filed upright in drawers as the Bertillon cards were. Superintendent Collins denied his suggestion. . . .
>
> The second problem with the English [Henry] System was their method of dividing fingerprint records into primary groups. Henry's method of attaching values to each of the ten fingers and then accruing those values for any finger in which a whorl pattern appeared used first the even and then the odd numbered digits, which was unnecessarily complex.
>
> What Parke proposed was to calculate the primary in a similar way, but using the patterns as they appeared in sequence on the fingerprint form—right hand first, then left hand.
>
> A person with the fingerprint patterns Loop, Loop, Arch, Whorl, Loop in the right hand and Whorl, Loop, Whorl, Loop, Loop in the left hand would, under Parke's system, have a primary classification of 3 over 21, whereas the same person, under the Henry System, would have a primary of 15 over 1. The only time a Henry

Primary would match one of Parke's was when whorls appeared in all ten fingers (32/32), or in none (1/1).[8]

3.6.3 FILING SYSTEMS

The classification process used determined where the card would be physically filed, with similarly classified cards housed together. The SID number provided a second control on the card, but the cards were filed based completely on classification. Identification sections would have at least two fingerprint files: a master fingerprint file and a secondary file. The master file held one tenprint card per individual. Usually this was the first or original tenprint card, the card to which the SID number was assigned. If the subject was subsequently fingerprinted, such as due to a re-arrest, that card would end up in the secondary file.

Because the master fingerprint file contained only one tenprint record per individual, the files were uniform and relatively easy to work with. The SID number indicated the location of the card in the secondary file, i.e., in the manual filing systems, the tenprint cards were filed by classification. In the semi-automated systems, the tenprint cards could be filed by SID number. The secondary file might have the same numbering sequence but required more space. These files contained not only subsequent tenprint cards but also other information such as mug shots and dispositions.

As the SID numbers were assigned, special number ranges might be reserved for special uses, such as for juveniles. Juveniles arrested for fingerprintable offenses have a higher percentage of records that are subsequently sealed by court order. Assigning these records to a unique location made it easier to find and remove the physical card as well as the electronic Rap Sheet.

Fingerprint cards were stored in various types of filing cabinets (see Fig. 3.5), including specialized rotary files that would move a tray of cards into a horizontal position for easier access. Physical cards required tremendous accountability for the location of the card. If the card was removed from the file, a marker would be inserted in its place. This marker, usually of a similar paper stock, documented who took the card, where it was, and when it would return. The cards themselves, being a paper product, were subject to fire, heat, humidity, and other environmental factors. They often became torn and worn.

Imagine clerical staff spending a career in this environment. Each staff member had to learn how to find a particular card in the maze of filing cabinets. They would follow certain procedures for card retrieval and were

---

[8] From "Origins of the New York State Bureau of Identification," by Michael Harling, http://www.correctionhistory.org/html/chronicl/dcjs/html/nyidbur3.html.

Figure 3.5

Typical Fingerprint Card Storage Cabinets

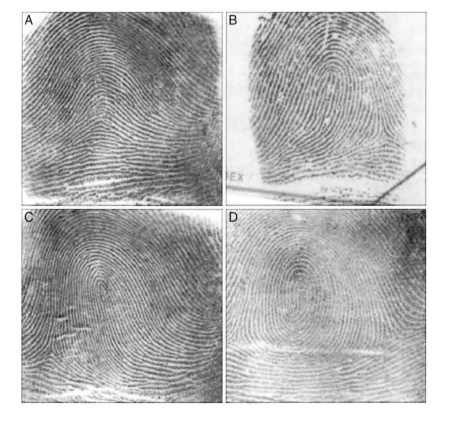

Figure 3.6

AFIS Pattern Types: (A) Arch; (B) Left Slant Loop; (C) Right Slant Loop; (D) Whorl

accountable for the physical return of the card to the proper location. After a successful apprenticeship, perhaps staff would be trained as fingerprint classifiers, learning all the rules of the Henry or American System.

AFIS systems changed all of this. With AFIS, pattern recognition software, as well as examiners, classifies images by one of four pattern types (whorl, arch, right slant loop, left slant loop (See Figure 3.6)) instead of by the Henry or American fingerprint classification rules. There are no secondary classifications; there are no complicated rules. AFIS coders can determine both the pattern type and minutiae placement.

In addition, with AFIS systems, fingerprint cards may or may not physically exist. If they do exist, they may be retained at an off-site facility. The images from the electronic cards can be displayed on a screen or printed onto card stock. AFIS examiners no longer have to wait for a physical tenprint card; the card information is as near as a computer terminal connected to the AFIS. The cards cannot be misfiled or subjected to deterioration due to the heat and humidity found in an office building. The information can be virtually retrieved, reviewed, and returned. There is no wasted paper and no file cabinets that must be searched through taking up space. This is one of the major advantages of AFIS.[9]

---

[9] For additional information on fingerprints, see the Onin web site, maintained by Ed German. Located at http://www.onin.com, it is an authoritative source of fingerprint information. See also the book by David R. Ashbaugh entitled *Quantitative–Qualitative Friction Ridge Analysis*.

CHAPTER 4

AFIS SUMMARY—
HOW THE SYSTEM WORKS

This chapter provides an overview of how Automated Fingerprint Identification Systems work through the interaction of various processing and databases. The chapter also notes some of the differences in tenprint versus latent print processing. Latent print processing includes not only a search of the latent print against the latent cognizant database, but also the search of new latent cognizant records against the unsolved latents. If desirable, an unsolved latent print can be searched against to the unsolved latents to identify a serial offender, if that person's identity is unknown. Also noted in this chapter are some of the changes to the identification business model that AFIS has introduced.

4.1 DATABASES

Identification systems may contain databases of one, two, three, or more records. Examples of these databases include the tenprint database, which contains information on two fingers; the latent cognizant database, which contains information on all ten fingers; and the unsolved latent database, which is the repository for latent print images not identified on AFIS. The tenprint and latent cognizant databases may contain millions of records, while the unsolved latent database may contain hundreds of thousands of records. Each database may be further segmented into an image, a matcher, and possibly an alpha database. Figure 4.1 shows an illustration of these databases.

The Computerized Criminal History (CCH) database contains information about the subject's activity for fingerprintable events. Although the term criminal history implies that only criminal activity is recorded, this is not always the case; any fingerprintable event is recorded in this database. For example, job applicants who have been fingerprinted as part of a background check have a history stored in this database. That history, or rap sheet, includes the date when the person was fingerprinted, the person's name and other biographical information, aliases, if any, and other identification information.

Figure 4.1
AFIS Databases

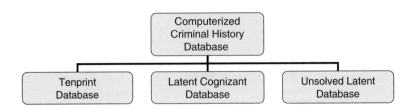

Why are there so many different databases? This depends on the purpose of the AFIS, advances in technology, cost, size of the database, etc. AFIS systems used exclusively in civil applications, such as for social services benefits, only need a one-record database. In this type of use, as people become eligible for benefits, they are enrolled in the database, which may contain images of only the two index fingers or the two thumbs. This type of search is fairly straightforward.

A brief note on the identification process is in order. Identification systems match finger image characteristics, not persons. When a person is arrested and fingerprinted, an AFIS search is conducted. If there is no match based on the finger image characteristics stored in the database (see Fig. 4.2), the record is assigned a state identification (SID) number. The CCH for the subject would include his or her name as it appears on the tenprint record or as it appears in the On-Line Booking System (OLBS), a computerized method of collecting and forwarding arrest history and information.

If the same person is arrested again but presents a different name, the CCH will return an identification with a criminal history that shows another name. That is, the finger images of the person now in custody match a person with another name, which means that both names belong to the same person. The arresting agency will have to determine which identity, if either, is correct. In the past, clever recidivists could use this ploy with some success, since not all of the criminal history searches were fingerprint based. This loophole is quickly closing as AFIS systems become more powerful and connected.

The tenprint (TPid), or identification, database contains the image record characteristics that are used for searching. There may be the records from two index fingers, the two thumbs, or other combinations. Some AFIS systems combine the index fingers and thumbs in their tenprint searches. The latent cognizant (TPlc), or criminal, database contains the finger image characteristics of all ten fingers. The image captures as much image characteristic information as possible, such as that contained in the nail-to-nail roll. The quality of these ten images is important, since they are associated with arrestees who may not be cooperative at the time the images are taken. For searching latent prints found at a crime scene, the need for a database that contains all ten images, of superior image quality, in a nail-to-nail roll, is readily apparent.

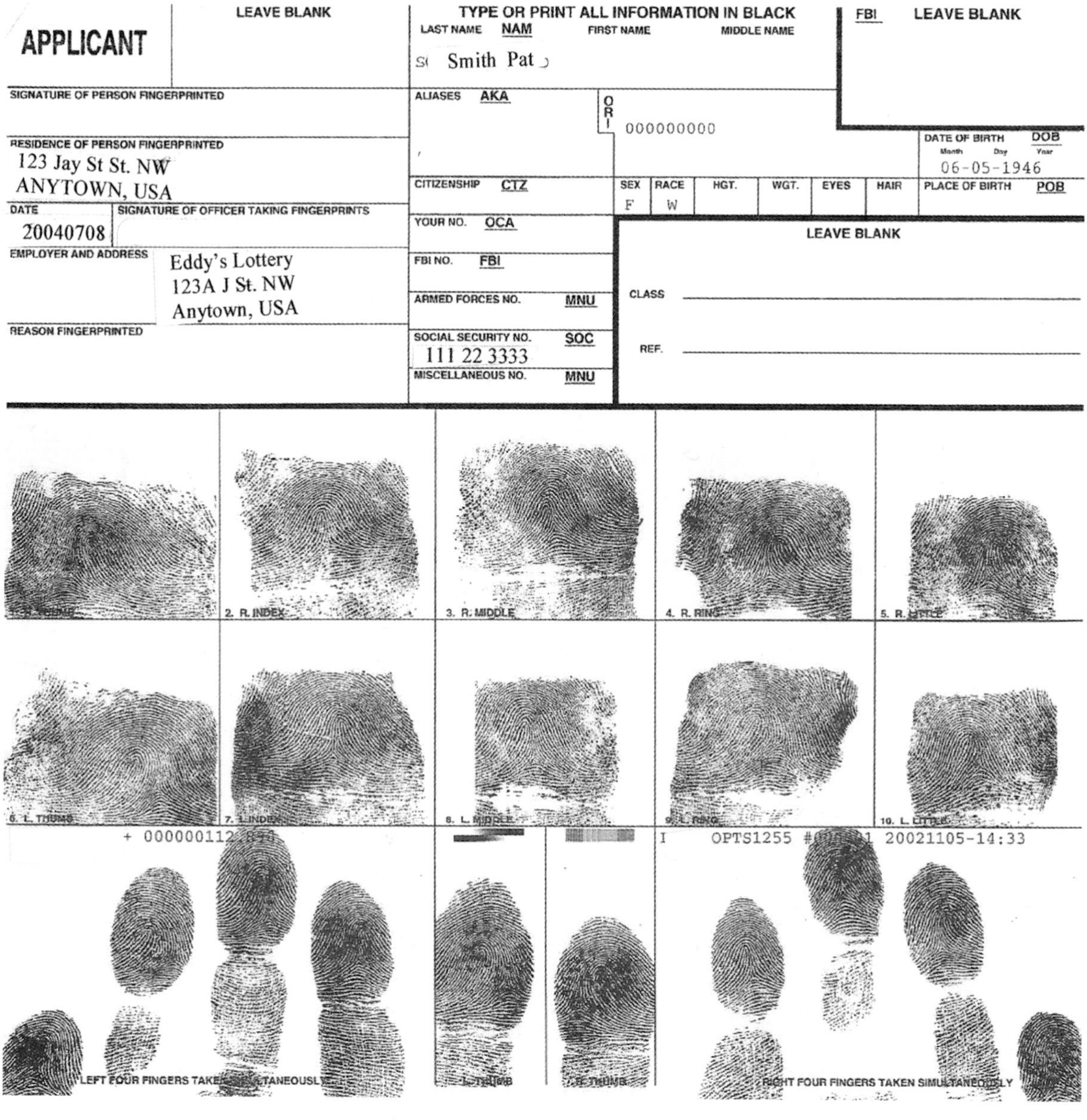
APPLICANT

LEAVE BLANK

TYPE OR PRINT ALL INFORMATION IN BLACK

LAST NAME NAM FIRST NAME MIDDLE NAME

Smith Pat

FBI LEAVE BLANK

SIGNATURE OF PERSON FINGERPRINTED

ALIASES AKA

ORI 000000000

RESIDENCE OF PERSON FINGERPRINTED

123 Jay St St. NW
ANYTOWN, USA

DATE OF BIRTH DOB Month Day Year 06-05-1946

CITIZENSHIP CTZ

SEX F | RACE W | HGT. | WGT. | EYES | HAIR | PLACE OF BIRTH POB

DATE 20040708

SIGNATURE OF OFFICER TAKING FINGERPRINTS

YOUR NO. OCA

LEAVE BLANK

EMPLOYER AND ADDRESS

Eddy's Lottery
123A J St. NW
Anytown, USA

FBI NO. FBI

ARMED FORCES NO. MNU

CLASS

REASON FINGERPRINTED

SOCIAL SECURITY NO. SOC 111 22 3333

REF.

MISCELLANEOUS NO. MNU

1. R. THUMB | 2. R. INDEX | 3. R. MIDDLE | 4. R. RING | 5. R. LITTLE

6. L. THUMB | 7. L. INDEX | 8. L. MIDDLE | 9. L. RING | 10. L. LITTLE

OPTS1255 20021105-14:33

LEFT FOUR FINGERS TAKEN SIMULTANEOUSLY | L. THUMB | R. THUMB | RIGHT FOUR FINGERS TAKEN SIMULTANEOUSLY

Figure 4.2
Fingerprint Card Data

With advances in technology, more rapid matcher speed, and relatively inexpensive storage, some vendors can now offer a single database that can be used for both civil and criminal applications. Using a "load balancing" algorithm, this type of AFIS can perform both tenprint and latent print searches in a designated priority or sequence. Other vendors prefer to separate their criminal and civil databases, and use a "binning" structure. The "binning" allows for a more rapid search of a database by limiting the search to only one segment of the database at a time, e.g., males with a whorl pattern on finger number 2.

Each system contains a minutiae database of these images. It is this minutiae database that is actually searched by the AFIS matcher. It includes finger image characteristics such as the minutiae location, ridge flow direction, and distance between minutiae points. Some systems also include ridge information. The extracted minutiae, direction of ridge flow, etc., of the submitted finger images are compared or matched against the records in the database of minutiae records.

Large state and federal agencies receive thousands of search requests every day. Some of these inquiries are for criminal processing as the result of an arrest; others are for civil processing, such as an application for a job, permit, or license. All of these submitted records are searched against the tenprint database. If a match occurs, the inquirer is sent the SID number and the criminal history. If there is no record matching the images in the tenprint file, a new SID number is assigned, the images are added to that file, and the inquirer is so advised. If the submission was related to a criminal inquiry, the images would also be uploaded to the latent cognizant (criminal) file.

In addition to the database used for known civil applicants and the criminal file, law enforcement agencies using AFIS also have an unsolved latent file. The unsolved file contains records from criminal cases for which no identification has been made following a latent print search. The expectation is that either the individual has never been enrolled in the AFIS database and consequently could not be identified, or the individual is in the database, but because of the low quality of the tenprint record and/or the latent prints, no identification could be made. At some time in the future, the image/minutiae on the database may be updated and a tenprint to unsolved latent search may be initiated with better success in making an identification. Or the matchers might be upgraded, resulting in increased accuracy in selecting candidates following a search.

4.2 PROCESSING OVERVIEW

4.2.1 TENPRINT

Consider the following simplified generic description of an arrest identification process. The process begins at a local police agency when an individual is arrested. The appropriate arrest information is entered into the local agency's booking system; fingerprints are taken by ink and roll or, more increasingly, are electronically captured on FBI-certified equipment. The proper finger placement and the fingerprint image quality are checked. The palms of each hand of the subject are placed on the platen of the livescan machine and those images are captured. Digital mug shots may be taken, along with descriptions of scars, marks, and tattoos (SMT), and entered into the system. If necessary, corrections are made. The images and biographic data can be mailed, faxed, or sent electronically to the state or local identification agency that operates the AFIS system. Because developmental efforts support electronic transmission, and an increasing percentage of arrest transactions are sent electronically, that method is described in this overview.

To send the information about the subject electronically, it must be locally formatted, following state and national standards, into an electronic arrest transaction that consists of the ten rolled finger images and four plain impression fingerprints, mug shots, SMT data, and the individual's arrest and biographic data. This is transmitted over secure data communication networks using secure encryption. A common variant is the secure purchase of a product over the Internet.

If an electronic bridge into AFIS is operational, no fingerprint card is printed at AFIS. Instead, the transaction information will be electronically saved and a temporary process control number (PCN) attached to the transaction. This PCN will be replaced by either an existing SID number if the subject is already in the system or a new SID number if this is the first tenprint record (see Figure 4.3).

The data is checked for completeness and proper format before it is accepted for further processing. If data is missing or incomplete, the image quality is

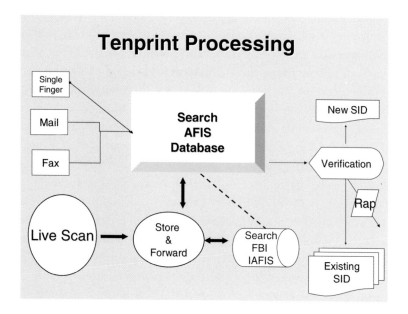

Figure 4.3

Tenprint Processing Overview

unacceptable, or the record is unacceptable, the inquiring agency is instructed to resubmit the record. Correcting the problem may require re-rolling the subject, completing all mandatory fields, retransmission, etc.

The arrest data is separated and sent to the CCH system to initiate the identification process. The individual fingerprints and the plain impressions are displayed on an AFIS workstation screen. A fingerprint technician then performs a number of operations, including validation of finger placement, image quality checking, pattern assignment, and image centering. The arrest transaction is entered into an updated and improved AFIS for searching against the state fingerprint database. Typically the two index fingers are searched, although some agencies may choose two other fingers, such as thumbs, or four fingers (index and thumbs) to improve the likelihood of making an identification.

The minutiae of the finger image characteristics are identified by the coder and the search is initiated. Possible matching images are presented on the computer screen next to the submitted image in a side-by-side format, as seen in Figure 4.4.

Candidates produced by AFIS may be confirmed by a verification/validation process. State identification results are electronically returned to the local police agency, including any criminal history and, if available, a mug shot. The rap sheets are mailed to those agencies not electronically connected to the AFIS.

In the past, arrest transactions were sent by mail to the FBI's Integrated Automated Fingerprint Identification System (IAFIS). It could take weeks to receive a response, and often the subject had long since left the area by the time the response was received. As more agencies adopt National Institute of Standards and Technology (NIST) transmission standards and the FBI transmission specifications, electronic forwarding is quickly becoming the preferred method.

By electronically accessing the IAFIS, local agencies are able to determine if a subject has a criminal history in another state. More importantly, the agency can determine if the subject is currently wanted in another state. Why is this information considered by some to be the most important part of arrest processing? A search of the state database produces a criminal history record for that state only. If this is the first time that the subject has been arrested or fingerprinted in the state, there would be no criminal history on file. It may be that the subject has provided his or her true name and has no criminal past, but a check of the IAFIS and Interstate Identification Index (III) may show that the subject has a record in another state, under a different name, and that there is an outstanding arrest warrant. Without this information the subject might have been released on bail based on only the original arrest. With this new information about the subject's criminal history, he or she will be held until a

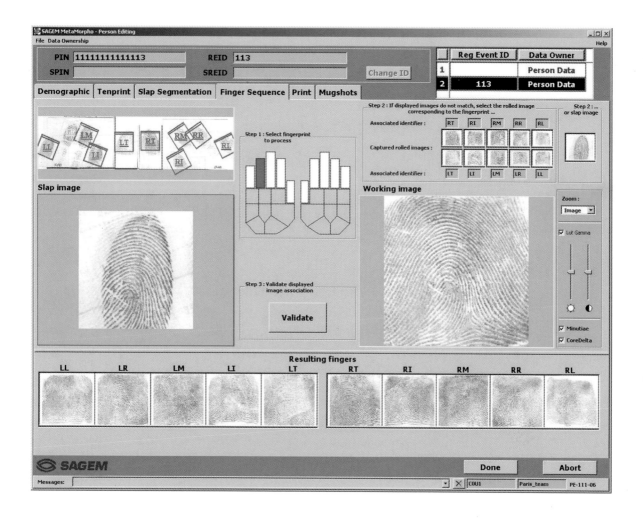

determination is made regarding the warrant from the other state or federal agency.

The increased accuracy of matchers, the improvements of coders, and the faster and less expensive AFIS systems are contributing to the adaptation of the "lights out" approach by many agencies. There is no industry definition of lights out, but it is understood to mean that the approach eliminates human intervention from one or more elements in the identification process. In its most complete application, lights out eliminates all human intervention from finger or palm image capture at the livescan station to the electronic delivery of a rap sheet and mug shot to the inquiring agency.

The transmission to the FBI also may include the individual's mug shots from the arrest portfolio, which will be stored in the III section of the FBI's IAFIS. The mug shots will also be saved on storage media, forming the basis for a mug shot system. In some cases, the agency may elect not to store the images but

Figure 4.4
Side-by-Side Comparison

instead maintain pointers to local agency storage systems for retrieval. SMT data will be kept in a database system and also forwarded to an FBI database.

Both tenprint and latent cognizant databases are used for investigative purposes. Since no paper fingerprint card exists, fingerprint images for each arrest are archived on storage media. A similar scenario takes place for other types of fingerprint submissions, e.g., civil applicant prints and inquiries. Many agencies maintain a separate civil processing unit, which exclusively handles non-criminal requests, many times an ink and roll tenprint card. Unlike criminal processing, in which time is critical, civil processing does not operate on a 24 hours a day, 7 days a week schedule. Also, records arriving for civil processing usually have a fee included to offset the cost to the local and state agencies and the FBI.

Other criminal justice agencies, such as the corrections department, may use the tenprint system to verify the identity of inmates. In this process, finger images of an inmate along with the minutiae of the SID number are compared against the AFIS database, and a bar code label that ties together the inmate record and DNA sample information is produced.

4.2.2 THE LATENT PRINT PROCESS

In the latent print process (see Fig. 4.5 for an overview), latent print cases are entered into the AFIS system at a central site or regional/remote site connected to AFIS.[1] The latent print may have been collected by a Crime Scene Specialist (CSS) who has special training to recognize and capture latent print images, or it may have been collected by a patrol officer who may be less skilled and who may have less equipment. Or the print may have been collected by another local agency and forwarded to the receiving agency for a search against their database. The latent image is evaluated by a trained latent examiner, and a determination is made as to whether the image is "of value," i.e., whether the image has enough identifiable characteristics to make a positive identification. If the image is determined to be of value, a search of the AFIS database is initiated.

The alphanumeric data related to the case is entered into the system. This data includes the case number, originating agency, county or region to search, crime type, the ID number of each latent print, and other information such as sex, pattern type, race, and finger number. Defaults are built into the system to provide a complete database search, known as the "cold search."

The latent fingerprint is manually positioned under either a digital camera or the scanner of a latent input workstation by a latent examiner, and the image

---

[1] This is the typical process. Agency policies and procedures may be different.

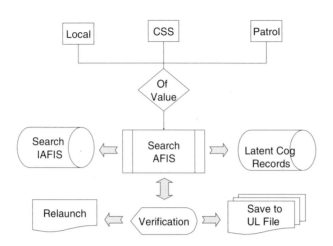

Figure 4.5
Latent Print Processing
Overview

is digitized. The examiner can check for image quality and if not satisfied, re-digitize the image. Next, the examiner, with the help of the coder, identifies and marks each minutia on the image of the fingerprint displayed on the input workstation, selects orientation, and repeats the process with each additional latent print.

The function of the coder is to identify or code the minutiae in the finger image. The ridge endings, bifurcations, and direction provide unique identification points. Intervening ridges between minutiae may also provide unique information. The minutiae points are identified by the coder and displayed on the screen. The examiner may choose to add additional minutiae points not found by the coder, or remove points considered marginal.

After all latents have been entered, the latent examiner checks the work and launches the case. The latent fingerprint is searched by the matchers against a latent cognizant database containing hundreds of thousands or even millions of images. Candidates for a match are made available at a verification workstation at the originating central or remote site and are retrieved for verification. Print images of the candidates are displayed side by side with the image of the latent print. Various functions assist in the verification process, including locked cursor movement and marking verification points. The latent and candidate images may also be sent to a high-quality image printer for an off-screen comparison. As part of their business practice, many agencies require that the identification of a latent print be confirmed by a second latent print examiner. The practices may also require that the identification be made from a comparison of the latent image against the printed fingerprint card.

It must be stressed that AFIS is only a tool used by the latent examiner. It is the latent examiner who determines if the latent image is of value, who selects the search criteria, and who examines the lists of candidates produced by the search. Finally, it is the latent examiner, following years of extensive training and experience, who makes the identification.

For latent print searching, the AFIS system eliminates the need to look at individual tenprint records selected by following the rules of the Henry or American Classification System. Instead of selecting tenprint candidates based on the fingerprint classification of the latent print, searching the CCH for a list of suitable candidates, and calling for and examining individual tenprint cards, AFIS does the sort. For latent print examiners, the AFIS system provided a quantum leap in latent print identification. Before AFIS, many latent print examiners had only suspect or elimination prints to compare against the latent print found at the crime scene. Larger police agencies may have had a filing cabinet of tenprint records of known offenders, classified by either the Henry or the American Classification System, and perhaps further divided by type of crime and location, i.e., burglary in midtown. If there was no suspect prints to compare, the latent print examiner would classify the latent print and check the files that corresponded to that classification. They might also check a file of other latent print images to see if there was a match and if the same unknown individual was still committing crimes. Other systems, such as Kodak's Mira Code and the Computer Assisted Latent Print System (CALPS), were used, but they were all of limited effectiveness and very labor intensive.

The following may be an extreme example, but it illustrates the difficulties of latent print identification before the advent of AFIS technology. A large metropolitan city was threatened by a serial killer, who was randomly shooting, and sometimes murdering, citizens. A latent print found at one of these murders was examined, and enough ridge detail was present to identify classification, pattern, and ridge count. Examiners queried the CCH for a list of matching records, with some addition and elimination on the number of ridges. A list of approximately 15,000 candidates was returned. The tenprint cards for all 15,000 were pulled, examined, and returned. The process took months. Today that same process, searching a much larger database, could be completed in minutes.

If a latent search results in no candidate or no match, the search parameters can be changed and the database searched again. For example, if the first attempt searched only the records of persons charged within a particular county, a second search, or relaunch, could include records from adjacent counties, all counties within a region, or within the entire state.

Latent examiners may perform as many individual searches as necessary. A latent case can have as many as 25 individual lifts, each of which may be launched (i.e., the minutiae are searched against the minutiae database) three times before being entered into the unsolved latent file. A search filtered by parameters such as county, sex, or crime group will search the matchers in times ranging from a few seconds to a few minutes. A cold search, i.e., a search without any parameters will take slightly longer.

Beginning in 1999, latent examiners could have their cases searched against the FBI's database with the implementation of the Remote Fingerprint Editing Software (RFES) terminal linking the offices with the FBI. The purpose of the RFES is to provide the fingerprint identification community with a software package that enables fingerprint examiners to perform immediate remote searches against the FBI's IAFIS on a 24/7 basis. This capability makes RFES an important aid in fighting crime on both the statewide and the national level. RFES provides access to 46 million fingerprint records (or 460 million fingerprint images) contributed to the FBI from states across the country.[2]

A parallel FBI development, the Universal Latent Workstation (ULW), allows latent print examiners to also search IAFIS as well as other databases. ULW creates a native feature set for vendors and IAFIS to allow searches from a single encoding. ULW translates the native search record (provided in ANSI/NIST format) into an IAFIS search, adds in the ridge counts, and allows edits of the record before submission. ULW requires e-mail connectivity to the Criminal Justice Information Services (CJIS) wide area network (WAN).[3]

4.2.3 UNSOLVED LATENT SEARCH

Not every latent print search will result in identification. While actual figures may vary, the rule of thumb is that only 10–15% of cases and 2–3% of latent print searches will result in an identification. Many latent print examiners will search the latent print more than one time to allow for differences in image capture, manual minutia placement, or other variables. After a reasonable number of additional searches, or relaunches, the examiner either deletes the AFIS case or saves the latent print information into the unsolved latent (UL) file.

The UL file, which is always smaller than the tenprint database, contains case information, case images(s), and minutiae. When a new tenprint inquiry is made, the two index fingers are searched against the tenprint file, and all ten fingers can be searched against the UL file. If there is enough minutiae match to produce a candidate, the latent print case will be marked for review by the examiner.

The exact details of this process may vary from agency to agency and vendor to vendor. Some systems only search new tenprint records, since the latent print has already been searched against the existing tenprint records in the database.

---

[2] http://www.fbi.gov/hq/cjisd/rfes.pdf.
[3] http://www.fbi.gov/hq/cjisd/ulw.htm.

Some search all tenprint records, with the notion that although the record and images already exist in the database, the newer images may differ slightly in terms of clarity, distortion, number of minutiae, etc. These new images may produce a minutiae match where none existed before.

4.2.4 LATENT/LATENT SEARCH

If no identification is made on the LT/TP searches, the latent print examiner still has other search options available. The latent print examiner could initiate a new search in which the unknown latent print is searched against a database of unknown latent prints. Also referred to as unsolved to unsolved searches, the latent/latent (LT/LT) searches provide an opportunity to determine if crimes are being committed by the same person, enough if the person remains unidentified.

Latent print examiners can initiate a LT/LT search, view the candidates and determine if one or more of the candidates matches the searched latent print. If there is a match, the examiner can notify the inquiring agency that another agency, or investigator within the same agency, is working on a case in which matching latent prints were found. This collaboration can ultimately lead to an identification and arrest.

4.3 WHY AFIS SYSTEMS WORK

The question of why AFIS systems work can be answered in several ways. They work because of the interaction of information systems, identification systems and subsystems, communication linkages, etc. They also work because of the dedication of agency administrators, researchers, programmers, and vendors, and because of the need for increased speed on information and the infusion of millions of dollars in federal funds.

Whereas a mailed fingerprint card was considered the fastest form of identification just a few years ago, now dedicated high-speed communication lines link computers to computers and confirm (or deny) identifications within minutes. The stereotypic rolling of an inked finger onto a tenprint card has been replaced with digital capture devices (livescan; see Fig. 4.6) that eliminate ink, eliminate paper, add mug shots and palm prints, and reduce errors. Concurrent advances of latent (crime scene) identification have led to the arrest of many criminals who in the past would never have been identified.

AFIS systems are attractive to agency managers because much of the clerical work previously performed, such as retrieving and classifying fingerprint cards, storing them in file cabinets, and looking for a misplaced or misfiled card, has

Figure 4.6
Livescan Station

either been reduced or eliminated. As in many other industries, the introduction of technology has reduced the number of employees who handle routine jobs. The personnel replaced by technology are retrained for other tasks, are removed from the workforce, or retire. These technologies also bring new opportunities for skilled workers such as computer programmers, managers, and program and policy analysts.

Consider the move of the FBI CJIS Division from Washington, DC to new facilities in West Virginia. With the introduction of IAFIS, there was no longer the need for the same staffing level for fingerprint cards as in the past. Also, many staff were reluctant to leave the Washington, DC area for West Virginia. Some chose to resign or transfer to another federal agency. Some retired. Some moved to West Virginia. And in West Virginia new opportunities arose for managers, administrators, and examiners.

Many agencies embrace the new technology as a way of replacing skilled personnel with the combination of a machine and less skilled personnel. Or put another way, the skill required to take impressions on a livescan machine, enter the data, and transmit the record information is far less than the skill required of a fingerprint classifier. Large cities can save millions of dollars when the booking process is completed by non-sworn personnel. If sworn personnel are used, supervisors can reduce the amount of overtime required by assigning prisoner booking to the next available officer instead of holding a sworn officer past the end of shift. The arresting officer's responsibility ends at the booking station, allowing this highly skilled officer to return to the street.

This move to automation, however, is not without its critics. Mixing civilian staff with sworn staff to perform nearly identical functions can create uneasiness. The sworn personnel may worry about their future, and the civilians may ask why their salary and benefits are so much lower than the sworn person right next to them doing the same job.

The move from paper to computers also requires a different skill set. Passwords, user codes, keyboards, and directories have replaced keys, pencils, and reticles. Achy muscles from standing too long at the file cabinets have been replaced by carpel tunnel syndrome from too much typing on a keyboard.

The key to the success of the AFIS system is the initial impression. A good nail-to-nail roll as seen in Figure 4.7 can contain over 100 minutiae points. These are the minutiae that are used in tenprint searches. These are also the minutiae that will be matched in a latent print search. Without the capture of as many minutiae as possible, AFIS cannot reach its potential.

4.4 WHY ARE SOME IDENTIFICATIONS MISSED?

A question that is occasionally (and now rarely) asked by administrators is why did their AFIS miss an identification that was made on another AFIS, possibly IAFIS? There are several possible explanations, most of which are the result of human error. The most common reason for a missed identification is that the image and minutiae on the local AFIS were of poor quality. This poor quality

Figure 4.7
Nail-to-Nail Roll and Plain Impression

Before AFIS	AFIS
Finger classification	Coder identifies minutiae
Fingerprint cards	Images on RAID storage
Magnifying glass	High-resolution monitors
Manual or semiautomated search	Fully automated search
Photo, mail, laser fax	Livescan
Response in hours, days	Images on RAID Storage
	Response in minutes

Table 4.1

AFIS Changed the Identification Business Model

is usually the result of careless or inattentive image capture by the booking officer or technician, resulting in reduced opportunities for identification.

Many forensic databases are populated with inked tenprint records that were converted at a pixel resolution of 500 pixels per inch (ppi). Newer conversions, at 1,000 ppi or higher, provide more definition and extract more minutiae, even from poor-quality images. If the local database has images at 500 ppi and the AFIS that made the identification has images at 1,000 ppi, the latter has more information to work with and thus a better chance of making the identification.

When subjects were fingerprinted using the ink and roll method, three sets of prints were taken. One card was retained for the local agency, one card was sent to the state identification bureau, and one card was sent to the FBI. The quality of the three cards could be vastly different, which could affect the results of the search. With livescan systems increasingly replacing inked and rolled tenprint cards, however, the subjects are rolled only once. The images that are sent to the state AFIS, IAFIS, and kept in the local repository are all identical.

Occasionally missed identifications are caused by a clerical error made by the booking officer on a critical piece of data, such as the sex of the subject. Because AFIS searches only those records matching the given parameters, this type of error would eliminate the subject from the search entirely. There are other explanations as well, including the software used for matching and coding the minutiae. While each vendor claims that their software is superior, there are differences in their coding and matching algorithms. While unlikely, a poor-quality record on the database might be identified by one vendor but not another. This is more of an exception than the rule.

Yet another consideration is the version of software used in various components of the AFIS system. AFIS systems that were installed 10 years ago probably had the records converted using software that was state-of-the-art at the time, but that has now been replaced with better, more accurate software. Some agencies have reconverted their entire databases using the newer coders and have replaced the older generation of matchers with faster, more accurate matchers. Not only are they more robust, but they are also easier to maintain with less down time.

Speedier responses, more accurate identifications, and cost savings can all be achieved with AFIS. The system, however, is only as good as the people using it.

CHAPTER 5

FROM PRINT TO IDENTIFICATION

This chapter provides further details on both tenprint and latent print processing. In addition, images of equipment used in the capture and search processes, as well as flow diagrams of AFIS processing, are supplied. The images, generously provided by Sagem Morpho, are representative of the generic design and features provided by all AFIS vendors. The chapter concludes with a discussion of the value of accurate and reliable reports, which can be obtained with AFIS systems.

5.1 AFIS COMPONENTS

The goal of the identification process is to make as many identifications as possible with the given resources. In the world of tenprint applications, this process is quantity driven, with the need to respond to a request with a complete criminal history or rap sheet within a limited time period (perhaps 3 hours). For latent print applications, the goal is to make as many identifications as possible by searching millions of records and producing a candidate list that is likely to contain a match to the latent print image.

Tenprint systems usually rely on the minutiae from two index fingers, two thumbs, or a combination of fingers and thumbs. While the system compares the minutiae, the examiner compares the side-by-side finger images on a monitor. Increasingly, AFIS administrators are adopting a "lights out" approach on some or all of the tenprint searches as the systems improve in accuracy. For example, it is now possible to search by using the patterns of all ten finger images, combined with the images of two index fingers and two thumbs, get a candidate with a high matching score, compare that with the results of a name search, and confirm the identification, all without human intervention or review.

In contrast, latent prints found at a crime scene are generally less complete than the nail-to-nail image found in the AFIS database. Criminals usually do not choose to leave all ten finger images (let alone nail-to-nail rolls!) at a crime scene. The search process for latent print applications thus requires a longer time period to complete due to the limited amount of finger image information available to the latent print examiner.

If making identifications is the reason for purchasing an AFIS system, then those operations that will maximize the performance of the AFIS system must be focused on. These performance metrics may include a faster response on routine inquiries, more accuracy in searches, fewer false positives, and fewer false negatives (missed identifications).

Searches may be conducted on databases other than the local AFIS database. A tenprint search of a state database, for example, may be forwarded to the FBI's Integrated Automated Fingerprint Identification System (IAFIS) to determine if there is an FBI number and a criminal history or warrant from another state. These transmissions are possible because of the introduction and adoption of national standards and specifications that describe what can be transmitted, the format for transmission, and the method for transmissions.

5.1.1 PHYSICAL LAYOUT OF AFIS

The diagram shown in Figure 5.1 is representative of a large-scale AFIS system configuration. This figure shows the main components of an AFIS system, including the matchers, coders, random array of independent drives (RAID) storage arrays, and various databases. The Ethernet connects the AFIS system to various input and output devices at other locations. A livescan is an example of an input device. The Ethernet also connects the AFIS system to the Computerized Criminal History (CCH) file.

5.1.2 AFIS HARDWARE

A card scan takes an image of a tenprint card much like a high-quality copier, capturing finger images for searches against the AFIS. The inquiring agency sends the resulting electronic images to the identification bureau (see Fig. 5.2), where they are electronically mated with the subject's biographical information, which was sent through the On-Line Booking System (OLBS). If the record was sent to the bureau by livescan, the scanner station or the quality control (QC) station, which handles records that need special processing, such as searches with missing or bandaged fingers, transposition of hands, or mismatch of pattern information, can be used to ensure the quality of the image. If the image does not meet the bureau's criteria, the bureau notifies the inquiring agency and requests resubmission or re-roll. The arrest and OLBS information remains captured, eliminating the need to re-enter this information.

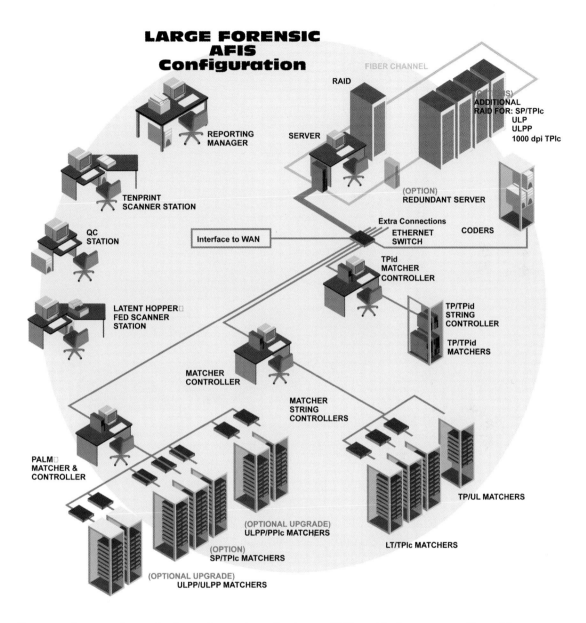

Figure 5.1
Large AFIS Configuration

Latent print examiners also have the option of using an FBI-certified scanner or other image capture device, such as a digital camera, to capture latent print images. This device is referred to as a latent print acquisition station (see Fig. 5.3) since the latent print image is being acquired for use in the AFIS search.

These workstations are networked together and can function as acquisition stations as well as verification stations that can display the results of an AFIS search. It is not unusual for the workstations to have functionality even if the matchers, which store extracted image characteristics, are not available. Sometimes referred to as "local mode," this allows latent print examiners to continue

Figure 5.2
AFIS Tenprint Station

to create latent print cases even if the workstation is not functionally connected to AFIS.

The tenprint and latent print workstations are very similar; they differ not in their hardware but in their software. In many cases, a workstation can be changed from latent print mode to tenprint mode based on the access rights of the user: a tenprint user who logged on would be granted access to the tenprint functionality, and a latent print examiner would be granted access to the latent print functionality. This flexibility allows more efficient use of the equipment based on need. For example, instead of purchasing ten latent print workstations and ten tenprint workstations, a location may need to purchase only 15 dual-use workstations. This results in reduced costs while providing improved efficiency. It also allows workstations to be used in a secondary function if another workstation becomes unusable.

The AFIS system administrator can assign access rights to examiners for various tenprint and latent print functionalities based on their job requirements, which determine what functionality each examiner is entitled to. A tenprint verifier might only be allowed access to the functions of case retrieval and verification of hit/no hit of records in the candidate list. This verifier would have no access rights to any tenprint acquisition or latent print functionality.

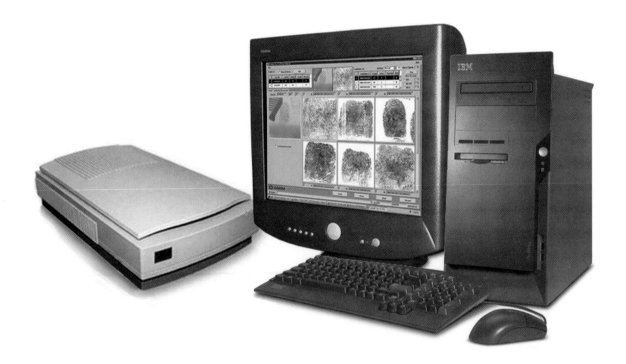

Figure 5.3

Latent Print Workstation

The AFIS administrator can also assign priority settings, which allow a tenprint or latent print manager to assign a higher priority than normal for processing a particular search, which allows the search to "jump to the head of the line" in the transaction queue and begin processing immediately.

For latent print applications, many agencies have digital photographic equipment that can capture the latent image with as much detail as possible (see Fig. 5.4). The equipment, whether purchased from the AFIS manufacturer as part of the AFIS package or as a separate component, typically consists of a planetary camera, computer equipment, and software. The software can remove or neutralize background colors or patterns, and overlaying latent print images can be made to appear separately. The software does not add to the latent image; rather, it removes background "noise" to more clearly reveal the latent print.

5.1.3 CODERS

The job of coders is to identify (i.e., extract) features from finger images such as minutiae, direction of ridge flow, distance between minutiae, and number of ridges between minutiae. In Figure 5.5, for example, the image on the left shows a plain impression without any minutiae placement, while the image on the right shows the minutiae placed by the coder following the proprietary algorithm of the AFIS vendor. Coders work either on the input workstation or on

Figure 5.4

Latent Print Digital Capture Device

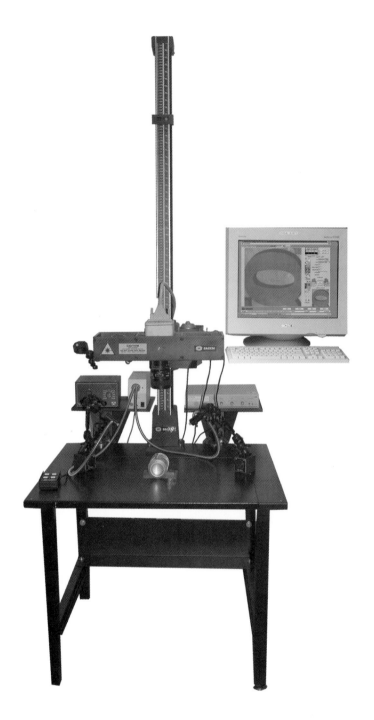

a separate computer. They have a key role in the identification process since they extract the image characteristics used by the matchers in searches. Incorrect feature marking can lead to false negatives, where a print is improperly matched.

5.1.4 RAID STORAGE

The redundant array of independent (or inexpensive) drives, or RAID, is a feature of AFIS that allows a number of smaller drives to be combined together to make a larger array, which provides additional features such as improved performance and data redundancy. The redundancy of smaller disks, faster input/output, increased capacity, and better security make RAID storage desirable for large AFIS systems.

Identification agencies that operate on a 24 hours a day, 7 days a week schedule cannot shut down for maintenance for an extended period of time. RAID allows more system reliability, since if one disk fails, it will have no impact on data reliability. To even further minimize the opportunity for system disruption, an agency may have a redundant or secondary RAID with the same or nearly the same information as contained on the primary RAID. New records are added to both the primary and the redundant RAID units. Many larger RAID arrays can even predict drive failure and contact the vendor, who then immediately ships a replacement, which can be installed in the array before the failure occurs.

The configuration in Figure 5.1 shows the option of RAID storage of tenprint images captured at 1,000 ppi. While NIST standards require a minimum

Figure 5.5

Placement of Minutiae by Coder

of 500 ppi for image capture, many agencies are opting to capture these images at higher resolutions, e.g., 1,000 ppi. Although these higher resolution images require four times as much storage and bandwidth for transmission, they provide much better clarity and ridge detail. Therefore, such AFIS configurations, made possible by the rapid advancements in the field of identification, the decrease in computer costs, improved system reliability, and a massive amount of state and federal funding, naturally have wide support among the members of the latent print community.

5.1.5 MATCHERS

In the configuration shown in Figure 5.1, the matchers, which house the extracted image characteristics, are located on the right and bottom. There are multiple sets of matchers for various types of searches. When a search is initiated, the extracted image characteristics of the search record are compared or searched against the extracted image characteristics already on file. Scores are assigned to the candidates produced by this search that indicate the relationship of the image characteristics on file to the image characteristics of the search print. If 75 minutiae of a search image exactly match 75 minutiae of an enrolled record in the matchers, the enrolled record would be given a very high score. It might have more than 75 minutiae, but the large number of matching minutiae creates an extremely high probability that the two images are from the same person.

As shown in Figure 5.1, there are three major components to the matcher subsystem: the matcher controllers, the string controllers, and the matchers themselves. Each has a specific function in the identification process.

The matcher controller is the computer that controls the operation of that matcher subsystem. Transactions from the AFIS system and responses back to it are channeled through the matcher controller.

Matchers may be arranged in an array, or string. The string of matchers contains all the image characteristics for the particular record type. For example, TPid matchers contain the image characteristics for all the tenprint records, that is, the two index fingers (or possibly two thumbs, or both) of everyone who has a tenprint record on file. These matchers are commercial-off-the-shelf (COTS) computers that reach a storage capacity on an estimated fill rate. When the matcher fills to a desired percentage, it is sealed from the addition of new records and a new matcher is added to the string. Many systems support two or more redundant matcher strings, which allow two searches to be conducted simultaneously, one searching through string 0 and the other through string 1. This redundancy allows the systems to meet throughput requirements for searches while also providing a backup should one string have to be shut down for maintenance, testing, or upgrade.

Tenprint to unsolved latent (TP/UL) matchers contain the image characteristics of latent print images that were searched on AFIS, but for which no identification was made. Depending on the needs of the identification agency, these matchers can be configured to search some or all of the tenprint records that are inserted into the database each day. This search may require slightly more time than a tenprint to tenprint (TP/TP) search. In TP/TP searches, only the index fingers (or thumbs or both) are used. Unlike latent prints, these tenprints are usually of good quality. In TP/UL searches, however, the image characteristics from all ten fingers of a new tenprint record may be searched against the entire database of latent print images, some of which will be of poor quality. Agency administrators can determine the number of searches allowed and the capacity of the unsolved latent file. Control of the file can also be achieved through periodic purging of records, for example, when the statute of limitations for the crime from which the latent print was retrieved ends. If not purged, these cases may drain resources that are better spent on active cases.

In the latent to tenprint (LT/TPlc) search, the image characteristics from the latent print are searched against the entire latent cognizant (or latent cog) database. This database, which contains the image characteristics of all ten fingers, may be a subset of the tenprint database or may be identical to the tenprint database, and it may contain more image records than the tenprint database. For example, if there are five million tenprint records on the tenprint database, then there are ten million image records (assuming the system uses the two index fingers) on the tenprint matchers. But if there is a three million record latent cog subset of these records with ten images for each record, then there are 30 million image records (three million records × ten fingers) on the latent cog matchers.

In addition to the two-finger tenprint matchers, the ten-finger latent cog matchers, and the single-finger unsolved latent matchers, there may also be matchers for palm prints (see Fig. 5.6). Palm images require a large amount of storage and transmission bandwidth. The AFIS configuration in Figure 5.1 shows palm print searches and storage with similar functionality to the tenprint storage and searches. AFIS may be configured to include a matcher string that can search palms against other palms in various ways. This function is of particular interest to latent print examiners, since palm impressions found at crime scenes can only be searched against other palm images. If there is database of known palm images to search against, the chances of making an identification from the evidence left at a crime scene greatly improves.

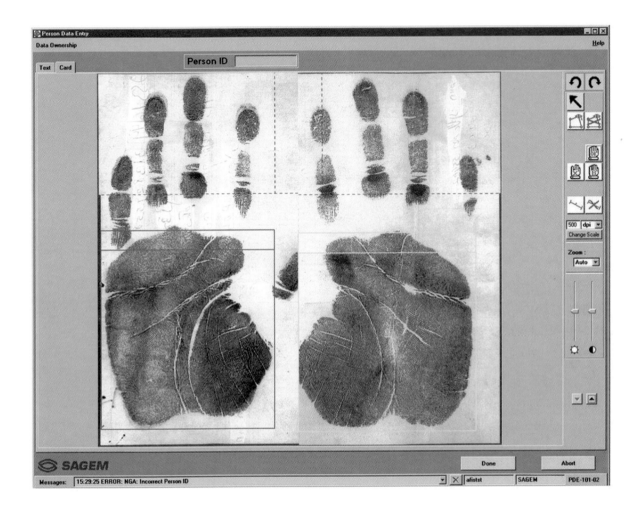

Figure 5.6

Livescan Palm Display

5.2 FINGERPRINT CARDS AND IMAGES

The fingerprint card shown in Figure 5.7 is representative of millions of fingerprint cards in existence. While the form of the card and the information it stores may have changed over the years, its key element is the accurate collection of finger images in a form that can be used for later comparison and identification. The identification process is based on the accurate collection of these finger images and the associated pedigree information. If the images are of poor quality but provide identifying minutia and ridge characteristics, an identification can be made even if the pedigree information is inaccurate or does not correspond to the true owner of the finger images. The identification is made based on the fingerprints, not on the demographic data.

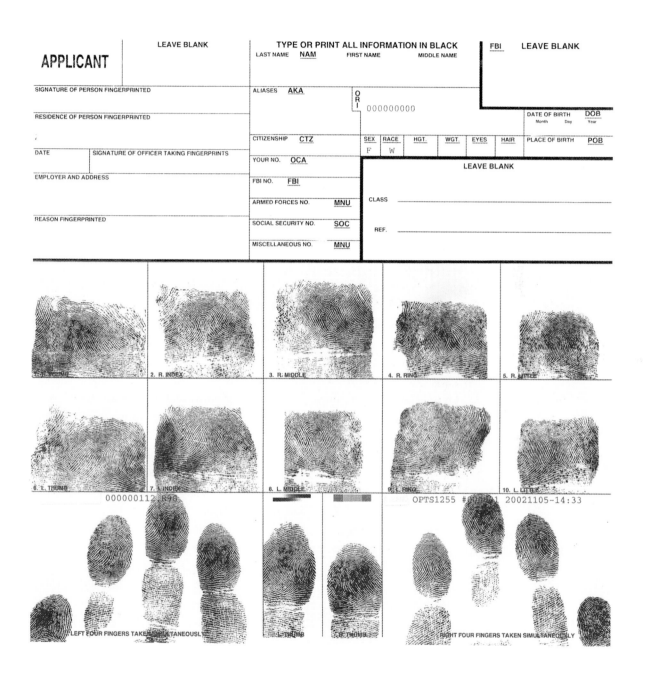

5.2.1 PAST PRACTICES

Until the advent of electronic image capture devices, such as livescan, all finger images were taken using special printer's ink, a glass or metal plate on which the ink was rolled, and a standardized fingerprint card. To ensure that the fibers

Figure 5.7

Tenprint Card

of the card absorbed the ink to maximize the quality of the print, the paper stock had to meet composition specifications. It had to be sufficiently strong to withstand numerous handlings by fingerprint examiners, fingerprint clerks, and indefinite file storage.

While the boxes in the first two rows of the fingerprint card contained the individual nail-to-nail rolled finger images, the four boxes in the lower portion of the card contained impressions of the fingers, which were referred to as flat, plain, or slapped impressions. The images in these boxes were captured by placing a group of four fingers onto the inked platen without any rolling, then pressing them onto the fingerprint card. After four fingers of both hands were captured, the thumbs were captured.

The large box on the lower left portion of the card shown in Figure 5.7 contains the plain impressions of fingers 7 through 10, which are the index finger through the little finger of the left hand. The next box contains the plain impression of finger 6, the left thumb. Moving on, the next box contains the image of the right thumb, finger 1, followed by the images of the remaining four fingers of the right hand, i.e., fingers 2 through 5. Look at the card and compare the images. Why are there two sets of images of the same two hands? What is different about the images? What is the same? Look closely.

One difference is that the images of the individual fingers are larger than those of the plain impressions. This is because the fingerprint technician taking the prints was attempting to capture as much finger detail as possible. The nail-to-nail roll captures the most information by including all the ridges, bifurcations, and minutiae from one edge of the fingernail to the other, and from the tip of the finger to the crease. The nail-to-nail roll also captures more minutiae at the very tip of the finger than does the plain impression. While the minutiae captured by the plain impressions are sufficient for tenprint identification purposes, latent print examiners needed as many minutiae as possible to search against. In many instances of car theft, for example, a latent impression from only a finger tip is found on the interior rear view mirror. The plain impression may contain more information below the first joint of the finger, but this was not typically used in tenprint identification and was not often found in latent prints.

The two sets of images were important for several reasons. The primary reason was so that a technician could quickly identify any finger sequence error, i.e., any finger that was rolled out of order and entered into the wrong box. If the image for finger 2 (right index) appeared in the box for finger 3 (right middle), it could result in a missed identification. Other mistakes were possible. Occasionally the finger images of one hand were entered into the boxes for the other hand, or the five fingers of one hand were erroneously entered twice and the fingers of the other hand were not rolled. Since the plain impressions of fingers 2 through 5 and 7 through 10 were taken as groups, it was easy for the experienced fingerprint technician to notice if the finger images in boxes one through five did not match the finger images in the lower right side of the fingerprint card.

This second set of images also acted as a backup set for the fingerprint examiner to use for identification comparison or to enter into an AFIS system if the primary set of images was not of sufficiently high quality. For example, if the rolled finger image for finger 5 (right little) was not clear, the technician could choose to use the image from the plain impression of finger 5 instead.

There were multiple types of fingerprint cards, but the two primary types were those used for civil searches and those used for criminal searches. The card in Figure 5.7 is an example of one used for civil purposes, such as job applications, background checks for licenses, or other non-criminal applications. In these instances, it was expected that the results of the search were needed as quickly as possible, since the applicant had a vested interest in the positive outcome of the search. In addition, the search needed to be done right the first time, because in such civil applications the applicant might be charged for the search and so would not want to pay again for a second search.

The criminal fingerprint card contained information regarding the charge, criminal code number, and arresting officer and other information relating to the criminal event that was the basis for fingerprinting the individual. Although the subjects in these cases perhaps were not as cooperative as those in civil cases in providing accurate personal information and clear finger images, the finger images from both civil and criminal fingerprint cards were expected to have the same quality. The FBI provides specific procedures for taking legible fingerprints.[1]

For identification processing, these cards were mailed or faxed to a central location where a criminal history check would be made. The search would be narrowed by using items such as the name and finger patterns (using either the Henry or the American Classification System). The results of the search would be sent, by mail or fax, to the inquiring agency.

Even with the introduction of fax machines and better communications, many states still did not operate a 24/7 identification bureau. Arrests made after the close of business were arraigned only on the current criminal charge without a fingerprint-based state criminal background check. A name check might be the only type of background check available, even though it was not unusual for the subject to provide a false name that had no criminal past connected to it. It was possible that the arresting agency might receive a criminal

---

[1] See http://www.fbi.gov/hq/cjisd/takingfps.html.

history that showed not only past misdeeds but also outstanding warrants only after the subject had been released following arraignment.

5.2.2 CURRENT PRACTICES

The advent of scanning has introduced a new set of variables into the identification process. In addition to the information contained on the physical fingerprint card, information is extracted from or added to the record through electronic processing. Card scanning and livescan are the primary scanning techniques.

5.2.2.1 Card Scanning

In card scanning, the information on the fingerprint card is converted into electronic media and can be transmitted over communication lines to AFIS using an FBI-certified scanner. This produces a high-quality image similar to that obtained from a high-end fax or copy machine. Although card scan images are clearer than the fax machine images they replaced, they may not contain the clarity and definition of livescan images or inked tenprint cards. Still, card scanning is a relatively inexpensive method for transmitting the finger images contained in the 14 image boxes on the card.

The arrest and pedigree information may come from another source, such as the OLBS. Care must be taken to ensure that the OLBS information matches the images transmitted, and that the card scan device is properly maintained. As with every device, proper training is required for optimum results.

Because the accurate capture and transmission of images is critical to the identification process, the FBI has developed an Image Quality Specification (IQS) for card scanners as well as livescan devices, fingerprint card printers, and other integrated products. To communicate with the FBI, agencies must use a device that has met their specifications and that appears on the FBI's list of certified products.[2]

5.2.2.2 Livescan

Livescan is rapidly replacing inked tenprint cards as the preferred input device. Livescan stations are available from each of the major AFIS vendors, as well as directly from manufacturers who will integrate the livescan units into the AFIS systems. The livescan device pictured in Figure 5.8 is typical of the devices on the market.

---

[2] See http://www.fbi.gov/hq/cjisd/iafis/cert.htm.

Figure 5.8
Capture of Images on a
Livescan

The livescan consists of a computer containing proprietary software that allows communication with AFIS, a keyboard to capture arrest and biometric data, a platen, and a screen. A camera may also be attached. For most operations, information about the subject who is being printed, such as pedigree information and charge and arrest information if a criminal case, is entered either by the technician or by the OLBS. Vendors may provide a pull-down menu to standardize the list of choices and provide uniformity to the process; this saves time as well.

One advantage of livescan machines is that the operator can preview captured images before accepting them (see Fig. 5.9). This can provide an improved level of confidence, since the finger image can be recaptured if the image quality of the first attempt is poor. Livescan also reduces incidences of either transposed or misplaced fingers by enabling a preview of minutia for each finger. The machine compares the minutia of each image, ensuring that no set of minutiae is repeated, i.e., that the same finger is not rolled more than once. Additionally, livescan compares the minutia of the rolled images with the minutia of the plain impressions to reduce the possibility of transposed hands or out-of-sequence fingers.

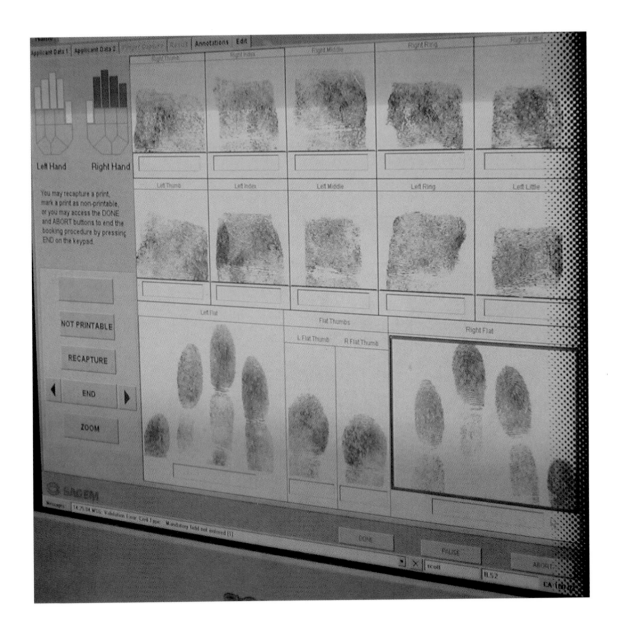

Figure 5.9

Images Captured on Livescan

5.2.3 IMPORTANCE OF HIGH-QUALITY IMAGES

Fingerprint images are captured at a resolution of 500 ppi (pixels per inch), 1,000 ppi, or another specified ppi. The higher the number of ppi, the more information is captured in the images. While not all of the information captured in a high ppi image may be needed by the AFIS matchers to match candidates, a high-resolution image is extremely useful in providing the greatest amount of ridge and valley detail.

The complete capture of this information is also extremely important. A nail-to-nail roll may be the only opportunity to capture image characteristics that may be used in the future to make a latent print identification. Without a complete nail-to-nail roll, the opportunity for latent print identification diminishes.

AFIS searches depend on the images captured. Most of the work performed by the AFIS systems can be done by the computer. The minutiae and ridge flow can be determined by electronic coders, and the electronic matchers can compare the characteristics of the submitted image with the characteristics of the images stored in the database. If the score is sufficiently high and other search parameters match (e.g., the name on fingerprint card matches the name on the CCH file), the system can declare a "lights out" identification without a human ever having looked at the images or the candidate list. An increasing number of AFIS agencies are using the "lights out" procedure, and to do this they are relying on the score of a fingerprint search that meets or exceeds an established threshold.

The quality of the images also has a tremendous effect on the likelihood of making a latent print identification on the subject at a later time. AFIS systems can store more than 100 individual minutiae points, the ridge flow and other characteristics. If the subject is fingerprinted with sufficient clarity such that 100 minutiae are captured in a nail-to-nail roll, then the AFIS has almost a complete record of the finger image. If at some time in the future the subject is fingerprinted again, there is a sufficient amount of information to compare against, particularly if the subsequent fingerprint capture is also of good quality. But what if the first capture is only of poor or fair quality?

If the captured image does not contain the minutiae and other characteristics available, the likelihood of making an identification in the future begins to diminish, particularly in a latent print search. Suppose that instead of 100 minutiae captured in the first printing, only 50 minutiae and image characteristics were captured, and the captured image is not the complete nail to nail, but just the upper half of the finger. This partial print image is added to the database. If a subsequent search of the same subject is made, his or her finger images would again be captured either on paper or electronically. If this capture is of fair quality, there would still be enough minutiae to make an identification. Tenprint searches also generally use two or more fingers, so fair images can produce an identification. The criminal history is forwarded to the submitting agency and the criminal history is updated with this new event. The tenprint identification process is complete. This, however, might not be enough for a subsequent latent print search.

Suppose the subject was engaged in a criminal activity such as a burglary and left a latent print at the scene of the crime. If that latent print came from the portion of the finger that had not been captured on the tenprint record, then would be no minutiae to match against. The perpetrator has a record on file, but there are not sufficient minutiae or image characteristics to make an identification. This can be very frustrating. To repeat, the identification technology is severely hampered if the booking officer does not take a nail-to-nail roll capturing good image characteristics.

5.2.4 INKED IMAGES VERSUS LIVESCAN IMAGES

The images captured with ink are considered by many (particularly by latent print examiners) to be preferable to images produced by an electronic scan. They hold that the impression produced by the ink-and-roll process by a trained officer on certified paper stock, when the ink is uniform in distribution and the finger is rolled from nail to nail, is the very best image possible. Inked cards are believed to contain more definition and more information than the image produced by a scan because of the levels of grayscale possible in the inked image and the retention of ink on the card.

The first generation of scanned images produced by livescan machines was captured at 500 ppi, a resolution with sufficient detail to complete a tenprint search, but not always enough for a latent print search or identification. Newer livescan devices capture images at 1,000 ppi, retaining four times as much information as the first generation. Newer generations of livescan machines also capture palm impressions, which may contain as much as ten times the size and minutiae as the individual finger images.

Scanned images usually go through a quality check on the livescan machine before the images are saved. Out-of-sequence fingers or hands, or low-quality images, can be corrected while the subject is still being printed. Since the transmission of the record to an AFIS immediately follows, the subject can be re-rolled if the transmission is garbled. Because of the transmission of scanned records, each image may have to be compressed prior to transmission and then decompressed in order to display the image, which may cause the image to lose some definition.

Which process is better process remains a topic of great debate and concern as electronic images begin to replace paper images.

5.2.5 IMAGE CAPTURE PROCESSES

As mentioned in Chapter 4, the information contained in the paper or electronic version of the tenprint card can be divided into three sections: alpha information, images, and minutiae. Alpha information, much of which will be kept in the CCH file, is descriptive information about the subject, including the name, address, reason for fingerprinting, charge, etc. This is the information produced on the rap sheet. Other information, such as sex, pattern, and Process Control Number (PCN), or later the SID (state identification) number, is stored in an alpha database. The images are stored in the image database, and the minutiae extracted from these records are stored on matchers.

The following image processing description is generic in nature (see Fig. 5.10 for an overview of the process). While many large agencies have switched to livescan, inked and rolled cards are still in use. Both will be described.

First, the subject is brought to the booking station for printing and identification. Pedigree and arrest information are entered, usually into some form of OLBS. If the agency has a livescan device, the information will appear on the screen, pre-filling the fields. This reduces the likelihood of input errors later in the identification process. If a physical tenprint card is used, this same information can be printed onto the card.

The fingerprint images are taken by rolling each finger and then taking the set of plain impressions. If this is done on a livescan machine, there are automatic quality control features, such as required fields, quality of the images (i.e., minimum number of minutiae present), and out-of-sequence finger notification. This last feature is completed by matching encoded minutiae of the finger images to ensure that they are not repeated. This also reduces the chances of

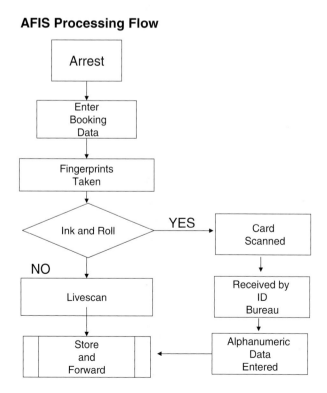

AFIS Processing Flow

Figure 5.10

Overview of Image Capture Process

transposed finger images. Livescan software can also provide a standardized list of options from pull-down menus. This speeds the process as well as makes it more consistent. In addition to the 14 finger images (one of each of the ten rolled fingers, one of each of the two plain thumb impressions, and one of each of the two remaining sets of fingers), the livescan can capture images of each of the two palms, as well as mug shots.

When the quality of the images has been approved and the data fields are complete, the record is electronically sent to the state and/or local identification bureaus. The record arrives at a "store and forward" server, where one copy is retained (stored) for search by the identification agency, and one copy is sent (forwarded) to IAFIS. The livescan device must meet the ANSI/NIST transmission standards for the data to be electronically forwarded through the AFIS and onto IAFIS; those agencies that are not fully compliant can forward the records to the FBI by mail. The livescan must also meet the FBI transmission specifications (EFTS) as well as any state or local EFTS, and it must comply with the FBI's wavelet scalar quantization (WSQ) grayscale fingerprint image compression specification. NIST transmission standards specify the record type and what is included in the record, for example, a finger image captured at 1,000 ppi. The FBI transmission specifications indicate the fields that must accompany that record, e.g., last name, first name, etc. WSQ specifies the compression and decompression of the image needed for electronic transmission. (Virtually all images are compressed and decompressed to permit reasonable transmission speeds.) States may add additional fields to the FBI EFTS in order to incorporate items of interest, such as the name of the county.

If the finger images were taken on a physical card with ink, once completed, either the card is sent to the state identification agency via mail or fax or the card is scanned and the record is electronically sent to the state agency. Once the record is received, the images can be matched to a record already created from the OLBS information. The images and data elements are assembled electronically into a single record that is sent to the store and forward server as described above.

5.3 AFIS NAME AND MINUTIAE SEARCHES

Once the state identification agency receives the record from the store and forward server, it may initiate two searches: a name search, which compares the name on the record with the names in the Master Name Index (MNI), and an AFIS minutiae search, which is based on image characteristics (see Fig. 5.11 for an overview). The search of the MNI produces a list of candidates and SID numbers.

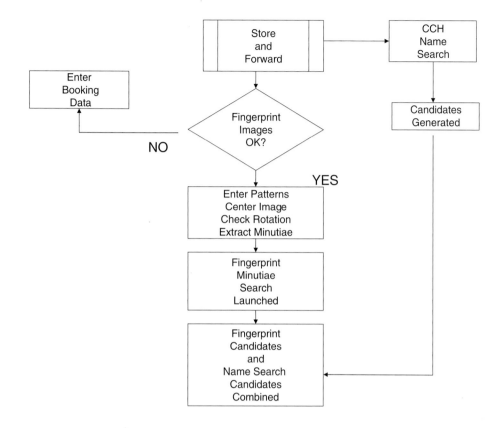

At the same time, the AFIS system can check the quality of the finger images. If the images do not meet the standards, e.g., are unusable, they are sent to a quality control unit for review. If it is confirmed that the images are not usable (e.g., blurred, transmission error), the booking agency may be asked to re-roll the subject. While this is usually possible with livescan-produced records because of the speed with which booking and review can be done, it is less likely to occur when the records arrive via card scan. For records that arrived by mail, the chances of a re-roll are almost nil.

If the quality of the images is acceptable, they are checked for patterns and centered, and it is ensured that the rotation is true (i.e., that the tip of the finger appears at the top). When these checks are complete, the coder extracts minutiae from the images and a tenprint to tenprint (TP/TP) search is launched. Tenprint matchers search those records that meet the pattern classification of the ten finger images, and then match the minutiae for two or more fingers. From this search a candidate list is produced. AFIS then combines the candidate list from the minutiae search with the list of candidates produced by searching the MNI and compares candidates (see Fig. 5.12).

Figure 5.11

Overview of Name and Minutiae Search

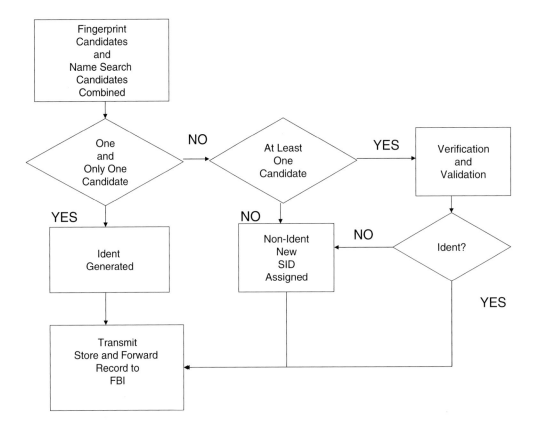

Figure 5.12

Ident/No Ident of name and minutiae search

If there is one and only one candidate from both the fingerprint search and the name search, an ident is generated. This identification information is forwarded to IAFIS through store and forward. If no candidate is generated from either of these searches, the record is considered a non-ident. A SID number is assigned, as this is considered the first enrollment of the subject into the state database. This record is then sent to IAFIS through store and forward.

If there is at least one candidate, the candidates are reviewed by trained examiners in a verification process. The return of multiple candidates may be due to multiple records for the same individual. These records will be consolidated into one record, usually the one with the first assigned SID number. This is repeated by a second examiner in a validation process independent of the decision of the first examiner. If the combined decision is that there is no identification, i.e., a matching record does not exist on the AFIS database, a new SID number is assigned and the record is sent to IAFIS through store and forward. If the combined decision is that there is an identification, the CCH will be updated with the new information. This information is also be sent to IAFIS through store and forward output.

The appearance of a SID number on a candidate list only shows the likelihood that the minutiae of the prints match the minutiae of a record on the database. State and local AFIS systems do not truly identify people; rather, they report that the characteristics of the finger images sent by the inquiring agency match the record of a person who has a record on the AFIS database. Whether the original name is the true name is not known.

The following is an example. The first time Chris is fingerprinted, the submitting agency sends an inquiry with Chris's prints to AFIS. Since Chris is not enrolled in AFIS, there is no record and thus no match. Chris's record is assigned the next SID number of 1234567H. Six months later, Chris is again fingerprinted in connection with a felony. When the booking officer asks Chris's name, he gives the name "Pat."

The inquiring agency submits "Pat's" fingerprint images to AFIS. The state agency reports that they have a fingerprint match for someone named Chris. Chris is therefore Pat, and may possibly use the name of someone else as well. Or perhaps neither Chris nor Pat is the subject's real name. The agency that fingerprinted Pat has to determine who Pat/Chris really is. AFIS determined that the finger images from Chris match the finger images from Pat, but making the real identity falls outside the responsibility of AFIS.

One viewpoint holds that it is not immediately important to know the name of a subject in custody. It is more important to determine whether the subject is wanted, has outstanding warrants, is dangerous, etc. There is another point to this example. To be nearly 100% certain of someone's history using only one biometric, fingerprints must be used. Regardless of whether names, social security numbers, dates of birth, or court records match, the only true, nearly absolute method for identification is to use fingerprints.

Misidentifications can happen, but they are increasingly rare. Having two or four clear finger images almost always produces the correct subject if the candidate is enrolled on the database. Can there really be errors in other identifiers such as date of birth and Social Security number? Of course. These errors are exploited in the relatively recent phenomenon of identity theft. Financial institutions, particularly credit companies, urge people to check their credit history regularly because of the very real possibility that someone has gathered sufficient non-biometric information about them to be able to assume their identity. Criminal justice systems cannot afford to make a misidentification. Unlike an error in one's credit report, which can be corrected relatively easily, a misidentification can have far greater consequences. Criminal charges may be imposed on the wrong person, or the criminal history of a non-criminal applicant may be missed, allowing an applicant to be placed in a position from which he or she should be barred.

Table 5.1

Tenprint Searches—Pre- and Post-AFIS

Process	Pre-AFIS	Post-AFIS
Acquisition of fingerprints	Ink + roll	Ink + roll, livescan
Transmission of fingerprint images	Mail, courier, or facsimile	Mail, courier, livescan, or group IV facsimile
Transmission of fingerprint data	Mail, courier, facsimile, or electronic interface	Mail, courier, facsimile, livescan, or electronic interface
Storage of fingerprint images	Inked images	Inked images captured on optical disks
Search processing	Name search followed by manual counting of ridges with magnifying glass	Name and fingerprint search using computerized matching and high-resolution monitors
Verification by	Examiner based upon manual examination with glass	Examiner using high-resolution monitors

5.4 TYPES OF AFIS SEARCHES

5.4.1 TENPRINT TO TENPRINT (TP/TP) SEARCHES

In pre-AFIS days, a clerk had to retrieve a tenprint card from the master fingerprint file, present it to the examiner for comparison, then return the card to the file. If another examiner needed that card, he or she had to either wait for the card to be returned to the file or retrieve another tenprint card on the same person from the jacket. Today, the candidate image is presented for side-by-side comparison with the subject image on high-quality computer monitors, and the examiner uses electronic tools to filter image data. Minutiae can be hidden, portions of the image magnified, and locked cursors can move across the two images simultaneously. See Table 5.1 for a comparison of pre- and post-AFIS tenprint search processes.

In tenprint searches, the use of two or possibly four finger images adds to the likelihood of making an identification. If two candidates appear, and their scores are high and similar, it may be due to a consolidation.[3]

The candidates produced in a TP/TP search are displayed on a candidate list in rank order. The tenprint examiner compares each AFIS-produced candidate against the subject image. While the matcher determines the relative placement of minutiae and patterns on the two images, the examiner can also check items such as ridge flow, core, and delta. This is the tenprint verification process.

Many AFIS systems require a duplication of this process, known as validation. In validation, a second examiner independently reviews the candidates, noting

---

[3] A consolidation consists of finger images from the same persons that were assigned different SID numbers. Not everyone is completely forthright when they are fingerprinted.

the placement of the minutiae, ridge flow, core, and delta. If both examiners agree on a decision, the result is considered final. If they agree that the candidate matches the inquiry, it is an ident. If they agree that the candidate is not an ident, and no other candidate is produced, the subject is assigned a new SID number and a rap sheet or criminal history is initiated. If the examiners differ in their opinions, a supervisor or other examiner will be summoned. If the images came from a livescan that is part of the booking process, the AFIS examiners may request that the subject be re-rolled if still in custody. This may produce a more clear set of prints from which to search. Another option is to search other fingers on AFIS and/or to treat the images as latent print images and search the latent cognizant database, if such a database is different from the tenprint database.

For most tenprint searches, only one candidate will appear on the candidate list. With improved coding, better matches, and faster throughput, the AFIS systems have become better at producing an exact match in the first position than in the past. Accuracy in image identification is a major selling point for AFIS vendors. This accuracy is reflected in the AFIS candidate list. Ideally, candidate lists will contain only the exact match, assuming the subject is enrolled on the database. If the output list has more than one candidate, the subject should appear in the first or second position of the list. No candidate list should be produced when the subject has not been enrolled on the database.

Tenprint searches are driven by a business model that requires a high degree of accuracy, a sufficiently large database with high-quality enrolled images and minutiae, and two or four good subject finger impressions to initiate the search. There may be an administrative or legal requirement to make an identification within a designated time period. For criminal processing, sometimes referred to as Priority 1 processing, a fast turnaround is required to ensure the retrieval of a rap sheet along with any wanted information or warrants prior to arraignment. For civil applications, the issue of speed may not be quite as pressing, but the search still must be concluded in a reasonable amount of time. Tenprint processing is quantity driven, with perhaps hundreds of thousands or even millions of transactions a year that must be completed accurately.

Some agencies are pursuing "lights out" tenprint searches. "Lights out" replaces human decisions with mathematical probabilities. In the extreme form, this means a tenprint search against the database with no human intention: no human who compares the candidates produced by the AFIS system; no human to validate the hit/no hit decision. The response and rap sheet are automatically sent to the inquiring agency. Agencies wishing to adopt the "lights out" procedure may begin with a limited application on certain types of tenprint searches, such as non-criminal AFIS searches that also match with the results of a name search of the MNI. Following evaluation, "lights out" may be extended to additional types of tenprint searches.

5.4.2 LATENT TO TENPRINT (LT/TP) SEARCHES

Because the latent print examiner does not work with the same volume or type of identification material as the tenprint examiner, latent print search procedures are somewhat different. Whereas the tenprint examiner has two or four impressions for a single search, the latent print examiner typically handles each latent print as a separate search. Whereas the tenprint examiner works with clear images that may have passed a quality check prior to transmission from a livescan device, the latent print examiner has only the images left behind at a crime scene, which may be smudged, have another latent print overlay, or be on a background that must be neutralized for the image to appear.

The output of the LT/TP search also differ from the TP/TP search. Like the tenprint examiner, the latent print examiner is presented with a candidate list. However, the latent print examiner may request that all candidates above a certain threshold, or a specific number of candidates, be presented for comparison. Because there are fewer minutiae to work with, the latent print examiner will look at matcher score, pattern, and ridge flow in addition to the placement of the minutiae in the side-by-side comparisons. If a candidate does match the latent print, the examiner may request that a card be printed or retrieved and compared with the latent print. The examiner may also request that a second or senior examiner confirm the ident.

If the first candidate does not match, the examiner continues on through the list of candidates above the threshold; if necessary, he or she may also look at candidates that are below the threshold. Given the combination of a low-quality latent print and low-quality minutiae on the enrolled image, it is possible that the score for the minutiae match could be below the threshold but still be within the requested list of candidates.

When two latent prints (or more) are searched on AFIS, the appearance of the same SID number on candidate lists for both images means that a candidate for the first latent print image also appeared as a candidate on the second image. This information can aid the examiner in making an identification. It may be, for example, that these images are fingers 2 and 3 (right hand index and middle fingers) of the same person left at the crime scene. Again, the AFIS search only provides information, not a determination, for the latent print examiner.

If the search does not produce an ident, the examiner may continue to search the latent print against the database by changing variables. Depending on the system, these variables could include geographic area searched, change in location of minutiae placement, change in number of minutiae placed, area of the latent print in which minutiae are extracted by coder or manually, or any combination of the above. These changes are encompassed in case level data such as geographic area, image data such as minutiae placement, and finger data such as finger number and pattern. Since capturing and loading the latent print image into AFIS may have taken a significant amount of time and thus ideally would not be repeated, the option of relaunching, or performing a second search, can be very appealing. The variables offer numerous search options. From a production standpoint, however, more time can be spent in searching through relaunches than in recapturing the image using photographic techniques.

If there is no ident after a reasonable number of searches have been completed, it may be because the subject had never been fingerprinted and enrolled in the searched database, or perhaps the subject is in the database but the image quality does not display sufficient minutiae to match against the minutiae from the latent image. In such cases, the examiner may move the case to the unsolved latent file, with the anticipation that the subject will be enrolled for the first time or enrolled with better images and minutiae in the future.

See Table 5.2 for a comparison of pre- and post-AFIS latent print search processes.

5.4.3 LATENT TO LATENT SEARCHES

The latent examiner may also initiate a latent/latent search. In this search, the examiner, recognizing that the latent print remains unidentified, looks for a match with another latent image from the unsolved latent file. If there is a match with a latent print in this file, the examiner can determine who initiated the search off the other latent print. By contacting the other inquiring agency,

Process	Pre-AFIS	Post-AFIS
Search time	Months	Minutes
Suspects or other identifying data	Required	Not required
Number of candidates	Thousands	Less than five candidates per search (average)
Verification time	2,100 hours	Minutes
Number of images compared against	Thousands	Millions
Searched by	Examiners	Computer
Verified by	Examiners	Examiners

Table 5.2

Latent Print Searches—Pre- and Post-AFIS

the examiners and investigators can determine if they have found a serial offender who has left latent prints at multiple crime scenes in either the same jurisdiction or multiple jurisdictions.

5.5 AFIS REPORTS

Every vendor can deliver a series of reports on various functions of the AFIS system. The topics of these reports range from the overall operation of the system, such as the amount of up-time, to very specific items, such as the amount of time an operator is logged onto the system. The reports may indicate the condition of the AFIS, with descriptions such as the average number of transactions in the system at any given time. The transactions covered could include the transactions received from remote livescan stations, those awaiting coding as searches, those in the matchers, and those awaiting images, verification, and validation. At the operator level, possible reports include the number of transactions by a specific operator, by a group of operators, by shift, or by transaction type (e.g., input verification, validation, etc.). There are a variety of methods to "data mine" a system that contains a complete, accurate, and reliable database.

It is the responsibility of the AFIS managers to learn the report capabilities of their AFIS system. It is also their responsibility to be certain that the information presented accurately represents the condition described. It is the responsibility of the vendor to train AFIS managers on the system's report capabilities and ensure that the reports are complete, accurate, and reliable. To be certain of this, a series of procedures that test the system must be initiated, such as monitoring a known series of transactions through the system and measuring the resulting reports. Are the numbers accurate? Was a transaction reported properly? Did it really take the processing time that the report states? For example, if a report is generated about the number of transactions in the anticipation queue, but it actually provides the number of images in the imaging queue, the report is wrong. Regardless of how impressive it might appear, the data must be verified during testing to assure both the reliability and accuracy of the information.

Along with each report, a data dictionary that not only explains the overall components and functions of the system but also provides a standard terminology must be provided. The data dictionary will help users understand the commonly used terminology and will reduce misunderstandings.

Reports are prepared for different employees for different purposes. First line supervisors may be concerned with the productivity of their staff in relation to the amount of time it takes them to perform their tasks. Managers may look for similar information about the productivity of teams or shifts rather than individuals. Administrators may want reports that indicate trends or opportunities for improvements. Researchers and policy makers may need data to support new initiatives and formulate policy. If the data is flawed or incomplete, the effort is wasted or offers false findings. There is no single report that can give all this information; individual, specific reports must be generated to answer these questions. In addition, employees must have the analytical skills to be able to draw conclusions from the reports, and they must be familiar enough with the process to know whether the reports do in fact reflect reality.

The challenge of reports is to use them to find not just what is, but what could be. Thinking like a business manager may show new opportunities that had not been considered previously. Reports can help find those opportunities.

5.5.1 TENPRINT REPORTS

Tenprint operations are usually production driven. Criminal inquiries must be responded to as quickly, accurately, and completely as possible. This rapid response may be needed for good public policy or the demand to keep current. Civil inquiries may have a fee associated with the search, so the individuals printed also become "customers." Report topics of interest to tenprint managers include throughput, up-time, average response time, and quantity of output per individual, group, and shift. The following is a brief list of reports that capture and present this information.

1. *Operator Activity:* This report covers the volume of transactions completed during a specific time period as well as the different types of transactions, for example, the number of tenprint records entered, verified, and checked by an operator. This information may help a supervisor determine if a team or shift is meeting standards. This report measures human interaction with AFIS.
2. *Workstation Activity:* This report provides information about the functionality of the various components of the AFIS system. It can tell managers whether the system components are operating at capacity or whether a different configuration should be considered, if there are sufficient workstations to meet peak demands, or if the workstations are working at only one-third or one-half of their capacities.
3. *AFIS Special Processing and Exception Reports:* These reports provide information not only on normal processing through the system, but also on any special processing or exception processing. If the special or exceptional processing becomes too extensive, it may take resources away from the normal processing. These reports can tell managers when and why these exceptions are occurring and how they can be avoided.

Additional reports such as the AFIS production summary report and the AFIS quality control production summary report round out the information available from the AFIS system.

5.5.2 LATENT PRINT REPORTS

The first question typically asked of the latent print abilities of an AFIS system is how many idents were made. After all, the purpose of an Automated Fingerprint Identification System is to support identifications. How many idents is a legitimate question. But is it the right question?

What about other questions, such as how many idents cleared cases, how many idents resulted from latent print to tenprint searches, and how many idents resulted from tenprint to unsolved latent print searches? While these are all identifications, they result from different search techniques and different processing. The development of latent print reports may require the capture of a search *reason* field on latent print searches. This is crucial in order for reports to have any merit. Without the search reason delimiter, automated reports could include ident information from tests and demonstrations mingled with results from normal latent searches.

Each report on the latent print system that is case related must include the search reason as a parameter. For example, reports that indicate the number of LT/TP searches launched or verified in a particular time period are presumed to include only those cases in which the search reason is a latent entry search. These reports must be able to provide information on any one of three levels: operator, site (each operator and site summary), or system (site summary, system summary), and they must be robust enough to capture information over time periods varying from days to years. Each report has options for reporting period, operator(s)/site(s), and field(s). Design criteria should include options for reports to be displayed at any terminal, produced on paper, or saved in ASCII or, increasingly, html format. In addition to the designed reports, there are provisions for ad hoc repots to be produced. The vendor has to provide training in the mechanics of producing these ad hoc reports.

Latent print reports are presented to three primary, but not mutually exclusive, audiences: first line supervisors, whose primary interests are throughput related; system administrators, whose interests are related to the effectiveness of the system, e.g., case closure; and a system improvement audience, whose goal is to enhance the efficiency of the system through improved identifications, higher throughput, and better practices.

The following four reports are examples of reports that should be available on a scheduled or ad hoc basis:

1. *AFIS Volumes:* This report provides latent print activity for all users on monthly, year-to-date, and cumulative bases by search reason.
2. *Idents by Actual Crime:* This report links an ident to the crime from which the latent print was acquired. Date, operator, and crime type variables are used.
3. *HIT Summary of Searches:* This report provides specific information on the latent case and the ident. It is useful in identifying commonalities of idents. Date, operator, and crime type variables are used.
4. *HIT Summary of SIDs:* This report provides specific information 'on the SID. It is useful in identifying commonalities of SID numbers. Date, operator, and crime type variables are used.

All of these reports can provide valuable information to the AFIS supervisors, managers, and policy makers. They can show both strengths and weakness, opportunities and threats.

CHAPTER 6

CURRENT ISSUES

The move to more fully automate identification practices has both planned and unplanned consequences. More groups of people are being fingerprinted as part of a background check than ever before, and the application of finger images to new areas is steadily increasing. These advances, however, are not always easy or fully integrated with other existing systems. This chapter describes some of these changes. It begins with a SWOT (strengths, weaknesses, opportunities, and threats) analysis of AFIS systems. One strength, for example, is the amazing accuracy of AFIS identifications; one weakness is the lack of complete interoperability between large identification systems such as the FBI's Integrated Automated Fingerprint Identification System (IAFIS) and the Department of Homeland Security's IDENT system.

DNA and fingerprint images in their current development are also described. These biometrics should be considered as complementary rather than competing identification methods. Also described in this chapter are examples of new civil applications of AFIS technology as well as the emergence of multistate and multinational identification systems.

6.1 SWOT ANALYSIS

There are many factors that determine how, and how well, AFIS systems are used, both now and in the future. They can be described in terms of strengths, weaknesses, opportunities, and threats—a SWOT analysis. A SWOT analysis is often used by businesses to examine areas of vulnerability and discover areas of opportunity.

After completing a SWOT analysis, a company may discover marketing opportunities that are not being fully exploited, or they may realize that their success is too dependent on just a handful of individuals. If those key employees leave the company for retirement, for another career, or possibly to work for the competition, could the company survive? A SWOT analysis helps companies examine the interaction of people and processes and make educated choices.

In another type of use, a SWOT analysis on a competing company might be initiated by a company interested in outperforming or taking over it. The analysis will inform the company of its competitor's strengths, weaknesses, opportunities, and threats, and how they can be used against the competitor. If it was found that the competitor was too dependent on a few key staff, for example, the company could then consider how to lure them away.

6.1.1 AFIS STRENGTHS

Automated Fingerprint Identification Systems have become a widely accepted method of identifying persons in a one-to-many (1:N) search. In both forensic and civil applications, AFIS systems offer incredibly high accuracy and a quick response, and in many cases provide a history. Depending on the number of fingers used and the size of the database, the accuracy rate can exceed 99.97%. That means that three people in 10,000 are not identified, but 9,997 of the 10,000 are. That number can be increased with the following situations:

- name search confirmation from the Master Name Index (MNI)
- searching multiple fingers
- multiple records of the same individual on the database
- more accurate matching algorithms
- more accurate coding algorithms
- better quality images on the database
- better images for comparison

The latest generation of AFIS matchers and coders, while state-of-the-art today, will be replaced by better, more accurate matchers and coders in the future. The same can be said for all the components of AFIS systems.

The systems are more reliable now than they were in the past. A request for proposals (RFP) will usually specify that the hardware and operating software be COTS—commercial-off-the-shelf components—which can be more easily repaired and replaced because of the standardization. This reduces both costs and downtime. For example, a new release in a COTS operating system software (e.g., upgrading from Windows 95 to Windows 98, Windows 2000, or Windows XP) can be more easily installed and configured than a new version of a custom-made operating system. Plus, application software from the AFIS vendor is more easily tested and introduced into a COTS operating system.

COTS hardware has reduced the need to use valuable computer room space for storage. AFIS administrators no longer have to keep a large inventory of equipment simply for use as spare parts—some of which might become outdated before it is ever used. Additional equipment can be configured into a small test system to test new application software before it is permanently installed on the operational system.

The computer equipment and software now in use are very reliable. New computers require less energy, generate less heat, last longer, and are less likely to break down before scheduled maintenance. They are also less expensive. Vendors are producing more reliable software that is less prone to bugs, or more politely, "undocumented features," that cause the system to fail.

The emergence of AFIS technology into other market areas has brought indirect benefits to the forensic AFIS community since it means more customers for AFIS products. More customers can translate into better products and better performance.

The strength of AFIS systems lies in the acceptance of AFIS as the benchmark for identification. Whether performed for a forensic application, such as an arrest or job application, or as a condition to receive government services, fingerprinting is very much accepted. It is not as invasive nor as expensive as other biometrics such as iris scanning or DNA testing, and the results are produced very quickly.

National and international standards have developed around fingerprint capture and transmission that permit any locale to collect, compress, transmit, and receive tenprint records and images. Networks such as the Criminal Justice Information Services (CJIS) wide area network (WAN) provide a communication system to IAFIS and other states and allow databases other than the local one to be searched with relative ease.

The identification of latent prints has increased geometrically with AFIS. AFIS systems can compare the image characteristics of a latent print against all the millions of records in the AFIS database and produce a list of candidates based on matching score. The training and experience of the latent examiner are used to make the ident, frequently by comparing the latent print or photo against the image on a tenprint card.

6.1.2 AFIS WEAKNESSES

6.1.2.1 Lack of Interoperability

As mentioned previously, one weakness of AFIS systems is that they are not completely interoperable. They do not function with the ease of automated teller machines that can connect to virtually any financial institution (usually for a small fee) and debit or credit an account. The database of millions of AFIS records available in one state is not immediately available to another state for searching. While a path does exist, through IAFIS, it does not connect every existing AFIS database. As has been discussed, a search of the local database for a criminal application (e.g., for an arrest) may return a "no hit," while the succeeding search of the IAFIS database results in a hit because of an arrest in another state and the issuance of an FBI number. (This presupposes that the arrest in the other state was for a fingerprintable offense that would be forwarded to the FBI. Many are not.) Access to other state databases is therefore quite important. Although the Interstate Identification Index (III) and the National Fingerprint File (NFF) make many out-of-state identifications possible, many challenges remain. For most agencies, searching other state databases is not a seamless process. The introduction of standards and the conversion of new tenprint records to a standards-compliant format will make such interactions more possible in the future.

Each of the major AFIS vendors has developed its own application software, and all of the software does not work on a single platform. Many versions of the application software are not backward-compatible, i.e., a software platform released in 1998 might not be able to communicate with application software from the same vendor that was installed in another system in 2001. Coupled with the differences in application software from different vendors, it becomes virtually impossible for one AFIS system to directly search a latent print on another AFIS system, with the exception of access through IAFIS.

This example might help to clarify the situation. Chevrolet manufactures transmissions for its cars, and Ford manufactures transmissions for its cars. These transmissions, however, cannot be interchanged. They perform essentially the same function, but are proprietary and unique to the manufacturer. In addition, the transmissions change over time, so that a 1998 Chevrolet transmission might not work in a 2004 Chevrolet.

Third-party vendors exist in both the automobile and the AFIS industries. In the automobile industry, the manufacturers of oil filters produce filters that are customized to each manufacturer. Likewise in the AFIS industry, manufacturers such as those specializing in image capture and transmission produce products that can be used by vendors and customers as part of the original AFIS system or as a feature subsequent to the installation. For example, livescan devices can be added to AFIS systems without necessarily installing new AFIS application software. The third-party application software in the livescan devices can be coded to interface with the existing AFIS and communicate with IAFIS through electronic fingerprint transmission specifications (EFTS). The move to COTS hardware and operating systems software has made a similar impact, but this is just the beginning.

Of particular importance is the impact this lack of interoperability has had in latent print identification. Latent print examiners are limited to searching their local databases with only restricted access to other databases. Because of the lack of interoperability and political will to make improvements, many latent print identifications that could be made are not. The record of a burglar, for example, may not be present on a local database because the burglar was never arrested in that locale. There may be a record in an adjoining state, with multiple entries, but the adjoining database cannot be searched because it operates with software from another vendor, the input structure is different, or there is no agreement allowing one state to search the other's database. Ideally, a latent print examiner should be able to search a hierarchy of databases from the local database, to the state, to IAFIS, and onto other states as necessary. And the process for those searches, while internally different as the searches move through different systems, should appear similar to the examiner. That does not happen in the current environment.

6.1.2.2 Lack of Integration at the Federal Level

Many people believe that agencies of the federal government such as the FBI and the Department of Homeland Security (DHS) rely on either one AFIS system or at least AFIS systems that are designed to the same specifications. Unfortunately, the systems used by most governmental agencies are neither interoperable nor integrated.

The FBI maintains records that adhere to the "gold standard" of ten rolled finger images (see Fig. 6.1). These nail-to-nail images, whether taken with ink or electronically, capture as much image detail as possible. They are used not only for tenprint identification purposes, but are also invaluable for latent print searches. They constitute a complete capture of the finger image surfaces.

The DHS adopted the U.S. Immigration and Naturalization Service identification system, the Automated Biometric Identification System (IDENT). IDENT is a two-finger system that allows agents to search the database in a few minutes, a much shorter time than the 2 hours required for an IAFIS search. While it is unreasonable to detain every person for 2 hours at the border while awaiting a background check, is it equally unreasonable to not press for an integrated system that can produce background information on a person in just a few minutes?

To reduce the time for checking the IAFIS database, an IDENT/IAFIS Integration Project was established to allow agents to submit all ten tenprint images to IAFIS and receive a response and rap sheet within 10 minutes. The faster response is possible due to a "lights out" search technique, in which the identification is based entirely on matching scores without human verification.

In June 2003, DHS Secretary Tom Ridge announced that the new "US-VISIT" (United States Visitor and Immigrant Status Indicator Technology) would replace an earlier Department of Justice program, the National Security Entry Exit System (NSEERS). This program requires that non-immigrant aliens from certain foreign countries be fingerprinted and photographed at the ports of

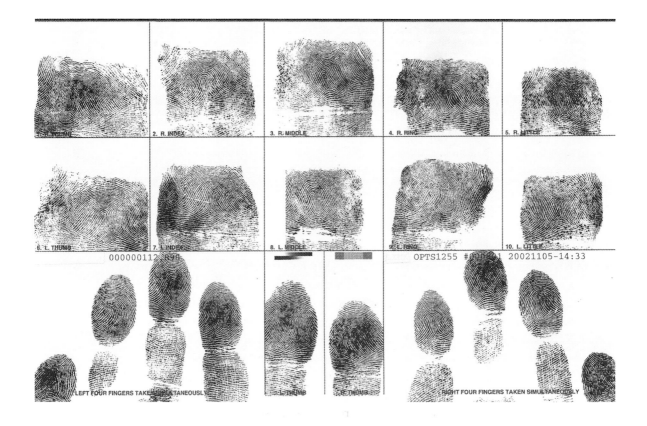

Figure 6.1
Tenprint Image

entry when they apply for admission to the United States. During the enrollment process, IDENT checks entrants against immigration records and information provided by the FBI. All aliens seeking admission at any of the 115 airports or 14 seaports nationwide with non-immigrant visas, regardless of nationality, will be affected by the first phase of US-VISIT, in which two plain finger impressions are captured and stored on a separate file at IDENT. By the end of 2005, US-VISIT will be installed at all land ports of entry.

A situation exists in which the two agencies that have the greatest influence on identification have systems that do not interoperate seamlessly. If it is important to fingerprint a foreign visitor for identification purposes, is it not important to collect the same amount of information as required for a teacher? Collecting only two images produces only 20% of the amount of image information that could be collected for later use, particularly for latent print applications. Even though a change in procedures to maintain the "gold standard" of ten rolled images, or as a compromise, ten plain impressions, would require more funding for IAFIS, this investment would provide the interoperability and security that is missing from the current plans.

The development of an additional database of only two fingers does not support the development of a hierarchy of AFIS searches in which local law enforcement agencies can search a tenprint record against the local, state, and federal databases.

6.1.2.3 Misunderstanding the System

Another weakness of AFIS systems is the possibility of misunderstanding of its functionality. AFIS systems function only as well as they are designed, implemented, and maintained. These systems are incredibly precise, and the databases can be searched in seconds, but their capabilities cannot be fully utilized if the AFIS administrators are not completely familiar with the system.

For example, managers and administrators may become upset because a hit was not made on their system even though a record existed for the subject. It is even more politically embarrassing when an identification is made on another system. The problem may not be with the AFIS system, however, but with the booking person who took the original tenprint images. The need to stress the importance of good image capture may lie beyond the span of control of the AFIS administrators, but the function is critical to the process.

Managers must know their system's capabilities and limitations and be advocates for its improvement. They must educate others, including those responsible for other components of AFIS, just how much AFIS relies on all the components of the identification process in order to make successful identifications. The media cannot be enlisted as the primary source of information about the workings of AFIS.

The decision to build or modify an AFIS system often involves trade-offs, and managers must be able to determine which trade-offs they are willing to make to get the best system for their needs at a price they can afford. The cost of capturing mug shots, for example, may prohibit the capture of palm prints. Likewise, faster retrieval may be considered more valuable than more storage of multiple sets of finger images. Managers must also keep in mind that the addition of a new feature, such as the ability to search palm images as part of a latent print process, may yield poorer-than-anticipated results because the corresponding increase in personnel needed was never considered.

6.1.2.4 Maintenance

New systems typically function as expected. The equipment is new; the software is state of the art, and all the moving parts work as designed. However, after a few hundred cycles, the equipment may begin to show signs of use. Drive motors in livescan machines may start to work just a little more slowly, or a computer microchip may fail. For example, an AFIS system that has an accuracy rate of 99.97% when new may exhibit some degradation in accuracy and throughput if the equipment is not maintained and calibrated as recommended by the manufacturer. Glass platens can become dirty or scratched, resulting in less-than-ideal digital images. Self-calibrating scanners can lose clarity as covers become torn, allowing spurious lighting onto a tenprint card that is being scanned. The computers that run the coder and matcher software have a limited life span and have to be replaced at scheduled intervals. Monitors can develop quirks that result in an inferior image display. The job of keeping an AFIS system well maintained is not insignificant. If proper maintenance is not performed, it can lead to equipment failures that are expensive and time-consuming to fix.

6.1.2.5 Training

All of the marvelous opportunities for improved identification processing are dependent on a staff that understands the system. The staff not only must know the characteristics of the system, but also must be able to exploit the existing performance and plan for improved services.

If an AFIS system is being purchased for the first time and the staff who will be using it have never before seen an AFIS system in operation, it might be useful to first arrange a demonstration. Few people buy a car without first taking a test drive; even fewer do so without having a driver's license. The same principals apply to buying an AFIS system: demonstrations and staff training should precede the purchase and implementation. Important questions to ask are who should be trained, what functions should they be trained in, and who will do the training. AFIS systems, for all their marvelous capacities, are entirely dependent on people. People program the computers, they enter the data and images, and in most cases make the verifications.

The staff who handled the old computer system operations will have to be trained in the computer requirements of the new AFIS system. Will the AFIS interface with an existing Computerized Criminal History (CCH) file to produce a pedigree or rap sheet in forensic applications? Will the AFIS vendor maintain the system and provide 24/7 uptime? Will responsibilities for AFIS be split between the vendor and the in-house staff? In one common arrangement, the in-house staff maintains the CCH, the vendor maintains the AFIS, and together they develop an interface between the two.

6.1.3 AFIS OPPORTUNITIES

The advances in AFIS that have been made in the past 10 years will probably seem old-fashioned when compared with the new AFIS opportunities.

6.1.3.1 Livescan

Better imaging will become standard as agencies move to a 1,000 pixels per inch (ppi) standard for all finger images and 500 ppi for all palm images. This additional clarity will be most welcomed by latent print examiners, because it will provide more detail of the finger characteristics for comparison. This is particularly important because inked and rolled cards are increasingly being replaced by digital images captured on livescan machines. Although the initial move from inked cards to 500 ppi digital images on the early livescan machines may have contributed to missed identifications if the booking officer was not precise, better image capture can compensate for lack of skill of the person doing the booking.

A "smart" livescan machine (see Fig. 6.2) is able to set an image quality threshold. Any image below the threshold would require that operator re-roll the subject or initiate an override to be able to accept and transmit the images.

Figure 6.2

Desktop Livescan with Camera

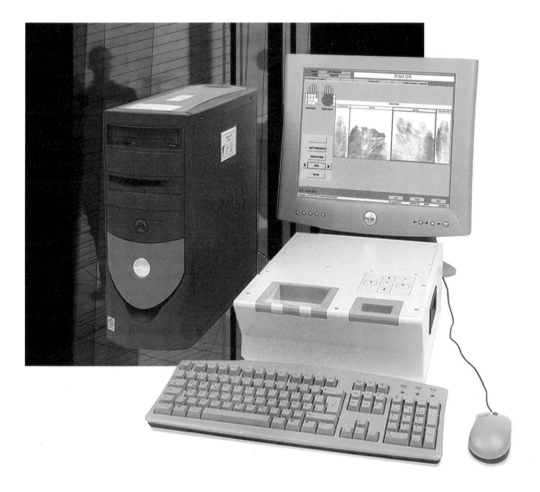

The capture speed of the 14 finger images can be improved so as to hasten the process in civil applications. If a nail-to-nail roll of the ten fingers and subsequent plain impressions is to remain the "gold standard," the process will have to be made faster. Only then will the capture of 14 impressions meet the timing requirements for civil applications such as US-VISIT.

Palm prints are now being taken as a part of the booking process on many livescan machines (see Fig. 6.3). Many agencies only capture palm impressions as part of a "major case file." In such cases, the palm images are typically kept with the crime folder, not with the corresponding fingerprint card, making it virtually impossible to tell if a person had ever had a palm print taken because it was never indexed with the fingerprint card. The increase in storage and bandwidth in current generation AFIS systems allows these huge files to be captured, compressed, and transmitted efficiently and inexpensively. The palm prints can have great value in latent print applications.

The newer livescan machines also have the ability to capture mug shots, also referred to as portraits. As with palm prints, standards exist for the capture, compression, and transmission of these digital images. The standards also call

Figure 6.3
Livescan Capture of Palm

for a uniform background with 18% gray, three points of lighting, and a facial aspect ratio (the size of the face in the field) of 55%. Mug shots have many uses. They can be printed onto a warrant to give the arresting officer a quick means of identifying the person. They can also, along with scar, mark, and tattoo (SMT) information, be used to create a photo array of suspects in an electronic lineup. This second biometric is used in addition to, not as a replacement for, the primary biometric, the fingerprint.

A fast livescan machine, coupled with additional bandwidth and minutiae storage, could replace applications that rely on names or other potentially false instruments. With livescan, identification and personal history are based on fingerprints, not on documents that can be forged or a name that can be altered. Livescan could be used in military applications, for example. Portable livescan machines could be used by trained soldiers to capture the finger images, palm prints, and even mug shots of captured enemy soldiers. In the movie "Navy Seals," Lt. (jg) Dale Hawkins (played by Charlie Sheen) took a photograph of a person he believed to be a non-combatant. He was asked by an intelligence officer, "Why did you let this man go?" He replied, "I had a bus to catch." If Lt. Hawkins had had a portable livescan, or better yet, a portable AFIS containing the prints of known offenders, he could have discovered that the alleged non-combatant was a terrorist. It may have made the movie less interesting, but it would have saved the lives of both service personnel and civilians. The standards and technology needed to make this happen are available now.

6.1.3.2 Interoperability

The political will that led to National Criminal History Improvement Program (NCHIP) funding for AFIS as well as to IAFIS must continue in order to support interoperability in forensic applications of AFIS, in both the criminal and civil processes. Opportunities are lost and identifications are missed each day because the AFIS systems cannot easily and directly communicate with each other.

6.1.3.3 Searching Plain Impressions

In April 2004, the Criminal Justice Information Services Division of the FBI published the National Fingerprint-Based Applicant Check Study (N-FACS). Its purpose was to determine the feasibility of searching IAFIS with plain (flat) impressions instead of with rolled impressions, and to make recommendations for enhancing the process. Among the findings and recommendations of the study is the following:[1]

---

[1] See National Fingerprint-Based Applicant Check Study (N-FACS), IAFIS-DOC-07054-1.0; CJIS Division, FBI.

This report fulfills the N-FACS mission by using various analytical studies and tests to assess the feasibility of implementing an alternative national flat fingerprint-based identification service within the FBI's IAFIS. All FBI testing conducted in support of the N-FACS was executed within the FBI's IAFIS or a similar Non-Operational Environment. The new four-plain-impression live-scan systems were evaluated in an operational setting with promising results. The N-FACS test results demonstrated the current capability to accept flat fingerprint submissions is feasible, but may adversely impact search accuracy, system processing, and image retention. The user community and the FBI should weigh the impact carefully.

Currently, rolled live-scan technology cannot capture all ten fingers expeditiously. Should rolled live-scan technology mature to such a capability, the FBI's CJIS Division views this additional data available from rolled fingerprints to be superior to the capabilities provided by flat-fingerprint impressions. Decisions must be made whether to pursue the new capability based on current assumptions or to explore changes to the IAFIS that would improve reliability and eliminate any risk of processing degradation.

Searching plain impressions when rolled impressions are not available is a better alternative than not searching at all. However, as is evident from the summary, a move away from the "gold standard" of ten rolled images may offer some opportunity, but ten rolled images remains the preferred vehicle.

6.1.4 AFIS THREATS

With all the positive aspects of AFIS in both forensic and civil applications, it may be difficult to consider possible threats, but threats to AFIS do indeed exist. Some of these threats are readily apparent, while others are not so obvious.

One obvious threat is the effect of the interruption of service, particularly in forensic applications. Systems that operate 24 hours a day, 7 days a week are designed to operate nonstop because the demand is nonstop. The need for redundancy is readily apparent, as is the need for backup, restore, and recovery procedures and practices. If an AFIS is taken out of service because of a natural or man-made disaster, how long will it take before some level of functionality can be restored? Simply having off-site backups for the databases is not sufficient. A fire in the building housing the AFIS may damage sensitive computers. Power may be interrupted for minutes or hours during a storm or disaster. The experience of preparation for the year 2000 (Y2K) problem made many agencies re-think their backup, recovery, and restore strategies. Those strategies should be continually reexamined.

The new AFIS are becoming more easy to use, but correspondingly more complex in their operation. On-site customization is being replaced by changes to the source files at the company's headquarters. This process allows for better control of the application software, but it also is a one-size-fits-all approach. This approach also requires that local software engineers become more dependent on the software engineers at the company's headquarters, who may be many time zones away and therefore not easy to reach.

This leads to the issue of who really knows the AFIS system. As a defensive measure, large AFIS agencies retain staff whose function is to understand the workings of the system as well as the vendor and to identify problems and resolutions in partnership with the vendor. Unfortunately, many of these agencies are losing the skilled staff who were part of the original AFIS installation team, who are leaving because of retirement, opportunities in other fields, or other reasons. Who will replace current AFIS management teams when they retire is a growing concern.

In the past, it was not uncommon for an employee to start as a fingerprint clerk, then be promoted to classifier or examiner. Along the way there may have been opportunities for supervisory responsibilities. The craft master level might be a position of an administrator in the identification agency. Good classifiers and examiners might also have furthered their skills as latent print examiners. In other words, there was a training ground for future administrators. That training ground, however, is evaporating.

Learning the complexities of the Henry Classification System is no longer necessary. There is little need to study ridge flows or tracings, or to argue over the second level pattern. Examiners no longer handle a stack of inked tenprint cards. Instead, they look at the images on their computer monitor and assume that the information presented is correct. The systems have developed so well that managers who do not have a fingerprint or systems background can assume that the AFIS system is working well simply because it is working. That is a very dangerous assumption.

Prior to 2000, there was a desperate need for COBOL programmers, most of whom had retired, to correct outdated computer programs (the Y2K problem). COBOL was so little used at that point that only a handful of people knew how to program with it. Agencies could find themselves in a similar situation with AFIS as the skill sets or design and testing are lost. This leaves the agency virtually at the mercy of vendors and their pricing structure.

The loss of tenprint examiners is second to the diminishing ranks of latent print examiners. Latent print examiners have a unique set of skills. The most important is their training and experience in making a latent print identification. The examiner compares a partial print with candidate images from tenprint records; this skill borders on the amazing. In addition, latent print examiners have to know how to use AFIS to produce the best candidate list that will contain the target. They may have to do this with no information other than the image itself. And, they may make the hit/no hit decision based only on this information.

The latent print examiners may also have to learn to use other computer systems and imaging software that will mask the finger image background, and they may be required to know the unique features of other AFIS systems. Understanding the features of latent print search computers such as the Universal Latent Workstation (ULW) or Remote Fingerprint Editing Software (RFES) allows the examiner access to the records on IAFIS.

Latent print examiners are also presented with more candidate images to choose from than in the past due to the ability of coding and matching software to present more candidates that to some degree match the image characteristics of the search print. More candidates, however, does not guarantee a latent print match or make the job any easier. In the past, when latent prints were compared only with elimination prints or suspect prints, the choices were much simpler.

Latent print examiners must also be able to articulate and explain their identifications in court. As defense attorneys challenge more latent print identifications through pre-trial hearings, latent print examiners are appearing in court more often. The identifications they make are no longer always accepted without question.

Keeping the cadre of latent print examiners across the nation will require funding and the political will to continue these positions. Too often, experienced latent print examiners have no promotional opportunities within their specialty and must transfer out to another assignment such as road patrol.

Another AFIS threat is litigation for a misidentification. Whereas a missed identification means that the tenprint submitted by an inquiring agency does not match a record that already exists on the database, a misidentification occurs when the wrong person is identified, and so the wrong criminal history is linked to that person. The embarrassment, possible incarceration, and almost certain resulting litigation are unpleasant for all involved.

Averting these threats will require funding resources, training, personnel, and the political will to succeed.

6.2 DNA AND FINGERPRINTS

Deoxyribonucleic acid (DNA) has been attracting much attention lately because of its remarkable accuracy in making a positive identification. DNA is extremely accurate in determining a match of a sample to an enrolled specimen. DNA evidence has freed prisoners wrongly convicted of crimes. Regardless of whether the freed inmates were originally convicted because of poor defense strategy, bad evidence, or misguided prosecutors, it was shown that their DNA did not match the evidence from the crime scene. Some believe that DNA will replace fingerprints as the most important identification medium. Will it? To answer that question, consider the steps in DNA sample collection and processing, and then make a comparison with that for fingerprints.

DNA is contained in hair, sweat, and nasal mucus as well as the fluids contained in a latent fingerprint. The frequency with which this evidence is recovered, under current practices, however, is too rare. For crimes in which bodily fluids are left behind as evidence, e.g., rape, the collection of a DNA specimen occurs at a hospital or other medical site that has the facilities to collect and preserve the specimen. This evidence, if not immediately identified, may become part of the unsolved DNA database of cases that have resulted in no match, waiting for a match to be made at a later date.

DNA samples collected from a group of individuals, such as convicted felons, can be sent to a state or private laboratory where they are searched against the DNA evidence from crimes already on file. While DNA is collected from inmates at a corrections reception center, not every police agency has the equipment and training to collect possible DNA evidence from a crime scene. Latent fingerprints, by contrast, are relatively easy to locate and collect. Also, not every community is prepared to commit the financial resources necessary to equip staff and maintain a lab with expensive equipment and highly trained and specialized personnel.

DNA analysis is subject to the same potential for misidentification and missed identification that exists in any process involving human intervention. Mistakes can be made in processing, recording information, transposing figures, or any of a number of different instances in which people become part of the process. Likewise, DNA testing equipment has to be regularly tested and calibrated to ensure that it still meets the same specifications as when it was originally installed. Sample collection devices have to be free of foreign material; chemicals used must remain pure and potent. Medical laboratories can make mistakes that, if not corrected, can lead to tragic results. When they do happen, a detailed review takes place in order to reduce the chances of that type of error in the future. The goal is to ultimately eliminate those mistakes altogether.

As of February 2004, there were 1,646,084 DNA profiles, consisting of 75,507 forensic profiles and 1,570,577 convicted offender profiles, stored on the National DNA Index System (NDIS). By comparison, the FBI's IAFIS holds over 46 million fingerprint records, with an annual submission of 12 million electronic prints and 4.5 million prints mailed on inked tenprint cards.

There is a wide difference of opinion regarding the collection and use of DNA. Proponents for expanding its use argue that taking a DNA sample at arrest is no different than taking fingerprints, a standard practice. Opponents argue that unlike fingerprints, DNA provides a wealth of information about a person's genetic makeup. This information could conceivably be used as a tool to gain information about other family members who have no direct association with the event for which the person was arrested. Unlike DNA, a fingerprint image has no associated link with any other family member. The unique friction ridges on a fingerprint developed due to pressure, not genetics.

6.3 THE MOVE FROM FORENSIC TO CIVIL APPLICATIONS

The early applications of AFIS technology were limited to the area of forensics. These original applications of AFIS, which relied on images from inked tenprint cards that were captured by digital cameras, increased not only the speed of the identification response, but also the level of accuracy. Identifications that took hours, days, or weeks pre-AFIS could now be concluded in minutes or hours. Latent print processing particularly benefited from this increase in response time and accuracy. The number of latent print identifications made after the introduction of AFIS was an exponential leap from the number made pre-AFIS, from a handful to thousands. Although the process was still very much linked to paper, the move to increased use of digital imaging was becoming apparent. The infusion of federal funding for state and local governments, the creation of IAFIS, and the immediate benefits in processing speeds and accuracy were attracting attention.

The markets that had first been dominated by large AFIS vendors were becoming of interest to smaller, more specialized companies. These companies could provide unique services such as application software or specialized hardware, such as livescan machines, that were competitive with the large vendors' products. This led to the large AFIS vendors entering into strategic alliances with niche companies, which provided for a more efficient, more competitive AFIS product while responding to competitive market forces. With more players in the field of AFIS technology, there were more minds looking for additional applications for the products.

As AFIS systems' electronic records began to replace the clerks who had classified and fielded the tenprint records, other components began to have similar effects. The introduction of livescan for the capture of finger images as well as pedigree information—along with mug shots and palm impressions—became a much less demanding process. Sworn personnel were no longer essential for fingerprinting a prisoner. Livescan machines do not require messy ink rollers and errors can be immediately corrected. Booking officers could be freed to return to patrol; less skilled personnel could handle the booking.

This turn of events saved money by relegating fingerprinting tasks to lower paid personnel. However, in some instances management failed to understand that the capture of the finger impressions, even with the livescan machines, was very much dependent on the operator. Constant pressure, a nail-to-nail roll, and image centering are just as necessary to the process whether it is performed by sworn personnel or clerical staff. Mistakes or lack of definition at this phase of the process must be avoided if AFIS is to meet its potential, particularly in latent print identifications.

From its creation in the criminal arena, AFIS began to move into the civil arena. There are a number of reasons for this migration, including the success in making identifications of arrestees and the increased use of these systems on vetting job applicants. The use of AFIS in the criminal or forensic arena underwrote much of the development costs of this new technology, and the millions of dollars invested in its development produced unexpected benefits. Government agencies found the technology valuable because of the increase of both throughput and the accuracy of identifications. There were significant reductions in staff costs as well, as the tedious work performed by clerks was gradually being taken over by computers.

The introduction of AFIS systems into applications that did not rely on a law enforcement database brought a new definition to the term "civil" applications. When AFIS was exclusively the domain of government law enforcement agencies, long-established terms such as "criminal" and "civil" had distinct meanings. A criminal search was an image search on someone who had been arrested or who was in some way connected with a criminal activity, while a civil search referred to a search on a person whose finger images were being compared with the same database used in the criminal searches, but the purpose was for a job application, not an arrest. In the case of the criminal arrest search, if a match was not found, the new record was almost always kept and the criminal history file was updated with the new information. For the job applicant, the record might be returned after the search. For the criminal there was no charge for the search; for the civil applicant, there might be a processing fee. In both instances a rap sheet would be sent to the submitting authority.

As the use of AFIS began to appear in applications that did not tie to a CCH file, the term "civil" began to evolve. AFIS split into "forensic" applications, which searched a law enforcement database, and "civil" applications, which were benefit related and less complex. The forensic applications are in the area of criminal identification, i.e., identifications that may be tied to a CCH database, including persons arrested for crimes as well as those who were fingerprinted as part of a job application. The forensic applications can be further subdivided into tenprint identification with a criminal component, tenprint identification with an applicant component, and latent print identification (see Fig. 6.4).

Civil applications of AFIS systems, such as determination of eligibility for welfare benefits, are different from the forensic applications in a number of ways. For instance, the new "civil" applications are usually a one-to-one (1:1) search, a verification function, rather than a one-to-many (1:N) search, an identification function. In the one-to-one search, as described earlier, the results are yes or no, pass or fail, match or no match. The subject needs to be enrolled only once and demographic updates to the record are not necessary, i.e., there is no forensic history of the person. The computer matches the person's name or identification number with the finger image and compares the most recent impression of the subject with the current impression. The search is performed against a relatively small database that may contain only one or two subject finger images instead of ten fingers. This type of searches can be called a "closed" search because the search is limited; it is also referred to as a "verification" search. Also, there is an inherent belief that the subject will cooperate since confirmation of identity is linked to the receipt of some benefit.

The criminal and civil systems differ in terms of their complexity and cost because of their differing purposes. Additionally, while the search databases for forensic applications are maintained for law enforcement purposes, the databases for civil applications are operated and maintained by non-law enforcement personnel. The requirements for record retention, confidentiality, and even accuracy can be very different for civil applications. The personnel who collect the demographic data and take the initial prints for civil applications do not need the same level of training as their counterparts in the law enforcement arena. Errors in processing can more easily be corrected because the network is more contained. These systems may only need to be operational on an 8:00 a.m. to 5:00 p.m. schedule, reducing stress on individual components

Figure 6.4

Forensic and Civil AFIS Applications

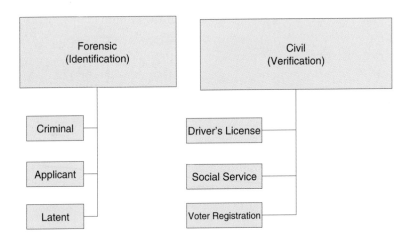

and personnel. Finally, unlike forensic applications, civil applications do not need to store entire images, only the digital representations and the template. See Table 6.1 for a summary of the major differences between forensic and civil AFIS applications.

The use of AFIS technology in civil applications, particularly public benefits programs, has not been without criticism. Anti-fingerprinting advocacy groups claim that requiring that individuals be fingerprinted to receive benefits to which they are lawfully entitled amounts to coercion and intimidation. They also claim that the idea of being fingerprinted, even if it means rolling only one or two fingers, has a chilling effect that will prevent eligible people from participating. Advocates of fingerprinting counter that the use of AFIS technology does not intimidate eligible persons, and it has helped to eliminate fraud. Whereas in the past a person may have registered for public benefits in one county, then registered for the same benefits in another county (either under the same or different name), such duplication has now been virtually eliminated. Counties and states claim to have saved millions of public dollars through the registration process. Once enrolled, the images are kept on a statewide database. Registration in any county constitutes enrollment onto the database. Another advantage of AFIS in public benefits applications is the reduction of administrative error. It is not difficult to prove that a person who claims eligibility for benefits has not been enrolled.

There are a growing number of civil applications that are using AFIS technology in innovative ways. For example, a school district in Pennsylvania experimented with using AFIS for a school lunch program. In the pilot program, all students were required to enroll one finger image, using a single-finger scanner like the one shown in Figure 6.5, and were given a personal identification number (PIN). Those students who paid for their lunch would deposit the money into their own account and use it to pay for their lunch purchases. Those

Forensic	Civil
Identification	Verification
One-to-many (1:N) searches	One-to-one (1:1) searches
Open search	Closed search
Candidate list	Match or no match
Linked to CCH	No AFIS history file
Connect to other AFIS	Stand alone
Capture 10 images	Capture one or two images
Latent print search	No other functionality
Store image, template	Store template only
Complex	Relatively simple
24/7	8:00 a.m.–5:00 p.m.

Table 6.1

Comparison of Forensic and Civil AFIS Applications

Figure 6.5
Single-Finger Reader

students who had their lunch subsidized would also have their lunch charged to their accounts, but the subsidy would cover the costs. The students' identities were authenticated by their finger image and PIN. The benefits of such a program include the following:

- It is less obvious which students have subsidized lunches, often a sensitive topic.
- More students who are eligible for subsidized lunches will purchase lunch.
- The PIN combined with a finger image reduces or eliminates fraud.
- Fewer opportunities for theft because less cash changes hands.
- Students do not need to carry their lunch money.

There are a growing number of businesses that are based on fingerprint technology. The May 2004 issue of *Entrepreneur* magazine lists the 50 top companies that started franchising since 1999. One of the top ten companies in this list provides children's identification products and services.[2]

In both forensic and civil applications, there is an increasing need to prove identity. Whether to confirm a background check following an arrest, to ensure that a job applicant has no past event that may preclude hiring, or to provide confirmation that a person is eligible for social benefits, AFIS systems will continue to evolve.

6.4 OTHER FRONTIERS

6.4.1 MULTIPLE AGENCIES SHARING AFIS TECHNOLOGY: WIN

When AFIS systems are networked together, it allows many smaller organizations the ability to pool their resources and create what becomes a much larger system in the end. In the mid-1980s, a number of western U.S. states and communities realized the need for AFIS, but were such small populations that it did not make sense for them to have individual installations. They worked together

---

[2] *Entrepreneur*, May 2004, p. 96.

to create the Western Identification Network (WIN), eventually composed of nine states, six federal agencies, and one locality. In 1988, they first met to create an AFIS system that would work across the member states. By 1989, Alaska, California, Idaho, Oregon, Nevada, Utah, Washington, and Wyoming had all appropriated money to pay for the new system. Soon after, the main AFIS was installed in Sacramento, California, with remote locations in Cheyenne, Salt Lake City, Boise, Carson City, Salem, and Portland. Alaska, California, and Washington already had their own AFIS system, and these existing systems were integrated with the main system, creating the first WIN in 1990. Integrating these systems boosted the fingerprint database from about 900,000 to over 14 million searchable records.

With WIN operational, more localities and federal agencies became involved. By 1992, Helena, Montana, the Immigration and Naturalization Service, the Postal Inspection Service, and the Secret Service all joined WIN. By the end of the 1990s, they were joined by the Internal Review Service, the FBI, the Drug Enforcement Agency, and the Alaska Department of Public Safety.

In 1998, WINPHO (for WIN-Photo) was created, which allowed mug shot and some Department of Motor Vehicles photos to be accessed in addition to an AFIS record. Members can access photo information over a secure Internet connection, using a standard World Wide Web browser; no specialized hardware or software is required. Ongoing funding for WIN is provided by user fees, charged on a cost-recovery basis. Any income is returned to the operation.

6.4.2 MULTIPLE NATIONS SHARING AFIS SYSTEMS: EURODAC

Eurodac got its start in 1991 as part of the Dublin Convention. A method was needed for members of the soon-to-be-created European Union (see Fig. 6.6) to track who was seeking asylum and where, and perhaps more importantly, to track asylum seekers who applied first in one country, then in another, and so on. Since the easiest way to track these individuals is via fingerprints, a common fingerprint transmission method had to be developed. By 1998, the scope of Eurodac had changed somewhat. Member states want to track not only asylum seekers, but also others who may have entered a country illegally. This would allow countries to quickly determine who was legitimately applying for asylum and who was not. Eurodac went live on January 15, 2003.

Eurodac is composed of a central unit that has a centralized database for comparing fingerprints. Information can be sent electronically between the member states and the database, but it can also be sent by physical means if necessary. Along with fingerprint images, data stored includes the country of origin, place and date of asylum application, gender, and a reference number. This data is collected for anyone over 14 years old, and is then sent directly to

Figure 6.6
Map of Europe

the central unit. The central unit generally handles all fingerprint comparisons within 24 hours except in the case of emergency.

For asylum seekers, data is kept for 10 years unless the individual is granted citizenship in any of the member states. When citizenship is granted, the information is erased. Those who have entered a country illegally will have their data stored for 2 years after their fingerprints were taken, but it will be erased if the person is granted a residence permit or leaves the European Union. Illegal aliens already in a country would have their fingerprints checked against Eurodac to ensure they do not have a pending asylum application, but in such cases Eurodac would not store the fingerprints or any other information regarding the illegal alien.

Countries within the European Union must make sure that fingerprints are lawfully obtained. Eurodac shares this responsibility, along with protecting the privacy rights of both the individuals fingerprinted and the member states. Additionally, each member country can appoint two representatives to an independent joint supervisory authority, which has the responsibility to ensure rights are not violated and to resolve implementation problems as Eurodac goes online. In order to ensure Eurodac's effectiveness, reports are given to the European Parliament after the first year of operation, the third year of operation, and every 6 years after that.

CHAPTER 7

BUYING AN AFIS SYSTEM: THE BASIC DOCUMENTS NEEDED

Peter T. Higgins and Kathleen M. Higgins
The Higgins-Hermansen Group, LLC

7.1 INTRODUCTION

Purchasing an automated fingerprint identification system (AFIS) can be a daunting task. It is a huge undertaking that can typically cost millions of dollars and years of staff time and effort. Each of the vendors you have considered has probably promised that their system is the very best—it will do everything that the police, the forensic team or the civil agency, and the public need it to do, and their system is faster and better than the other vendors' offerings. Plus, your colleagues likely have systems from different vendors and have strongly held views on their experiences.

Selecting the AFIS that is best suited for a specific community is dependent on a number of different steps and involves a great number of individuals within the community, many of whom (e.g., a state's network manager) will never use the system or even care how it functions, as a biometric system, once it is installed. Getting the cooperation and input from each of these individuals at the earliest stages of the project and maintaining their cooperation throughout the design, development, implementation, and testing phases is critical to the project's success.

7.2 THE NEED FOR A DISCIPLINED APPROACH

An AFIS provides an automated way to search fingerprints, latent images, and palm prints. While all AFIS employ standard computer hardware, and some employ special purpose accelerator boards, the soul of these machines is software that contains the algorithms and other mathematical magic. The major AFIS vendors all offer a core commercial product that is normally modified or augmented as part of a procurement to reflect the interfaces and business rules of the customer, be it a criminal justice or civil agency. The basic foundation of hardware and software is typically referred to as a commercial-off-the-shelf (COTS) system. The integration of COTS systems with customer networks and business rules is part of the discipline of software engineering.

AFIS software engineering has been a challenged industry since its inception. Many AFIS are initially disappointments, and there are far more contentious discussions about payments being withheld until systems work as anticipated than the industry would care to admit. One lesson to be learned is that there is more to purchasing an AFIS than picking the lowest price or the best match rate in a limited test environment, also known as a benchmark.

The stories of failures and cost and schedule overruns in the systems development and software engineering arenas are legendary. In the mid-1980s, the U.S. Department of Defense (DOD) decided to study the issue to determine if there was anything that separated the successful projects from the rest. Carnegie Mellon University (CMU) was selected to perform the study. DOD established a center of excellence at CMU, the Software Engineering Institute (SEI), which is still actively studying and reporting on this field.

The SEI demonstrated a clear correlation between the maturity of a business's processes and the quality of its products. They then modeled the levels of maturity to enable government procurement and program offices and industry to evaluate the maturity, and thus the likely success, of a development effort undertaken by a corporate division or an entire company. This model is known as the capability maturity model (CMM).

The CMM has five levels of maturity, levels 1 through 5. Very few companies achieve level 5—or even aim for it. At the lowest level, level 1, there are few or no defined processes, and any established processes are poorly documented and not routinely followed. To move up from level 2 to level 5, it is not sufficient to simply have policies; the policies must be written, disseminated, understood, updated based on experience, and followed. Coupled with the CMM elements, there are system engineering elements that play a role in success. The most important relate to the requirements and the design phase of a project.

Standardized, quality-oriented software development based on mature processes has been shown to reduce the time to delivery, the number of latent defects, and the overall cost. More recently, the SEI published studies on the procurement and integration of COTS systems. The major difference between developing a new system from scratch and integrating one based on COTS is that "the requirements process must become more flexible, yielding to the realities of commercial products."[1] Later in this chapter, we will see how this should be taken into consideration in the specification of requirements for procurement of an AFIS.

A corollary to the SEI findings is that an agency or department purchasing an AFIS needs well-defined processes of its own to ensure that they convey their requirements clearly to their users and the vendor, that they manage the design

---

[1] "COTS-Based System." www.sei.cmu.edu.

process properly, and that they test the product thoroughly. While there is a CMU model that permits the measurement of the maturity of a procurement organization, it is unlikely that an agency that is not normally involved in the large-scale computer system procurement business would spend the time and resources to develop and maintain such skills in-house.

This chapter explains how to apply the lessons from the SEI and from many AFIS procurements to increase the probability of a successful procurement—one you can be proud of and that provides years of quality service.

7.3 OVERALL STRATEGY

There are logical phases to any AFIS procurement (or any other large procurement activity), and there are structured ways to approach each of them. The overall process can be cleanly divided into three phases:

1. Pre-acquisition
2. Acquisition
3. Development and deployment

The activities in each phase should be structured to address the appropriate issues as thoroughly and rapidly as possible. One way to do this is to use a structured decision tree to focus on the development of appropriate decisions and to document them. What is a decision tree? It is a series of questions that are intended to open your mind to possibilities, narrow down decisions, and ensure completeness of the process. The questions are based on years of procurement experience and common sense, but still follow the age-old basics: who, what, why, where, when, and how.

A decision tree provides a way to make and document decisions. Like a customer satisfaction survey instrument, answers can filter out inappropriate questions. Think of a customer survey that instructs "If your answer to question 8 is No, then skip to question 13." In our case, a good example would be "If you are not going to search latent fingerprints, skip to question 22."

Do not think of a static set of questions that can simply be sent to stakeholders in the mail when buying an AFIS. The biggest challenge is likely to be their lack of up-to-date knowledge about AFIS technology and procurement options. While the questions can evoke new thinking, it takes an expert to effectively work through the questions with the stakeholders. This is because program managers typically buy just one AFIS in a lifetime, yet the technology, standards, and products evolve relentlessly. The requirement specifications and source selection criteria are unique for each situation and cannot just be updated from the last procurement or from another agency's procurement.

7.4 PRE-ACQUISITION PHASE

For this phase the basic questions in our decision tree revolve around the following:

- What is our goal?
  - What will the system do, who will use it, where will it be placed, and what services will it provide and to whom?
- Who will manage the project?
  - Who will assist them, including consultants?
- Where, how, and when will we get funding?
  - In what fiscal years will we be purchasing the system?
  - Is funding available for travel to vendor sites and for consultants?
  - What are the out-year costs of ownership and can we afford them?
- What is our acquisition strategy?
  - Sole source or competition?

Obviously, the pre-acquisition phase questions and answers are very dependent on agency policy, procurement and privacy laws, and overall priorities and strategies. The key stakeholders include contracts, finance, management, policy, users, legal, specialists, and the vendors. The state-of-the-art approach is to gather the key stakeholders in a conference room for a few days and go through the decision tree questions, explaining each one based on the response of the audience. Details on how this can be done productively are presented later in this chapter. Note that this chapter does not provide a complete decision tree family of questions but rather shows how to build and apply one that is appropriate to your activity.

Pre-acquisition documents include a concept of operations (ConOps) and an acquisition strategy. The next two sections address these documents.

7.4.1 CONCEPT OF OPERATIONS DOCUMENT

Before any significant steps can be taken in the development of the AFIS project, the project development team should prepare a detailed concept of operations (ConOps) document. The ConOps is a statement of why the system is needed, providing a general description of how it is expected to work, who will use it, and when it will be installed.

If armed with the right questions and tools, a ConOps can be written in 3 days. Starting with an outline and a white board connected to a computer, a facilitator can solicit high-level ideas for each ConOps topical area, capture them on the board, and later that same day convert them to Keynote™ or PowerPoint™ slides. On the second day, the team can review the slides and see their input from day one presented to them in an organized way. This will evoke corrections, additions, and deletions. After the facilitator updates the slides, they are reviewed a second time and updated again, as appropriate. On the third day, the facilitators can flesh out the material in the slides to a ten or so page ConOps that can be signed off and approved that week. The slides can then be updated, as appropriate, and used to brief those not present at the meeting.

At this point, it is critical to share the ConOps with potential vendors to determine if it needs to be changed to make your wants and needs match up with their COTS products. This can help control costs, reduce risk, and permit the vendors an early look at your needs. One way to do this is to hold a meeting where the slides are presented to all the vendors and copies of the ConOps are distributed. Follow up by inviting each vendor to an informal meeting to permit them to comment on your ConOps before it is converted into a requirements specification, when contracting rules are likely to prohibit further informal communication with potential vendors.

In preparing the ConOps, the following outline is a useful starting point. The list should be tailored to the needs of the individual jurisdiction and modified over time as experience dictates.

- Purpose and intended use of the AFIS—civil, criminal, applicants, homeland defense, etc., as well as highlights on users, customers per service offered, etc. [what and who]
- Timeframe for contract award, deployment, and numbers of years of intended use [when]
- Deliverables to include any converted records, equipment, training, and documentation [what]
- Functionality—identification, verification, latents, palms, etc. [what]
- Transactions—based on ANSI NIST standards, etc.; both AFIS searches and responses [what]
- Hours of operations of the AFIS—staffed versus lights out [when]
- Staffing per shift [who]
- Workloads in terms of transactions per day, priorities, and capacities for storage [what]
- Performance in terms of response time, throughput, and maximum acceptable matching error rates [how]
- Gateways to other systems such as other AFIS and criminal history systems [what]
- Open issues and next steps

Once approved, the ConOps will act as the base document from which subsequent requirements specifications, source selection plans, and master schedules will be developed. A detailed ConOps will help the project development team focus its efforts and ensure that all approved functionality is included in sufficient detail to allow the vendors to propose appropriate systems. The ConOps will also be used to ensure that additional, non-approved functionality is not added to the requirements. Any approved changes should be added to the ConOps so it remains up to date.

An example of the knowledge required to do this successfully can be seen in the performance–response time area. If you need an AFIS response in 10 seconds to support a border security capability, do not specify a response time of 10 seconds. It is fairly easy for almost any AFIS to give a 10-second response time if there are no other searches running in the AFIS. However, in normal operations there will be multiple transactions arriving at some non-Gaussian arrival rates, queuing delays, simultaneous searches, throughput tradeoffs, and possible contention from higher priority transactions. The ConOps, and later the requirements documentation, should address this by specifying the average response time for 95% of the transactions with a minimum queue length of so many transactions at each priority level. The vendors have complex models that can translate these numbers into the number of fingers to be matched, the number of matchers, the match rate per second for each matcher, and the allocation of queues to matchers.

7.4.2 ACQUISITION STRATEGY DOCUMENT

Before you can get permission to procure an AFIS, secure funding, or release a request for proposals (RFP), you will need to document your acquisition strategy. As with the ConOps, a facilitator can lead you through the process of creating this document in a few days. The scope of the acquisition strategy document is, for a large part, a function of local policy and practice. A good list of topics to cover should include the following:

- Scope of the project—list the high-level tasks to be contracted [what]
- Sources to be invited to bid [who and how]
- How will it be acquired—open competition or sole source? [how]
- What type of contract will be used—firm fixed price or cost plus fee? [how]
- Budgeting and funding, including an estimate of anticipated costs by fiscal year [how and when]
- Priority and linkage to the appropriate strategic plan [why]
- Local management information standards and requirements (e.g., use of XML for certain interfaces) [how]
- Test and evaluation before and after shipment [how and who]
- Logistics considerations to include shipment, training, and facility implications such as power and air conditioning [what]

- Government furnished property, information, or access to government facilities and information systems [what]
- Security considerations—what level of clearance, if any, will be required for contractors and government personnel on the project? [who and what]
- Project milestones to include preparation of acquisition phase documents, their approval, and release [when]
- Who will run the acquisition? [who]
- Who approved the Con Ops? [who]

As part of developing an acquisition strategy, many decisions will have to be made. Some of the key decisions can be addressed with a decision tree. They include the following:

- Should there be a benchmark or not?
- How should vendors be distinguished by use of mandatory versus rated requirements?
- Should the evaluators be given a chance to see the bidders as part of an oral presentation or not?[2]
- What weights should be assigned to the following vendor proposal constituents: price, experience, benchmark results, orals presentation quality, and rated requirements?

The next subsection addresses the pros and cons of benchmarking.

7.4.3 BENCHMARKING

A benchmark is a documented procedure that will measure an AFIS in the execution of a well-defined set or sets of tasks. Many different aspects of an AFIS, ranging from response time and false match rate to ease of the user interface, can be measured. It is assumed that these metrics relate to the anticipated performance in a particular application. Thus, there is a need to carefully align any benchmark with the particulars of the intended use. Obviously, nobody else's benchmark results are fully indicative of results you would experience. A well-defined benchmark can be applied to several vendors' systems so that comparisons can be made between different proposed systems based on your anticipated use and your data.

An ANSI-IAI Standard for Benchmarking AFIS Systems was published in 1985. Since it was not reviewed and updated at the end of the 5-year nominal life of ANSI standards, it was dropped. It is still worth reading just to know what performance metrics can be benchmarked.

---

[2] An outline for an oral presentation can be found in Ch. 9 of *Biometrics: Identity Assurance in the Information Age*, Woodward, Orlans, and Higgins, 2002, by Osborne, a McGraw Hill Company.

The decision of whether to perform a benchmark and when to do it has to factor in costs in travel and staff and consultant time, the purpose, and the potential value added. Benchmarking is a management decision that needs to be made early. The less familiarity you have with state-of-the-art AFIS, the more appealing and important a benchmark becomes.

Benchmarks require test background files and a rigorous plan. It is very hard to tell exactly what is going on in an AFIS undergoing a benchmark. Such factors as how many fingers are actually being searched, what threshold score is being used, and which filters, if any, are in use are nearly impossible to independently ascertain. You will find that you are at the mercy of the vendor for answers to these and other issues. If you do decide to benchmark, then it is imperative that you have a significantly large database with data from your own users. If you are using single fingers, the number of records needed is different from that required for tenprint searches.

Once the number of tenprint records in a repository reaches approximately 400,000, the false match rate starts to go up. Rarely, however, will you have the luxury of such a large benchmark database to be used for each vendor, as it can take almost a minute to extract the minutiae from one set of ten rolled impressions. Extracting the data from 500,000 records would take about 9 months on one machine; nine dedicated machines working around the clock could complete the task in 1 month. It is unreasonable to ask each vendor to dedicate that much hardware for such a long time for benchmark preparation. If you cannot provide at least 100,000 of your own tenprint records for a background file, then you should consider an alternative approach, other than letting the vendors each provide their own hand-tailored background data. The best alternative for tenprint benchmarking would be along the lines of 3,000 to 4,000 tenprint records run against 3,000 to 4,000 different tenprint records from the same people.

At some point the error rate for binning by pattern type starts to be eclipsed by the false match rate. The exact point is different for each system and each database, but no benchmark is likely to be large enough to reach that point—yet your system is likely to cross that threshold on the first day of operations. Unfortunately, benchmarks tend to mask this and other issues.

There are three approaches for using the results of benchmarking:

1. Pre-filter the list of bidders.
2. Use in evaluation of proposals.
3. Verify the apparent "winner's" proposal claims.

A benchmark should be based on the anticipated size and functionality of your system to the extent possible. As noted previously, size is often a major stumbling block that cannot be overcome. But it is important to use your own data, run the benchmark at the vendors' factories, and benchmark each vendor against a standard. The benchmark should focus on the following:

- Ease of user interfaces
- Basic functional and administrative features
- Lights out versus best practices
- Reliability, relative reliability, and accuracy versus labor content to compute a value factor

While there is no best practice for benchmarks, it is illustrative to look at the FBI's approach to benchmarking IAFIS. They had already converted their cards to digital records and were paying the vendors for the benchmark time and effort, thus the enormous background file.

- 300 latents were checked against a 500,000 record background file
  - Hand-built "ground truth sets" were based on minutiae comparisons
  - 30 of the 300 were compared using the same feature extractions for all vendors
  - Vendor-extracted minutiae were compared against known minutiae
- Two latent sets and two tenprint sets were developed
  - Latents: some with a limit on the number of minutiae and some with all available minutiae
  - Tenprints: first searched masking some minutiae and then with all minutiae

A benchmark plan should cover the

- Purpose
- Scope
- Source of sample data
- Tests to be run
- Evaluation procedures
- Pass/fail or rated criteria
- Personnel to be assigned and their roles and responsibilities

The benchmark plan should set limits on

- The location of benchmark sites
- Time, in both hours per day and days
- How early the background data will be available

There will be many benchmark challenges. Many of your unique, mandatory requirements are not likely to be available at benchmark sites, such as local interface protocols and systems or the latest ANSI/NIST implementation. Your small test databases will not reflect the realities of error rates in large databases. Since it is likely that not all of your required functionality will be available in the COTS product to be benchmarked, you should consider that an 80% (or some other less-than-100%) threshold be used for successful functionality demonstration, as opposed to reliability and accuracy metrics.

7.5 ACQUISITION PHASE

For the acquisition phase, the basic questions in our decision tree revolve around the following:

- What are the tasks for the vendor to perform?
  - How will we specify them?
- What are the requirements for the system to be purchased?
  - How will they be specified?
  - What workflows need to be defined?
- How will we select the best value vendor?
  - What will we tell the vendors to include in their proposals?
  - Who will evaluate the proposals?

Like those of the pre-acquisition phase, the questions and answers of the acquisition phase are very dependent on agency policy, procurement and privacy laws, and overall priorities and strategies. The key stakeholders include contracts, finance, management, policy, users, legal, specialists, and the vendors.

To document the decisions and the answers to our decision tree questions, two major documents are prepared in the acquisition phase:

1. The source selection plan
2. The request for proposals (RFP), which consists of:
   - Statement of work (SOW)
   - Requirements specification
   - Proposal preparation instructions
   - Terms and conditions

In the following sections, the source selection plan, the SOW, and the requirements specification are addressed.

7.5.1 SOURCE SELECTION PLAN

A clear and detailed source selection plan will give the source selection team a basis from which they can differentiate one proposal from another and highlight the strengths and weaknesses of the different proposals.

The source selection plan must reflect the RFP. If the proposal preparation instructions do not ask for a certain type of information (e.g., location of training), then that should not be an evaluation criterion. The source selection plan as well as the RFP should be based on the decisions made in the preacquisition phase and documented in the ConOps and acquisition strategy. As the complexity of the procurement and the RFP increase, so too does the need for an increased involvement of experts and users in the source selection process.

Those assigned to source selection will need to dedicate a couple of weeks to reading, analyzing, and documenting the strengths, weaknesses, and open issues associated with all of the submitted proposals. Clarifications are typically sent to the bidders when a proposal is too ambiguous, appears to have overlooked a requirement, etc. It is a local policy decision if vendors can submit wholesale changes to their proposals in response to a clarification request.

The source selection process requires the *a priori* selection of evaluation criteria and relative weights. The plan documents process and the associated evaluation forms. Evaluation criteria for rated requirements should provide examples of excellent, very good, acceptable, and poor ratings. Otherwise, there will be too many subjective considerations based on personal levels of expectations. Likewise, reviewers will tend to be harsher on the first or last proposal, as they become more aware of the state of proposal writing. Prior to seeing the proposals, reviewers should take a short training course with a few examples of appropriate ratings explained to them.

When setting the relative weights for cost, technical expertise, management, oral presentations, and benchmarking, be sure to leave enough weight for the last of these so that the winner is not likely to have already been selected before considering the benchmark results. Cost should not be weighted too high, as the lowest bidder is not always the one who understands what you want. You have to balance cost and likelihood of success.

7.5.2 STATEMENT OF WORK (SOW)

Working from the high-level plans for AFIS functionality spelled out in the ConOps document, the project development team must generate a detailed requirements specification document that lists all of the functional requirements that the system must be able to perform once it is delivered, tested, and installed. In many instances, the requirements specification document becomes an integral part of the SOW that is included in the RFP or request for bid (RFB) packages that are made available to the potential vendors.

It is critically important to clearly distinguish the requirements for the vendor from those for the system to be purchased. You are not just purchasing a COTS product; you are purchasing services from the vendor, including training, integration, shipping, and installation. The SOW tells the vendor what you want the vendor to do. It should be organized around a work breakdown structure (WBS) to which the vendor should align their work and work products.

A typical WBS for an AFIS procurement could look like this:

1. Project management: reporting, reviews, master schedule, WBS dictionary, etc.
2. Design and integration: design documents and reviews, and necessary software coding, procurement of all components and their integration, factory acceptance testing, etc.
3. Delivery, installation, and training: facility impact analysis, packing, shipping, unpacking, wiring, integration with local systems and communications, transition planning and support, training, on-site acceptance testing, etc.
4. Warrantee and maintenance services
5. Card or other file conversion effort: standards, reports, output, data ownership, etc.

Each SOW task should identify any deliverables associated with it.[3]

7.5.3 REQUIREMENTS SPECIFICATION

Project definition is one of the most crucial steps in successful project development. Until the government understands exactly what it wants the AFIS to do and how it wants it to accomplish these tasks, the requirements specification (requirements spec) cannot be developed. The conversations with the vendors during the ConOps development process are critical to ensuring that your requirements are achievable, reasonable, and understood. The requirements spec will form the core of any RFP that is released to potential bidders.

Developing a detailed and unambiguous requirements specification document is a complex process that generally requires cooperation and input from all members of the project development team. Requirements specification

---

[3] For a further discussion of deliverables and SOW and WBS definitions, see Ch. 9 of *Biometrics: Identity Assurance in the Information Age*, Woodward, Orlans, and Higgins, 2002, by Osborne, a McGraw Hill Company.

documents typically go through several iterations before they are deemed clear enough to release to vendors—the process from first draft to final document can take several months to complete.

To reduce the possibility of creating ambiguous statements within the requirements specification document, the team assigned with generating the document should meet with the contracting officer assigned to the project to discuss rules and requirements that are typically contained in standard terms and conditions sections of the RFP package to ensure that requirements spelled out in the requirements spec and subsequent SOW do not conflict. In some instances, items that may logically be contained in the requirements specification document may already be covered in the government's standard contracting package. In those instances, the requirements document should reference the specific section and paragraph in the terms and conditions that are part of the RFP package.

The requirements specification document is where you specify the capabilities of the system to be delivered and relate them to the automated and semi-automated workflows you will be following. It should echo the ConOps but have more granularity and detail. The document typically has the following outline:

1. Introductory material, including table of contents, change history, reference documents, standards, and other high-level information.
2. Contextual information, such as the current environment and interfaces, planned changes in policy, interfaces, volumes of transactions, etc.
3. Functional performance (throughput, response time, availability, etc.), interface protocols and data rates, and storage requirements, using "WILL" statements for informational purposes and "SHALL" statements for system requirements. This can be arranged by workflow, by functional area, or by subsystem.
4. Appendices, as appropriate, including a glossary of terms and abbreviations.

The requirements should be labeled with their evaluation classification so the vendors know which ones to spend additional time responding to. The classes are as follows:

- Mandatory requirements: those requirements that the vendor must address in their proposal. Evaluation of mandatory requirements is generally on a pass/fail basis. Failure to address any one mandatory requirement may result in the proposal being removed from consideration.
- Rated requirements: those requirements for which a vendor may present a solution that can be rated as providing a more creative approach to the requirement than was anticipated. Developing rating schemes that can be

substantiated requires significant efforts on the part of the project development team.

- Optional requirements: if optional requirements were part of the SOW and the requirements spec, these must be evaluated as to cost, time required, and overall benefit to the project.

The purchaser should avoid overspecifying the system, but understand that if you do not specify something, you will get the default COTS capability in that area. For instance, if you state that the "system SHALL provide a latent case management system," you cannot then fail the vendor at acceptance test time when the latent case system turns out to be more basic and limited than you had imagined. The alternative is to include a rated requirement for a latent case management system (LCMS), add a proposal preparation requirement that the vendors submit their COTS LCMS documentation, and then rate the depth and quality of that documentation.

As previously noted, requirements specs must be clear, complete, and unambiguous. To ensure that they meet all of these requirements, it is useful if the document itself is highly structured and formatted to incorporate the following:

- A list of assumptions that have been made by the project development team in preparing the requirements specification.
- A list of compliance standards that must be met by the vendors, e.g., national or local requirements for electrical standards, image compression and transmission, etc.
- A description of the expected users of the system.
- Requirements that must be met by the vendor should be contained in separate SHALL statements. For example: "The card scan workflow SHALL permit an operator to adjust the contrast/brightness of a fingerprint image during the quality control process."
- Each requirement, and each informational statement, should be individually numbered to allow the proposal reviewers to track compliance with each of the requirements.

7.6 DEVELOPMENT AND DEPLOYMENT PHASE

For the development and deployment phase, the basic questions in our decision tree include the following:

- How well is the vendor performing the SOW tasks?
  - Are they on schedule?
  - Do they understand the nuances of your needs?

- How well is the vendor's product conforming to the requirements spec?
  - Are the interfaces all understood and documented?
  - Has each requirement been allocated to a COTS or developmental item?

In the development and deployment phase, the documents are prepared by the successful offerer. The SOW defined the documents for the vendor to deliver and the scope of those documents. During this phase, the government team needs to review the documents for completeness, accuracy, conformance to the requirements spec, the SOW, and the requirements spec, etc. The typical development phase documents include the following:

- System design
  - Components and networks, including speed, memory, protocols, capacities, etc.
  - Detailed design, including all of your requirements and all second-level design information such as model of latent workstation and its compliance with the Appendix F Quality Specification and with all requirements allocated to components
  - Workflows, including administrative workflows even if they are to be staffed by the vendor
  - Interfaces with livescans, card scanners, Records Management Systems, Computerized Criminal History Systems, other AFIS, the FBI's CJIS WAN, if applicable, etc.
  - Reports that can be generated, including those that are automatically prepared and printed at the end of each month and quarter
  - Backup and continuity of operations plans, scenarios, and limitations
  - Requirements traceability and verification matrix that maps the requirements to the design and to the verification methods
- Test plans with test cases, requirements, and design details allocated to test cases, test methods, etc.
- Card conversion plan, including location and approach for data entry, card scanning, quality checks, and loading into the operational environment
- Integration and transition plan
  - Factory integration
  - Site integration
  - Installation
  - Transition
  - Training
- Project management plan and master schedule
  - Configuration control plan
  - Design review(s)

- Customer interface and status reporting
- COTS product update approach
- Bill of materials

There should be a formal design review a few months into the project to ensure that all stakeholders are aware of and agree with what is being developed. In addition, there should be frequent meetings, alternating between the vendor's facility and the purchaser's facility, where status can be assessed and open issues addressed.

7.7 CONCLUSION

If a disciplined and well-documented process is followed, there are less likely to be disconnects of vision and disappointments after delivery. Understand that if you want a copy of another agency's AFIS, just say so; otherwise, specify what you want and demand documentation that is aligned with your requirements and a process that is responsive to your statement of work.

CHAPTER 8

STANDARDS AND INTEROPERABILITY

To meet the challenges of interoperability, equipment, software, and systems must be compatible. All systems do not necessarily have to consist of interchangeable parts, but the more adherence there is to uniformity and standardization, the easier it will be to communicate and exchange information. This chapter looks at the development of standards by the American National Standards Institute/National Institute of Standards and Technology (ANSI/NIST) and the FBI for equipment and transmissions, as well as the administrative issues that have to be addressed if systems are to communicate. The chapter concludes with a case study of how identification rates can be interpreted in various ways due to the current lack of standardization.

8.1 SYSTEM CHALLENGES TO INTEROPERABILITY

Finger and palm images, textual descriptive data, SMT (scars, marks, and tattoos) data, and other information useful for identification purposes may be collected from flatbed scanners, livescan devices, palm print readers, etc. Scanners may be used to digitize photos, sketches, or pictures. Depending on the image, the digital representation may contain either color or grayscale pixels. The images may be compressed before transmission and decompressed afterward. All of these procedures have worked well without a requirement for interoperability. Vendors developed, and agencies purchased, systems that were unique to their own applications; the technology did not allow much cross-communication.

Between 1970 and 1985, the first AFIS systems were developed. During this long period, various approaches to AFIS development were used, not all of which were successful. This was before National Criminal History Improvement Program (NCHIP) funding, during which time agencies were dependent on local or state rather than federal funding for their programs. Many of the early AFIS applications were stand-alone systems that were depended on inked ten-print cards. The operations were based on proprietary software from a limited number of vendors. For these reasons, there was no opportunity for information to be exchanged electronically.

To meet the need of a framework for the interchange of fingerprint data, ANSI and the (then) National Bureau of Standards produced the ANSI/NBS-ICST 1-1986 *Fingerprint Identification—Data Format for the Information Exchange.* This standard and subsequent standards define the content, format, and units of measurement for the exchange of fingerprint information between AFIS systems and an interface with IAFIS. The standard defined four types of records and emphasized the development of a standard minutiae encoding format. The four record types were the following:

- Type 1: Textual data transaction type, header, file content specifications, subject descriptive and arrest data
- Type 2: Fingerprint minutiae data
- Type 3: Fingerprint images (low-resolution: 10 pixels/mm)
- Type 4: Fingerprint images (high-resolution: 20 pixels/mm)

The 1986 standard was not widely accepted, however, because the minutiae encoding did not accommodate existing proprietary formats. The FBI National Crime Information Center (NCIC) Advisory Policy Board (APB) recommended that the FBI establish a new standard for electronic image communication. Between 1990 and 1992 government and AFIS vendors worked to develop it. Building on the 1986 standard, the new standard, ANSI/NIST-CSL 1-1993, incorporated a user-defined text record and created separate images for binary (black-and-white only) and grayscale fingerprint images. It also created a user-defined image record and addressed image compression and decompression methods.

Following the introduction of this standard, NIST began to address the need to accommodate SMT information as well as subject photographs (mug shots). An addendum to the 1993 standard was created with the introduction of ANSI/NIST-ITL 1A-1997. This standard contained a total of 10 record types:

- Type 1: Transaction information
- Type 2: Descriptive text (user-defined)
- Type 3: Fingerprint image data (low-resolution grayscale)
- Type 4: Fingerprint image data (high-resolution grayscale)
- Type 5: Fingerprint image data (low-resolution binary)
- Type 6: Fingerprint image data (high-resolution binary)
- Type 7: Image data (user-defined)
- Type 8: Signature image data
- Type 9: Minutiae data
- Type 10: Facial and SMT image data

Record	Contents	Type of Data
Type 1	Transaction information	ASCII
Type 2	Descriptive text (user-defined)	ASCII
Type 3	Fingerprint Image data (low-resolution grayscale)	Binary
Type 4	Fingerprint Image data (high-resolution grayscale)	Binary
Type 5	Fingerprint image data (low-resolution binary)	Binary
Type 6	Fingerprint image data (high-resolution binary)	Binary
Type 7	Image data (user-defined)	Binary
Type 8	Signature image data	Binary
Type 9	Minutiae data	ASCII
Type 10	Facial and SMT image data	ASCII/Binary
Type 11	Reserved for future use	—
Type 12	Reserved for future use	—
Type 13	Latent image data (variable-resolution)	ASCII/Binary
Type 14	Tenprint fingerprint impressions (variable-resolution)	ASCII/Binary
Type 15	Palm print image data (variable-resolution)	ASCII/Binary
Type 16	User-defined testing image data (variable-resolution)	ASCII/Binary

Table 8.1

Record Types Used in the ANSI/NIST-ITL 1-2003 Standard

As AFIS systems become more robust, new opportunities for data exchange became possible, including the exchange of latent print and palm print image data. These opportunities were addressed in ANSI/NIST-ITL 1-2003,[1] which replaced earlier versions of the standard. In this standard, the number of logical record types grew to 16. The records are defined in Table 8.1. These last changes were particularly important for the latent print community, since they standardized the transmission standards for latent prints, allowing their transmission across networks in a standardized fashion.

In the 2003 standard, record types 1, 2, and 9 use ASCII textual information fields; record types 3, 4, 5, 6, 7, and 8 use binary information; and record types 10, 13, 14, 15, and 16 use a combination of ASCII and binary. The tagged-field records, which are logical records containing unique ASCII field identifies for variable-length data fields that are capable of being parsed based on the contents of the first two fields,[2] contain ASCII tagged textual fields and binary, grayscale, or color image data. Two additional record types are reserved for inclusion at a future date.

The following list summarizes each of the 16 different logical record types used in the 2003 standard (also see Table 8.1).

1. Type 1: transaction record. The type 1 record is mandatory for each transaction. It provides information about the type and use or purpose of the transaction, a list of each logical record included in the file, the source or originator of the physical record, and other useful information.

---

[1] Available from ftp://sequoyah.nist.gov/pub/nist_internal_reports/sp500-245-a16.pdf.
[2] ANSI/NIST_ILT 2000, p. 3.

2. Type 2: user-defined descriptive record text. The type 2 record contains user-defined textual fields that provide textual information about the identification and description of the subject of the fingerprint information.

3. Type 3: low-resolution grayscale record. The type 3 record is used to exchange low-resolution grayscale fingerprint image data information that was scanned at no less than the minimum scanning resolution, then scaled down, subsampled, or interpolated.

4. Type 4: high-resolution grayscale record. The type 4 record contains and is used to exchange high-resolution grayscale fingerprint data, which may be in a compressed form. There are typically 14 of these high-resolution records in a file: the ten rolled impressions, the two thumb plain impressions, and the plain impressions of each of the remaining sets of four fingers on each hand.

5. Type 5: low-resolution binary record. The type 5 record contains and is used to exchange low-resolution binary fingerprint image data. There are typically 14 of these high-resolution records in a file: the ten rolled impressions, the two thumb plain impressions, and the plain impressions of each of the remaining sets of four fingers on each hand.

6. Type 6: high-resolution binary record. The type 6 record contains and is used to exchange high-resolution binary fingerprint image data. There are typically 14 of these high-resolution records in a file: the ten rolled impressions, the two thumb plain impressions, and the plain impressions of each of the remaining sets of four fingers on each hand.

7. Type 7: user-defined image data record. The type 7 record allows the sender and recipient to define image data not defined elsewhere in the standard. Such images could include soles, toes, or ear impressions.

8. Type 8: signature image data record. The type 8 record contains or is used to exchange scanned high-resolution binary or vectored signature image data. A series of binary numbers expresses the vectored signature data.

9. Type 9: minutiae record. The type 9 record provides for remote searching of latent prints. More specifically, the type 9 record is a logical record that contains and is used to exchange encoded geometric and topological minutiae from a finger or palm. Each record contains processed image data from which the location and orientation descriptors of extracted minutiae are listed. It must contain the minutiae data from a fingerprint, palm, or latent print.

10. Type 10: facial and scar, mark, and tattoo (SMT) image record. The type 10 tagged-field image record contains and is used to exchange facial and SMT image data together with the textual information related to the digitized image. Sources for the images may include a scanned photograph, a live image captured on a digital camera, or a digitized "freeze frame" from a video camera.

11. Type 11: record reserved for future use.

12. Type 12: record reserved for future use.

13. Type 13: variable-resolution latent image record. The type 13 tagged-field image record contains and can be used to exchange variable-resolution latent fingerprint and palm print image records along with fixed and user-defined textual information fields related to the digitized image. The scanning resolution must be a minimum of 19.69 pp/mm (500 ppi). However, the standard further states, "It is strongly recommended that the minimum scanning resolution (or effective scanning resolution) and transmission rate for latent images be 39.38 pp/mm plus or minus 0.40 pp/mm (1,000 ppi plus or minus 10 ppi)." Also, the latent image data shall be uncompressed or the output from a lossless compression algorithm. There is no limit on the number of latent records in a transaction.

14. Type 14: variable-resolution tenprint image record. The type 14 tagged-field image record contains and can be used to exchange variable-resolution tenprint fingerprint image records along with fixed and user-defined textual information fields related to the digitized image. The fingerprint images can be either rolled or plain impressions. The scanning resolution must be a minimum of 19.69 pp/mm (500 ppi). However, the standard further states, "It is strongly recommended that the minimum scanning resolution (or effective scanning resolution) and transmission rate for latent images be 39.38 pp/mm plus or minus 0.40 pp/mm (1,000 ppi plus or minus 10 ppi)." Also, the tenprint image data may be compressed. There are typically 14 of these variable-resolution records in a file: the ten rolled impressions, the two thumb plain impressions, and the plain impressions of each of the remaining sets of four fingers on each hand.

15. Type 15: variable-resolution palm print image record. The type 15 tagged-field image record contains and can be used to exchange variable-resolution palm print image records along with fixed and user-defined textual information fields related to the digitized image. The scanning resolution is not specified. Images scanned at 19.69 pp/mm (500 ppi) may be exchanged as a type 15 record. However, the standard further states, "It is strongly recommended that the minimum scanning resolution (or effective scanning resolution) and transmission rate for palm print images be 39.38 pp/mm plus or minus 0.40 pp/mm (1,000 ppi plus or minus 10 ppi)." Also, the palm print image data may be compressed. There may be six of these records in a file: two full palm prints or four partial palms, and two writer's palm, which is the area on the side of the palm that normally rests against the paper when writing.

16. Type 16: user-defined testing image record. The type 16 record is for developmental purposes and the exchange of miscellaneous images. It is a tagged-field version of the type 7 user-defined logical record, and is intended for an image not specified or described elsewhere in the standard. The scanning resolution is not specified.

The standard is reviewed every 5 years. If there are sufficient changes to the current standard, a new standard is released.

8.2 ELECTRONIC FINGERPRINT TRANSMISSION SPECIFICATION (EFTS)

The ANSI standard defines the content, format, and units of measurement for the exchange of fingerprint information between AFIS systems and an interface with IAFIS. The Electronic Fingerprint Transmission Specification (EFTS)[3] defines that interface. It specifies the file and record content, format, and data codes necessary for the exchange of fingerprint identification information between federal, state, and local users and the FBI. It provides a description of all requests and responses associated with electronic fingerprint identification services, including tenprint, latent, and fingerprint image services.

To ensure that existing protocols are not adversely affected, EFTS honors these protocols. It uses a process that provides for coordinated enhancements within the various systems while maintaining reliable interoperability. This process is based on the tagged-field structure and two key concepts.

The first concept states that field definitions cannot change over time or from system to system. If a change is needed, a new field is defined and assigned a new tag number. The second concept states that the new field cannot be made mandatory for established functionality; it can only enhance functionality for those systems wishing to incorporate it. With this process in place, every system on the network has the opportunity to enhance its own system on its own schedule, and no system is ever forced to make a change in order to maintain current functionality.

This has led to many states developing their own EFTS. Building on the FBI EFTS, the states are allowed to collect additional information in their versions of the EFTS by adding a new tagged field with a new tag number. The information in these new tagged fields is used in the state AFIS system, but the fields are stripped off before transmission to IAFIS.

As part of its commitment to ensure image quality, the EFTS includes two image quality specifications (IQS) as appendices: *Appendix F: IAFIS Image Quality Specifications*, and the less stringent *Appendix G: Interim IAFIS Image Quality Specifications for Scanners*. To ensure that only equipment that meets the requirements of Appendix F or Appendix G is used, the FBI Communication and Technology Branch of the CJIS Division undertakes testing of equipment claimed by the manufacturer to meet the specifications. If the equipment meets the requirements of Appendix F or Appendix G, it is listed as certified for

---

[3] http://www.fbi.gov/hq/cjisd/iafis/efts70/cover.htm.

compliance with the FBI's Integrated Automated Fingerprint Identification System image quality specifications. Such equipment includes livescan systems, fingerprint card scan systems, fingerprint card printers (grayscale), and integrated products.

8.3 WAVELET SCALAR QUANTIZATION

The Wavelet Scalar Quantization (WSQ) grayscale fingerprint image compression algorithm is the standard for the exchange of fingerprint images. The WSQ specification defines a class of image encoders and a single-image decoder with sufficient generality to decode compressed image data from any WSQ-compliant encoder. This allows future development while maintaining existing compatibility. WSQ compliance provides for interoperability between state and local systems and between these systems and the FBI.

NIST[4] has developed a range of functionality for decoders and encoders. In order to obtain certification, a WSQ decoder must implement the full range of functionality, including the reconstruction of images using odd and even length filters and imbedded restart codes. These requirements are contained in Part I of the WSQ, titled "Requirement and Guidelines."

A WSQ-compliant encoder must meet the specific parameter values contained in Part III of the WSQ specification. To test for compliance with the WSQ specification, the output from the equipment tested is compared with the output from a double precision reference implementation developed at NIST. Prior to a request for testing WSQ compliance, vendors are directed to conduct self tests on their equipment. These tests would incorporate the NIST reference set, which can be downloaded. Following a successful self-test, the vendor may apply to the FBI for final testing and certification. More details can be found at the NIST WSQ web site.

8.4 MANAGEMENT CHALLENGES TO INTEROPERABILITY

State and local AFIS systems do not always directly communicate with each other. Most AFIS systems were developed independently with the vendor's proprietary software. Some cities have AFIS systems that not only are independent of the state system, but also are made and supported by different vendors. The systems may differ in their hardware configurations, expectations of throughput, staffing levels, and even hours of operations. The policies for the access and retention of records could be different, as well as the agency with responsibility for operating of the system.

---

[4] http://www.itl.nist.gov/iad/894.03/fing/cert_gui.html.

The state AFIS systems do communicate through a hierarchy with IAFIS, but they do not communicate with each other directly. States can send inquiries to the FBI's Interstate Identification Index (III). If a record is found, the state holding the record forwards the criminal history to the FBI, and the FBI forwards the criminal history back to the inquiring state.

Currently, one state cannot directly search records on another state's AFIS system. This has particular significance in the latent print community, since the lack of direct access limits latent print searches on the local or state AFIS system. This scenario is not entirely different from the early days of information exchange in the financial sector. When the banking industry began electronic processing, customers moved from paper transactions to electronic transactions within the bank. It became possible to check account balances and withdraw money through credit cards and debit cards. Telephone banking emerged, and now there are virtual banks that have no brick-and-mortar buildings for customer transactions. It is possible to view an account from any location where there is a phone, a computer, or ATM access.

Banks that are competitors in many of their business transactions find it profitable to be cooperative in certain transactions and share data. Consider the following. A visitor from the United States travels to Paris. Instead of taking U.S. dollars to the currency exchange, the visitor finds an ATM nearby on Blvd. St. Michele. The visitor inserts the debit card, selects English as the preferred language, follows the English instructions, and withdraws several hundred dollars' worth of Euros. The visitor's credit union debits the account by the equivalent amount in U.S. dollars, plus the interchange fee. By allowing a withdrawal from an ATM on Blvd. St. Michele in Paris (in Euros), the bank that owns the ATM collects a fee. In addition, the network collects a fee, the visitor's credit union collects a fee, and the visitor receives cash in the local currency with assurances that the transaction is private and secure. Plus, the exchange rate is better than that found at the local currency exchange. The financial system is interoperable.

AFIS systems have not yet reached that level of cooperation and integration. There are standards in place for the collection and transmission of tenprint records and images to the FBI, and AFIS vendors use these standards and specifications when building the individual AFIS systems. However, local and state systems may not be able to communicate and share information because they have not completely embraced the standards in their internal processing and thus are unable to communicate with each other. More importantly, states have not found political and economic advantages to expend the large sums needed to make these systems interoperable.

Now a return to the banking analogy. Before the advent of ATMs and electronic funds, each bank had its own method of recording transactional data. It took many days for a check to clear because the various banks involved had to verify and approve the transaction. Now that each of the major financial institutions has agreed on a set of standards, the process has become much more streamlined. Checks clear quickly, financial institutions can cut their costs by not reinventing the existing practices, and customers can now access their money from almost anywhere on the globe.

Efforts are underway to improve AFIS systems' interoperability through technical resources. Various "black boxes," which to some degree allow images and data from one set of native records to be searched on another database, have been created. These searches, particularly in the area of latent prints, may require the introduction of "sneakernet" to physically move the data from point A to point B, search the point B database, and return the results to point A.

Many of the technical issues will be resolved as more agencies begin to follow the NIST transmission standards and the FBI transmission specifications. In 1998, the AFIS Committee of the International Association for Identification, chaired by Peter Higgins, and AFIS vendors demonstrated the possibility of searching a latent print on various databases.[5] This proof of concept was the first organized attempt to provide an automated electronic latent print search of multiple databases beyond IAFIS. While not elegant, it confirmed that the concept was viable.

Prior to the introduction of AFIS systems, agencies providing identification services developed their own standards and business practices to meet their needs and the needs of the submitting agencies. Standards for transmission and specification did not exist in the developing stages of AFIS technology. Agencies relied on existing practices in those areas where AFIS systems were not mature, or where there were financial limitations. For example, the standardized electronic capture of finger images, mug shots, and alpha data is fairly routine on newer AFIS systems; the expense to upgrade equipment and revise processing procedures to include these on older systems is significant. AFIS vendors, in response to governmental needs, are working to develop systems that can be interconnected, allowing access to systems in other agencies built by other vendors.

The management challenges to interoperability may exceed the technical challenges. In addition to any programming or modification of existing hardware that may be required, both the host and user agency will have to enter into an agreement that has passed through legal and administrative review. The host agency will protect its assets and allow use of its system only on a limited basis. It will demand assurances that the systems are being used as agreed, and

[5] For a complete report see Appendix or http://onin.com/iaiafis/IAI_AFIS_071998_Report.pdf.

the data integrity remains intact. It will also audit for any questionable use and may terminate the agreement within a short time.

Beyond the technological issues, what are the management issues that challenge interoperability? There are several, including foreign access to a database, amount of transaction time for foreign inquiries, usage agreements, indemnifications, security, firewalls, etc. All of these issues can be resolved with time, money, and political drive. The following sections discuss some of these management issues.

8.4.1 SECURITY

Whenever remote access to a database is considered, a primary concern is the security of the information system and databases. As long as the system is a closed system, or one in which access beyond the network is severely restricted, security is manageable. Providing access to outside interests presents additional threats, which come from access to the infrastructure as well as access to the information.

Just as with any network, expansion into foreign environments heightens the need for "defense in depth." The host agency must not only continue to ensure its own system integrity, but must also ensure the integrity of participating agencies and personnel.

In the ATM example above, the security of the system is maintained by the participating financial institutions. The identity of the card holder is confirmed with the use of the debit card and the associated personal identification number (PIN). However, since these transactions can be compromised, the financial institutions limit the risk per transaction by limiting the amount of money that can be electronically withdrawn.

While the equipment and technology of the host agency may be standardized and commercial off the shelf (COTS), the participating agency may have customized hardware and software, and/or special protocols that need to be reconfigured to be compatible with the host agency. Many related issues may then arise, such as who will pay for the hardware and/or software changes necessary to allow access to the host agency. Additional firewalls and anti-virus software may have to be installed; new user codes and passwords have to be assigned to the new personnel; training and audits are needed, etc. The cost can be significant for each party. How can these expenses be justified in times of financial belt-tightening?

In addition to the issue of security of the network is the security of the information. Will the information be used for the intended purpose? Will the data be safeguarded in the same spirit as at the host agency? What are the opportunities for misuse or abuse? A recent article on data sharing of a government database operated by a private vendor points up the problem. In January 2004, Associated Press reporter Brian Bergstein reported,

> Other states expressed worries about security. An open-records request in Georgia uncovered an Oct. 2 memo, for example, in which motor-vehicle department staffers noted that Seisint had promised "that every effort will be taken to make the database and the data transfer safe and secure. However, the potential for abuse still exists."
>
> The Florida files include an Oct. 7 letter in which Deputy Superintendent Mark Oxley of the Louisiana state police wrote that his agency would not participate because of "lingering concerns" about the security of the records that would be sent to the database. He also questioned the "ever-broadening scope extending far beyond the original counterterrorism mission."
>
> However, Oxley added that "most disappointing of all" was that Louisiana had to learn from news reports that Seisint's founder, Hank Asher, had admitted piloting flights for cocaine smugglers in the 1980s. Asher has resigned from Seisint's board.
>
> Questions about Matrix still loom even in member states. New York has not shared any records because of questions about long-term funding and privacy laws, said Lynn Rasic, a spokeswoman for the governor's office.

If these databases are breached for malicious or fraudulent purposes, both public trust and data integrity might be lost. If an agency chooses to share data, it must be careful about both the integrity and intent of the requesting agency, and it must maintain ongoing audits of the use of the data by the requesting agency. If the host agency permits another agency to access its database, it might limit the time volume of access. For example, the host agency might not want to have its own transactions delayed due to foreign transactions in the system, so it might restrict foreign transactions to a time of day when the host transactions are low, or a day of the week when these foreign transactions are at a low point. There will need to be assurances that the foreign transactions, when they are allowed, follow the format of the host searches and do not take longer than the time for a host transaction. Ideally, the foreign transaction should flow through the system with the same characteristics as a native transaction; this would be another example of interoperability.

8.4.2 TYPE OF SEARCH PERMITTED

The agencies also have to agree on the types of searches to be run, whether they are civil searches or forensic searches. If they are forensic searches, options include tenprint to tenprint searches, latent to tenprint searches, tenprint to unsolved latent searches, or latent to unsolved latent searches. For tenprint searches, there may be limitations on the type of inquiry, i.e., the inquiry of the requesting agency must conform to the statutes or policies of the host agency. This, for example, might include the purging of records sealed by court order.

8.4.3 INDEMNIFICATION

The user agency, to the extent permitted by state or federal law, would agree to indemnify and save harmless the host agency, its officers and employees, from and against any and all claims, demands, actions, suits, and proceedings brought by others arising out of the terms of this agreement founded upon the negligence or other tortious conduct of the user agency. This would include, but not be limited to, any liability for loss or damage by reason of any claim of false imprisonment for false arrest.

8.4.4 AGREEMENT TO MAINTAIN RECORDS

The host agency may require that the user agency maintain a log of searches against the host agency and that these logs are subject to audit by the host agency.

8.4.5 CHARGES

Generally, any communications charges are the responsibility of the user agency. This is also applicable for trouble-shooting communication problems. Maintenance of special communications equipment is also the user agency's responsibility.

8.4.6 SUSPENSION OF SERVICES AND AGREEMENT TERMINATION

Services might be suspended if there is a violation of law or regulation, such as the violation of an administrative regulation. If no resolution to the problem can be found, the agreement would be terminated after 30 days. This allows time for any appeal in the decision to terminate and provides a reasonable exit period.

8.5 A CASE STUDY: THE ISSUE OF HIT RATE FOR LATENT PRINTS

Ask several latent examiners or supervisors their hit rate is for latent print identifications, and they will respond with several different answers. One may say that the hit rate is 10%, another may respond that the rate is 15%, and yet another may say that the rate is actually 20%. Who is wrong? Who is right? Why is there such a difference in their answers?[6]

Hit rates have different meanings for different people. A latent print supervisor may want to include all activity since it speaks to the use of staffing resources. A mid-level manager may be more interested in the number of cases in which an identification has been made. The agency chief executive officer might be more interested in the number of individuals identified and the cases cleared. The term hit rate, or ident rate, does not specify if the rate refers to the number of latent print identifications, the number of cases that have a latent print ident, or the number of searches on the AFIS systems to produce the ident. The problem centers on what should be used as the numerator and what as the denominator in the equation that yields the hit rate. In addition, the ways to get that numerator and denominator vary.

This section examines various factors that lead to different interpretations of these rates and the parameters that contribute to these differences, including the conditions under which the latent prints are captured at the crime scene, the expertise of the officer at the scene, how the latent print is processed, and whether the rates are based on cases or individual latent finger images. This section also compares the latent print processing practices of two agencies. Both are assumed to be staffed with competent personnel dedicated to keeping the citizenry safe. The differences lie in the procedures they use, the levels of expertise at key decision points, and who uses the information.

There is no national reporting center that collects latent print identification data. As a result, there are no national standards or definitions, such as those associated with the uniform crime report (UCR). The UCR collects specific crime-related information from law enforcement agencies. The uniformity of crime reporting provides some level of assurance that each reporting agency, regardless of size, is reporting the same crime type the same way. The uniformity can also allow comparisons of the effects on local reported crime due to a change in police policies.

There is no national or industry-wide standard for latent print identifications. In addition to differences in rate interpretation by staff within an agency, there are differences in counting latent print identifications between agencies. The method of counting does not negate the value of the latent print identification, but it may mask opportunities to replicate true increases in the number of identifications.

---

[6] This chapter assumes the continuity of evidence is maintained throughout all transactions.

8.5.1 OBTAINING LATENT PRINTS

According to many television shows, police departments have specially trained personnel armed with very sophisticated equipment who can descend on a crime scene within a matter of minutes after discovery. The evidence they collect is put into a plastic bag and whisked to "the lab," and within a very short time the perpetrator is identified and the rap sheet is being sent down "from the state." That is the popular media version, but the facts lie somewhere else.

To understand the problem of statistical application of latent print hit rate, one must look at the very beginning of the process. This section examines the latent print capture and entry practices of two hypothetical agencies. Questions to consider about these practices include the following:

1. Where do the lifts come from?
2. Who lifts the latent prints at a crime scene?
3. What types of crimes usually have lifts collected?
4. Are elimination prints taken?
5. Who searches the latent prints on the system?

Each of these questions is discussed in the sections below.

8.5.1.1 Where Do the Lifts Come From?

While generally thought of as the originating department, the agency that retrieved the prints might search other AFIS systems in addition to their own "native" AFIS. A search of the criminal IAFIS database by a non-federal agency would be an example. (As a professional courtesy, identification agencies will search latent prints against their database at the request of another law enforcement agency. Typically done on an available time and resource basis, searching latent prints on other databases is an encouraged practice.) So the answer to the question of where the latent prints come from depends on whether the latent prints were retrieved by an agency that launched a latent to tenprint search on their own AFIS system, or whether the identification was made as a result of another law enforcement agency submitting the latent print for search.

Who is considered to have made the latent print identification in such as case: the submitting agency, the agency that made the ident, or both? The agency that originally collected the latent images certainly can claim that their latent prints led to the identification and therefore the case. The agency that searched the latent print on their AFIS system invested staff time, talent, and expertise into making the ident. The managers in these departments would like to report that they made the identification (perhaps the "big break") on the case. Who is entitled to claim credit for the identification?

8.5.1.2 Who Lifts the Latent Prints at the Crime Scene?

Imagine the evidence technicians in their white protective suits combing a crime scene looking for every piece of evidence, including hair and blood (DNA), fibers (lab), and latent fingerprints (AFIS). Does every local police department have this technology, investment in personnel and equipment, and sophisticated laboratory? Probably not. What a typical department most likely has are trained evidence technicians, crime scene investigators, or others, perhaps some with latent fingerprint training, who know what to look for and what to discard. Or perhaps they have officers trained in the preservation of evidence who are taught to bring back to the office anything that looks like evidence.

Personnel trained in fingerprint identification who work a crime scene have the experience to look at an image and decide if it is "of value," i.e., if there is sufficient ridge structure to effect a positive identification. With this knowledge, a crime scene technician trained in fingerprints from Agency A may discard finger images that are of "no value" and, alternatively, see ridge structure in what might appear to the untrained eye as merely a smudge. The technician without fingerprint training from Agency B, however, collects every piece of evidence he or she can find, with the notion that it will be sorted out later. In some departments, the crime scene specialist is also the fingerprint expert and so knows exactly what to look for and how to process the latent print images. Figure 8.1 describes two of many decisions that affect the statistical reporting of latent print identification. It shows how two agencies with competent staff process a total of 100 latent prints found at ten crime scenes.

In this example, there are ten identical crime scenes investigated by two evidence collectors; one, a crime scene specialist at Agency A who has latent

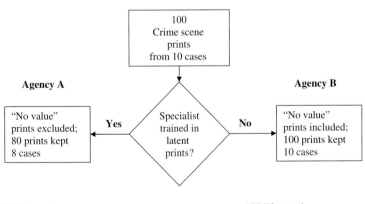

Figure 8.1

Latent Prints from Crime Scene

Agency A

"No value" prints excluded; 80 prints kept 8 cases

Yes

100 Crime scene prints from 10 cases

Specialist trained in latent prints?

No

Agency B

"No value" prints included; 100 prints kept 10 cases

100 lifts at crime scene
20 of no value, 80 of value
80 lifts taken to headquarters

100 lifts at crime scene
No value determination made
100 lifts taken to headquarters

fingerprint training, a second from Agency B who does not have that training. Experience will show that the specialist from Agency A will cull out those images that have insufficient ridge structure to effect a positive identification. Likewise, this specialist may see ridge detail not noticed by the untrained eye. What appears as a smudge may have sufficient detail to make an identification. From the 100 crime scene prints, the specialist trained in fingerprint identification will select fewer prints for searching because he or she has discarded those images not suitable for searching. In this example, the fingerprint-trained specialist finds 80 latent prints "of value" for searching on the AFIS system. The specialist without the fingerprint training from Agency B collects every latent image, regardless of the amount of ridge structure present, intending to allow the fingerprint technicians at headquarters determine whether the image is "of value." Therefore, this technician has selected all 100 images.

These differences in data will affect the final statistics. Agency A, with the fingerprint-trained evidence technician, has 80 latent prints to search on the AFIS system, while Agency B has 100. If each agency makes identifications on the same ten images, the first department will have a fingerprint hit rate of 12.5% (ten identifications divided by 80 latent prints), while the second department will have a fingerprint hit rate of 10% (ten identifications divided by 100 latent prints). Is one right and the other wrong? Does it make a difference?

8.5.1.3 What Types of Crimes Usually Have Lifts Collected?

Fingerprints are not lifted from every crime scene. Due to resource limitations such as staffing not every crime scene that is likely to contain latent prints is searched by a forensic team. There may be a dollar threshold on stolen property that is used to determine if an evidence collection team will be used. Crimes such as homicide nearly always have technicians present at the crime scene to collect evidence.

8.5.1.4 Are Elimination Prints Taken?

In addition to the latent prints found at the crime scene, departments may take elimination prints, which are prints of persons who have a legitimate reason for being at the crime site that are used to eliminate them as suspects. In the case of a burglary, elimination prints might be taken of the homeowner, family members, and other persons who had a legitimate reason for being at the crime scene, most likely before the time of the crime. Police officials, who of course are also present at the scene of the crime, usually already have their fingerprints stored on the AFIS system. As part of a background check, police applicants are fingerprinted and their finger images are kept on file. The expertise required of the fingerprint examiner who makes identifications on elimination prints is no less than the expertise required to make any latent print identification.

In Figure 8.2, the effect of taking elimination prints is highlighted. Agency A takes elimination prints at the crime scene, but Agency B does not. When the technicians from Agency A return to headquarters, they make a manual comparison of the 80 prints they have taken with the elimination prints. They make 20 identifications without the use of the AFIS system. They close two cases with these identifications, i.e., in two of the ten cases, the only latent prints found at the crime scene were identified as belonging to persons who had a legitimate reason for being there. Of the original 100 images the technicians examined at ten crime scenes, 20 were determined to be of no value. Assume these 20 represented all the images in two cases. The elimination prints identified another 20 latents and closed two additional cases from further latent print searches. At this point, the team from Agency A has 60 latent images remaining from six cases. The technicians at Agency B did not take elimination prints from anyone present at the crime scene. They still have 100 latent prints taken from ten crime scenes.

If asked for a statistical report at this time, the staff at Agency A could report that they made identifications on 20 out of 80 latent prints (100 images minus 20 images of no value) in eight cases, a hit rate of 25% before any AFIS searches. Agency B has 100 latent images, value undetermined, and has not taken any elimination prints. Their hit rate for 100 images thus far is zero.

As illustrated in Figure 8.3, when the teams from the two agencies return to their headquarters, each team has a different number of images from the crime scene to search. The team from Agency A has 60 images, while the team from Agency B has 100. With the computer imaging equipment available, the team from Agency A determines that only 50 of the 60 latent images are of value; similarly, Agency B eliminates 30 of the 100 latent images, leaving 70 latent images for them to search.

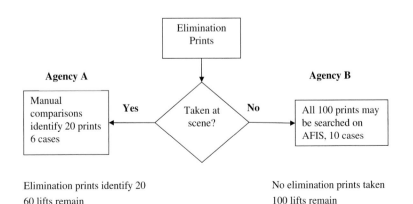

Figure 8.2

Use of Elimination Prints

Figure 8.3

*Prints Remaining After
Elimination Prints*

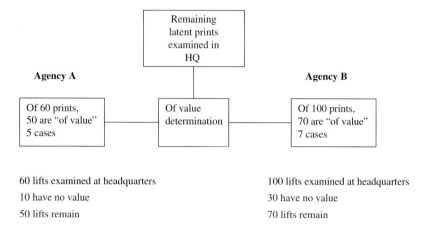

60 lifts examined at headquarters

10 have no value

50 lifts remain

100 lifts examined at headquarters

30 have no value

70 lifts remain

Time for a statistical recap. Both agencies went to ten crime scenes and looked at 100 latent images. Agency A considered 20 from two crime scenes to be of no value and did not process them any further. The number of latent images retrieved from the eight remaining crime scenes is 80. This is the base for any further comparisons. Agency B did not make any quality determination at the ten crime scenes and retained all 100 latent images. Their base for further comparisons is 100 latents from ten crime scenes. Agency A has 20% fewer latent images to search than Agency B, and their images are of reasonably good quality. The quality of each of the 100 images for Agency B is unknown. The denominator for Agency A is 80, and the denominator for Agency B is 100. With the use of the elimination print process, however, Agency A reduced this denominator to 60. Agency A could also claim a 25% identification rate (20 elimination prints identified from the group of 80, i.e., 20 divided by 80). Agency B has an identification rate of 0%.

Back at headquarters, both teams used photographic technology for a better view of the latent images. The technicians from Agency A removed an additional ten images that were of no value. The Agency B technicians removed 30 images that were not of value. The denominator of Agency A is now 50, and the denominator of Agency B is now 70.

Next, Agency A searches the remaining 50 latent images on the AFIS systems, while Agency B searches their 70 prints. As shown in Figure 8.4, each agency makes 25 identifications that close three cases.

What is the resulting ident or hit rate for each agency? There is no simple answer. The hit rate for Agency A may be

- 56% of latents (20 elimination print idents plus 25 AFIS idents from 80 latent images)
- 62% of cases (45 idents in five of the eight cases)

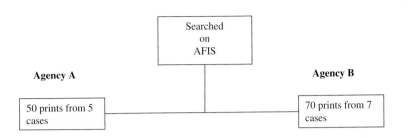

Figure 8.4

Latent Prints Searched on the AFIS System

- 50% of AFIS searches
- 25% of cases are cleared by elimination prints

The hit rate for Agency B may be

- 35% of latents (25 AFIS idents of 70 latents searched on the AFIS system)
- 57% of cases (25 idents in three of the seven cases)
- 35% of AFIS searches
- 0% cleared by elimination prints

This example demonstrates the possible differences in statistical reports depending on the way in which the latent images taken from the crime scene were processed. The variation does not speak to the dedication and resolve of the evidence technicians and crime scene specialists who work on the identification process. If the purpose of this statistical information is to provide a clear picture of current operations and provide opportunities for improvement, then some of the differences between the two agencies are relatively minor. What does become apparent is the effect of elimination prints in improving the identification rate.

8.5.1.5 Who Searches the Latent Prints on the System?

For clarity, in the example above, it was assumed that the AFIS operators were equally proficient in using the AFIS system. However, this is not always the case. If an agency has latent print examiners whose responsibilities are limited to latent print searching, not latent print collection, they can specialize in the technical skills useful for identifying the greatest number of minutiae in the latent print. That is, by concentrating on using the AFIS system as a search tool and knowing the unique features of the AFIS system, the latent print examiner would be able to make more identifications than an examiner who uses the AFIS system only occasionally. Latent print examiners whose primary responsibility is to work on AFIS systems might, for example, have some idea of how the AFIS system performs its search or matching function and thus can exploit the features of the system to find as many minutiae as possible. Such features could include use of light filters, use of offset lighting, searching only a portion of the database, or some other technique that could improve the likelihood of a match.

If the crime scene examiner is also the latent print examiner, the amount of time spent on each function is limited by the amount of time spent on the other function. Spending time at a crime scene results in fewer hours for searching the AFIS system for a match.

8.5.2 THE SEARCH DATABASE

Once the latent print is collected and digitized by the latent print examiner, it is searched against the AFIS database. The database may be as small as a few thousand records or as large as several million. It may be specific to some common characteristic, e.g., a search of all tenprint and criminal records on file, or it may be a subset of a larger database, such as only those tenprint records with an arrest. Questions that might be asked about the characteristics of the AFIS database include the following:

1. What are the criteria for inclusion in the search database?
2. Was the best card selected for conversion?
3. How many records are stored on the latent cognizant database?
4. How many records are added, deleted, or updated annually?

Each of these questions is discussed in the sections below.

8.5.2.1 What Are the Criteria for Inclusion in the Search Database?

If the database is a criminal or forensic database, it holds the records of all persons fingerprinted for a criminal offense and certain other categories. In general, the database for searching latent prints includes the images of individuals whose finger images are likely to appear at a crime scene. In addition to those previously arrested and fingerprinted, the prints of law enforcement personnel and other public officers may be included in the database.

The reason for including criminal offenders in the database is apparent, but what is the reason for including law enforcement and other personnel? Latent fingerprints found at the crime scene may include those of law enforcement personnel who were not strictly adhering to preserving the scene. In the aftermath of September 11, many agencies are including the finger images of all personnel whose latent prints might appear at a crime scene, including firefighters.

8.5.2.2 Was the Best Card Selected for Conversion?

It may seem like this is a question that does not need to be asked, but it must. In an earlier discussion, it was noted that a criminal record may contain several events, e.g., arrests, each of which may be associated with a fingerprint capture. If a person had been arrested only once, there would only be one tenprint card in the master fingerprint file. If that person had been arrested more than once, there would be several sets of finger images of the same person in the file, and the finger images on each card would not necessarily be identical. Conditions such as finger pressure, amount of ink, cooperation of the person being fingerprinted, and skill of the person taking the finger images can all contribute to the amount of finger image data recorded.

For each roll or electronic capture there should be enough minutiae and ridge flow to match with another image. If the image is of poor quality, or if a transmission error between the capture device and the database occurred, the finger can be re-rolled to produce an image of acceptable quality. A good finger image capture can result in as many as 100 or more individual minutiae points.

Assume two agencies have similar tenprint records needing to be converted into electronic images. The first agency feels that whatever card is identified as the master tenprint record for the person (perhaps the first tenprint card, perhaps the most recent) is the card that should be converted. The other agency first reviews each tenprint record and then selects the best quality card to be converted. This quality control step will provide a superior database, but it is an expensive process since it involves personnel and considerable time.

AFIS software usually includes a feature that allows, either manually or automatically, the replacement of a lower quality image with a better quality image. Another feature offered by AFIS vendors is the creation of a virtual card made of the best images from several tenprint records. The advances in AFIS technology have permitted the creation and maintenance of a database that contains every image of every tenprint record, regardless of the number of tenprint records a person has on file. For a subject who has been arrested eight times, for example, all 80 images (ten fingers × eight tenprint cards) can be searched. To do so requires vast storage farms and extremely fast matchers, but it is an option currently offered by AFIS vendors.

8.5.2.3 How Many Records Are Stored on the Latent Cognizant Database?

The larger the database, the greater the opportunity to make a latent print identification. If the subject has never been enrolled, i.e., has never had prints taken for this agency, there is no chance of making an identification. If the agency has a large database, there is at least a chance of making the ident if the person has been enrolled.

The recent push for improved national security has caused the number and type of persons being fingerprinted, both for criminal and civil purposes, to increase. A few years ago firefighters were not printed; now they are. Employees such as child care workers, mental health aides, etc., are now being fingerprinted and their records are retained on a database.

8.5.2.4 How Many Records Are Added, Deleted, or Updated Annually?

How much does the database change every year? New records are created for subjects who were never fingerprinted in the past, additional tenprint records are added for new events such as arrests, and records are deleted. Records may be deleted due to notification of death, court order, age limitation, or being in a category no longer considered appropriate for fingerprint image retention.

The addition of new records presents new opportunities for making an identification that was not possible in the past. If the owner of a latent print had not been enrolled in the database, there was no chance of making the identification. If, however, the subject was arrested after the search has been completed, there are at least two options for re-searching the latent print. The first is the tenprint to unsolved search, in which new records are automatically searched against a database consisting of latent images that were not identified on an AFIS search. These images are maintained on a separate database. When a new record meets a threshold score, a message is sent to the examiner to look at the case. The second option is to recapture, or relaunch, a latent print search at some time after the original search. This option is valuable since there may have been a new addition to the database during that time period that did produce a candidate in the UL/TP file. There may also have been changes to the structure of the database itself, which would allow a more exacting search and match than was previously possible.

The preceding paragraphs have described human and electronic parameters that may affect the latent print identification. Who collects the latent print evidence at the crime scene, taking elimination prints, the quality and number of records on the AFIS database are all factors that affect the number of identifications made both with AFIS technology and by other means. The next section describes some of the influences on determining the statistics of reporting identifications.

8.5.3 COUNTING LATENT PRINT IDENTIFICATIONS

What is considered an ident? For criminal processing purposes, an ident is a latent print image that is matched by standard techniques against a known print image. Counting idents is another matter. Assume an agency collects 100 latent prints from 80 crime scenes for 80 cases. From these 100 latent prints, the latent print examiners make 50 identifications on 40 unique individuals. Consider also that each of these latent prints were searched an average of two times on the AFIS system. What is the hit rate? The following factors have to be included to answer this question:

1. How many unique cases were entered?
2. How many latent searches were launched?
3. How many idents were made as a result of these searches?
4. How are multiple idents on a single case counted?
5. Is the hit rate calculated by the number of unique cases, multiple searches of the same case, or all latents received?
6. Are data management system reports used to calculate a hit rate?
7. If so, how are test/demos controlled?

8.5.3.1 How Many Unique Cases Were Entered?
In this example, there are 80 crime scenes and 80 cases. Any statistic using cases has to refer to 80 cases.

8.5.3.2 How Many Latent Searches Were Launched?
Personnel collected 100 latent prints from these 80 crime scenes. Each print was searched on the AFIS system an average of two times. Some searches produced an ident after the first search; others may have been searched two or more times before being entered into the unsolved latent file. There are 200 searches for these 100 latent prints.

8.5.3.3 How Many Idents Were Made as a Result of These Searches?
There are 50 latent prints that are identified from 40 unique individuals. Forty individuals were identified from 50 latent prints.

8.5.3.4 How Are Multiple Idents on a Single Case Counted?
If a crime scene produces two or more latent prints, and both of these prints are associated with the same individual, for reporting purposes is this considered one ident or two? For example, if two latent prints considered to be of value are found, searched on the AFIS system, and found to be the number 2 and 3 fingers of the same person, how should this be counted?

Consider the same case, but with eight latent prints, five of which are ultimately linked to three individuals. Are there five idents or three idents? Five idents (the number of latent prints identified on the AFIS system) divided by the number of latent prints collected (eight latent prints) yield a hit rate of 5/8, or 63%. Three idents (the number of individuals) divided by the number of latent prints collected (eight latent prints) yields a hit rate of 3/8, or 37%. Five or three idents made in one case; case closed at 100%.

8.5.3.5 Is the Hit Rate Calculated by the Number of Unique Cases, Multiple Searches of the Same Case, or All Latents Received?

If the hit rate is calculated by the number of unique latent print cases, it will be a much higher rate than a hit rate based on the number of idents against the number of latent prints collected. A hit rate of 10% is considered standard. In the example above, if any one if the eight latent prints is identified on the AFIS system, the case has an ident.

If the hit rate is calculated by using the number of all latent prints received, this would necessarily include those prints determined not to be "of value." If the agency has crime scene investigators who could eliminate images which were not "of value," the number of latent prints would be smaller, but they would be of better quality than the images collected by investigators without fingerprint training.

8.5.3.6 Are Data Management System Reports Used to Calculate a Hit Rate?

While very advantageous in a tenprint processing environment, statistics produced by data management systems have to be reviewed for duplication, testing, and other search factors. The three functional areas of latent print capture and entry practices, database characteristics, and identification statistics provide a continuum from gathering latent images at a crime scene to searching, identification, and tabulation of the search results. While each agency might perform these tasks in a slightly different manner, the combination of these individual differences has a significant impact on the final search results and how they are reported.

To reiterate a statement from the beginning of this section, there is no right way to report idents, nor is there a national standard for reporting idents. Until there is, opportunities for improvements will be missed because the technical language and concepts are not fully developed.

8.5.4 NEW YORK STATE SURVEY

In the late 1990s, the New York State Division of Criminal Justice Services (NYS DCJS) conducted a survey of latent print procedures of other identification agencies based on the three functional areas of latent print capture and entry practices, database characteristics and identification statistics. Under the direction of NYS DCJS Deputy Commissioner Leo Carroll, the goal of the survey was to determine why some agencies were reporting such a wide range of identification rates, and whether information could be gathered that would increase the total number of latent print identifications. The findings of this survey were presented to the Sagem Users Group, published in the Sagem newsletter, and presented by the author at the 1999 Educational Conference of the International Association for Identification.

Fifteen AFIS managers were asked to complete a questionnaire about their identification practices and policies. The questions ranged from how latent prints were captured at crime scenes to how they were counted at the conclusion of an AFIS search. From the answers provided some conclusions can be drawn. Almost immediately it became apparent that the managers participating in the survey represented two major user groups: police departments and multi-jurisdictional state agencies. The police departments collectively had far more investigative personnel than the state agencies, and had more direct influence on the evidence collection process. In general, the law enforcement agencies collected the latent prints and either forwarded them to the state system or used the state AFIS system for their latent print searches.

Law enforcement managers are familiar with the practices of their departments and how they interact with the state AFIS system. They may not, however, be as familiar with the technical aspects of the AFIS system as the state administrators are. For example, it is not necessary to know the size of the AFIS database to use an AFIS system as a search tool any more than it is necessary to understand the bank interchange process to use a debit card in Paris.

The responding states do not all have the same responsibility with regard to criminal investigation and may have a slightly different focus. State AFIS users have provided information as it applies on a state level. For example, database size, entry practices, hit rates are provided for the entire state AFIS network, not just the practices employed by a single agency.

The areas of most interest were how the idents are counted and how the hit rate is determined. There was no uniformity in the answers. The survey asked the following question:

How do you count your latent identifications?

1. **One** ident per case, regardless of number of lifts hit.
2. **Multiple** idents per case, only if more than one individual is identified with lifts from that one case.
3. **Number** of latent prints hit (i.e., three lifts hit in one case from the same SID produces three latent idents).

Six respondents chose option 1, four, option 2, and five, option 3. The method chosen has a serious impact on how many idents are counted per case. For example, if four different individuals are identified in one case, those idents would be reported as one hit under option 1, four under option 2, and four under option 3. In another example, if four lifts in one case result in the identification of the same individual, it would be counted as one hit under option 1, one under option 2, but four under option 3.

The calculation of the number of idents becomes even more complex when the method used to calculate a hit rate is considered. The survey asked the following:

Which of the following is used to determine a hit rate:

1. **All** latent cases received by the site/latent unit (regardless of whether they were searched on an AFIS system).
2. Only **Unique** cases searched on AFIS systems regardless of number of times searched on AFIS systems (one case received and entered on an AFIS system regardless of the number of searches performed equals one case).
3. **Multiple** searches of the same case (one case received, entered on an AFIS system, and searched five times equals five cases).

Three users choose option 1 and calculate their hit rate on the number of all latent cases received regardless of whether they are searched on an AFIS system. Nine users use option 2 and calculate their hit rate on the number of unique cases entered ignoring any additional searches of the same case. Three users selected option 3 and based their hit rate to include multiple searches of the same case. (See Tables 8.2 and 8.3.) What are the consequences of these choices? Some agencies use a very narrow definition, counting only one ident regardless of the number of lifts hit, while others take a more broad approach. Also, some agencies include all latent cases in their ident rate regardless of whether they were searched on an AFIS system. What is the effect of different latent entry practices, different databases, and different ident hit rate calculations?

What are some of the factors beyond count that may contribute to a higher ident rate?

- Better control of what is collected at the crime scene
- An evidence technician collected the latent image at the crime scene
- Search parameters were optimized
- The best card was selected for conversion
- Database size and volatility
- Accuracy of the matchers
- Accuracy of the coders

As a practical application, Table 8.4 provides a comparison of the responses from two agencies, one a local police department, the second a state agency.

Table 8.2

Latent Print Count and Hit Rates

Agency	Number of Records in Lat Cog Database	Number of Latent Cases	Number of Latents Searched	Number of Idents	Ident Count[a]	Hit Rate[b]	Notes
Police Dept 1	183,000	?	844	79	One	All	
Police Dept 2	150,000	1,100	2,830	220	# Hit	Unique	550 idents over 2.5 years
Police Dept 3	15,000	—	1,218	195	# Hit	All	
Police Dept 4	190,500	1,600	1,600	375	One	Unique	
Police Dept 5	200,000	2,119	5,337	1,061	# Hit	Include	
Police Dept 6	700,000	4,732	12,450	1,374	Multiple	Unique	656 unique Individuals
Police Dept 7	245,000	—	—	—	One	Unique	
Police Dept 8	245,000	410	1,230	127	One	Unique	91/127
State 1	741,000	3,700	6,200	419	# Hit	Unique	
State 2	220,000	2,465	4,943	357	# Hit	Multiple	Tracked by image, not case
State 3	1,028,000	4,700	8,015	569	Multiple	Unique	505 cases, 569 latents
State 4	684,000	1,055	1,748	271	Multiple	Unique	
State 5	1,089,000	7,168	21,504	781	Multiple	All	
State 6	1,500,000	30,000	50,000	704	Multiple	Multiple	
State 7	641,000	725	4,860	158	One	Unique	86 cases, 158 idents
Totals	7,831,500	59,774	122,779	6,690			

[a] Count: One, one ident per case regardless of number of lifts hit; multiple, multiple idents per case only if more than one individual is identified with lifts from that one case; # hit, number of latent prints hit (i.e., three lifts hit in one case from the same SID produces three latent idents).
[b] Hit rate: All, all latent cases received by the site/latent unit (regardless whether searched on AFIS); unique, only unique cases searched on AFIS regardless of number of times searched on AFIS (one case received, entered on AFIS regardless of the number of searches performed = one case); multiple, includes multiple searches of the same case (one case received, entered on AFIS, searched five times = five cases).

The local department is referred to as Agency 1 and the state department as State 1.

What are some of the differences between these two agencies?

- The local agency collects its own latent prints, assuring a more direct level of continuity and this is usually lifted by an evidence technician.
- Agency 1 uses the lifts, State 1 has photos, one step removed from the evidence.
- Agency 1 always has the person who lifts the prints at the crime scene follow the case through AFIS; State 1 does not.
- The two agencies use different techniques that employ system search parameters.

Table 8.3

Idents as a Percent of Latent Cases and Latent Searches

Agency	Number of Records in Lat Cog Database	Number of Latent Cases	Number of Latents Searched	Number of Idents	Idents as Percentage of Cases	Idents as Percentage of Searches
Police Dept 1	183,000	Unk	844	79	—	9%
Police Dept 2	150,000	1,100	2,830	220	20%	8%
Police Dept 3	15,000	—	1,218	195	—	16%
Police Dept 4	190,500	1,600	1,600	375	23%	23%
Police Dept 5	200,000	2,119	5,337	1,061	50%	20%
Police Dept 6	700,000	4,732	12,450	1,374	29%	11%
Police Dept 7	245,000	—	—	—	—	—
Police Dept 8	245,000	410	1,230	127	31%	10%
State 1	741,000	3,700	6,200	419	11%	7%
State 2	220,000	2,465	4,943	357	14%	7%
State 3	1,028,000	4,700	8,015	569	12%	7%
State 4	684,000	1,055	1,748	271	26%	16%
State 5	1,089,000	7,168	21,504	781	11%	4%
State 6	1,500,000	30,000	50,000	704	2%	1%
State 7	641,000	725	4,860	158	22%	3%
Total	7,831,500	59,774	122,779	6,690	11%	5%

Table 8.4

Comparison of Two Approaches

Function	Agency 1	State 1
Latents from own agency	100%	0%
Lifted by evidence technician	Always	Usually
Type of latents	Lifts	Photo
Lifter enters cases on AFIS	Always	Never
Search parameters	Searches based on pattern, finger number	Broad, then narrow
Relaunch procedures	Examiner's option	1–3 times per case
LC database size	250,000	1,500,000
TP database size	250,000	4,300,000
Best card converted	Yes	No
Linked to CCH	No	Yes
Updates	Unknown	340,000
New records annually	10,000–15,000	325,000
Records deleted	0	105,000
Latent idents counted	One ident per case	Multiple idents
Ident rate	Only unique cases searched on AFIS	Includes multiple searches
Number of cases	410	30,000
Number of searches	1,230	50,000
Number of idents	125	700
Idents as percentage of cases	30.98%	2.35%[a]
Idents as percentage of searches	10.33%	1.41%
Palm prints	10–15% of Lifts	Not entered
Palm prints as percentage of idents	5–7%	None

[a] State 1 has an ident rate of 11% when idents are counted as a percentage of new cases.

- Standard practice in one agency is to relaunch the lift 2–3 times, but this is the examiner's option at the other agency.
- Different sizes of databases.
- Agency 1 has a reported hit rate of 31% of cases; State 1 has 2% for all cases received, but 11% for new cases.
- Agency 1 has a 10% ident rate when compared against the number of searches, while State 1 has a 1.5% ident rate.

As is evident from this example, there are various methods employed to count idents and determine a hit rate. What is the preferred method? Without the agreement as to a uniform method for reporting ident counts and rates, it becomes nearly impossible to compare idents in any meaningful way. This situation is perhaps not that different from the problems faced by the FBI in collecting crime data. Until the development of the uniform crime report, there was no practical method for comparing crime rates and measuring success or weakness.

More recent developments in crime mapping technology, combined with standard definitions in a data dictionary, allow participants to make valid comparisons and look for methods of improvements, to "sing from the same sheet of music." In addition, the various methods used in reporting may mask opportunities to improve idents that may become apparent if all users agree to the same reporting techniques.

CHAPTER 9

CONTRACTUAL ISSUES REGARDING THE PURCHASE OF AN AUTOMATED FINGERPRINT IDENTIFICATION SYSTEM

Lisa K. Fox, Senior Attorney

9.1 INTRODUCTION

This chapter identifies various topics to consider and explore when procuring an Automatic Fingerprint Identification System (AFIS or System). Procurement of an AFIS is a time-consuming and complicated undertaking. Critical to its success is a thorough understanding of the business needs driving the AFIS procurement and the obligations imposed by the procurement process.

Information technology procurement in general, and AFIS procurement in specific, requires substantial amounts of planning and dedication of resources to increase the probability of success. Unlike purchases of commodities with standard specifications, well-understood expectations of performance, and minimal risk associated with errors, an AFIS procurement may involve a series of unknowns, or half-knowns, and a wide range of assumptions. An AFIS may not be usable if specific performance criteria are not met. Procurement of an AFIS involves a substantial expenditure of funds for a proprietary system, the operation of which can have a direct and critical impact on people's lives. Generally, once a vendor's technology is implemented, it is uncommon for a user to change either the vendor or the technology due in part to the large expenses associated with creating the database. Further, as technology improves, a vendor may present relatively inexpensive options for migrating to the more advanced technology, thereby decreasing the probability of vendor change.

This chapter does not discuss actual terms and conditions for an AFIS solicitation or resulting contract. Much material exists on this subject, and there is too much variation dependent upon the nature of the AFIS and the applicable statutory and regulatory requirements. Instead, based on the author's personal experiences in the AFIS procurement environment, it identifies topics that a governmental employee, such as a program analyst and manager, should explore and consider, with suggestions for addressing these concepts. It also identifies selected topics that are not ordinarily the focus of an AFIS procurement, but that can have a major impact on the process. While written specifically with respect to competitive procurements, the identified concepts must also be addressed within a non-competitive acquisition. Thus, this chapter is of value to governmental entities seeking an AFIS via non-competitive means.

As is true in most specializations, terminology has specific definitions and meanings in the procurement arena. For the purposes of this chapter, specific definitions are avoided, as it is not possible to consider all the possibilities and terminology is used in a generic sense. The terms "contract" and "agreement" are used interchangeably, as are the terms "procurement," "purchase," and "acquisition." For purposes of convenience, the entity acquiring the AFIS is referred to as "government" or "government entity" or "governmental agency" (or some variation), fully recognizing that such procurement could be made by any level of government. "Vendor" is used to generally reference the entity that supplies AFIS regardless of the stage of the procurement. The terms "solicitation" and "request for proposal" or "RFP" are interchangeably used to describe the public document that defines the kind of AFIS sought and the associated terms and conditions for its acquisition. The term "parties" collectively references the governmental agency and vendor.

Further, acknowledging that not even a fraction of the laws and requirements applying to governmental procurement could be discussed, New York state and federal requirements are cited as examples of various concepts, as appropriate.

Finally, this chapter is not intended to provide legal advice. Instead, the goal is to identify and raise issues for consideration within an AFIS procurement. While specific suggestions are presented, ultimately any action must be based on a thorough examination and understanding of the specifics involved in a given procurement after consultation with legal counsel and approval by the authorized decision makers for the jurisdiction.

9.2 PREPARING TO ACQUIRE AN AFIS

Automated fingerprint identification system (AFIS or System) technology is a type of information technology that is commonly used for the identification of persons, dead or alive. While the intended use of AFIS will govern the functionality needed, there are topics common to all AFIS procurements.

Functional needs dictate how a procurement is designed. For example, if the procurement is for a public benefits system, the governmental entity will determine if it will acquire services to operate the AFIS, including the enrollment process. Generally speaking, a vendor would not handle the enrollment process for forensic applications, since enrollment occurs within the context of criminal justice activities. Thus, the services obtained under the two procurements greatly differ.

The initial planning and decisions made in an AFIS procurement have ramifications throughout the procurement and form the basis for the entire project. A decision about a funding source may impact the development of needed customizations. The evaluation criteria may overemphasize the importance of one factor and exclude another. The failure to request different licensing rights may impact the provision of disaster recovery or the overall costs for operating the AFIS.

Thus, the most important step in preparing to acquire an AFIS is the planning stage. The failure to fully consider the possibilities and business needs for an AFIS can be fatal to a project. While the government may ultimately acquire an AFIS through a procurement, if that AFIS does not satisfy its business needs or does not provide the foundation for meeting the future business needs, the procurement may need to be repeated, at a great cost to the government. It is far better to thoroughly explore the AFIS technology and needs initially. Chapter 7 outlines the types of issues that must be considered when defining the AFIS needs.

9.3 SPECIAL CONSIDERATIONS FOR PUBLIC PROCUREMENT

Public procurement is the expenditure of public funds with the goal of fulfilling a defined governmental mission, and in general it carries with it special considerations. Public funds are directly expended not only for the procurement, but also for the salaries and associated costs of the government employees undertaking the procurement. Governmental entities have scores of procurement requirements and different control structures, ranging from statutes and regulations to general guidelines and policies. There are also requirements and limitations placed on government employees' actions with unique meaning within the context of procurement. Public procurement may also function as an economic development tool, increasing the visibility of the procurement and the need to ensure the appropriate utilization of limited governmental resources.

While it is not possible to address, even in part, the vast array of procurement requirements, the litmus test to apply is whether the actions are fair and supported by the records. For example, the concept of fairness is present in the idea that everyone should have access to the same information about the procurement. This concept of fairness underlies the public notice requirements for a procurement, the kinds of information included in a competitive solicitation, and the manner in which the evaluation criteria is developed.

By its nature, public procurement is a lengthy process, and information technology (IT) procurement tends to be even longer because of the extra effort needed to carefully analyze the business needs of government and define the scope of the procurement. Adequate time and resources must be dedicated to ensure a successful acquisition.

9.3.1 GENERAL REQUIREMENTS FOR GOVERNMENTAL ACTION

As an action of the government, a procurement must comply with the array of general rules applicable to any governmental action. Final governmental decisions are open for public review, so freedom of information laws or sunshine laws must be complied with during the procurement process. The general theory is that the final information maintained by the government should be available upon request. In addition to the solicitation, the submitted proposals and evaluations may be subject to the statutory requirements on the release of information. The public access laws, however, generally recognize the need to balance the interests of the public in knowing what its government is doing with the property and privacy interests of vendors.

This balancing of interests is especially relevant in light of the proprietary nature of AFIS technology and the significant financial investment made in an AFIS. As part of the procurement process, a governmental entity may request information about specific AFIS technology from a vendor that is of a confidential or proprietary nature. The proprietary information may be critical for a government to thoroughly evaluate whether the technology meets its business needs. Similarly, in light of the significant investment made in the AFIS, a government may also require detailed and confidential information about the financial status of a vendor, such as copies of audited financial statements. Consideration must be given to how your government's requirements treat this information under its public access laws. This information must be clearly communicated to the vendor so that informed decisions can be made about the procurement, including what risks, if any, are associated with the possible public release of such information. Many jurisdictions provide a specific statutory framework for a vendor to exempt its proprietary information from public release. Such framework must be understood and incorporated into the request for proposals (RFP).

Records retention requirements must also be considered. While far from glamorous, records retention requirements are the foundation of governmental operations and form the basis for future evaluations of the procurement. For example, suppose that Agency A releases a competitive procurement for an AFIS and awards the contract to Vendor B. The System is implemented and things go along fine. Toward the end of the contract term, the parties decide to pursue the development of a non-competitive contract for the future. A control agency, however, may wish to revisit aspects of that initial competitive procurement, especially if a competitor has contested the new non-competitive contract. Agency A may need to recreate the initial competitive bid, and in order to do that, the original records must be available.

The government is ultimately responsible to its taxpayers for its expenditures. Its actions should reinforce and support the public's trust, while balancing the needs of government with fairness to others. This general concept of fairness is woven throughout the procurement process, including the information gathering stage, defining the nature and form of the public procurement, and developing the terms and conditions for the public procurement.

9.3.2 REQUIREMENTS IMPOSED ON THE ACTIONS OF GOVERNMENTAL EMPLOYEES

As alluded to above, procurement is simply one activity undertaken by governmental employees and is subject to the general rules imposed on employees' actions. Consideration must be given to how the governmental entity's ethical requirements impact the public procurement process. As a general rule, most governments require its employees to comply with a code of ethics. Public employees are held to a higher standard of behavior since they are making decisions that affect public welfare and the public purse. For example, in New York State, Public Officers Law sections 73, 73-a, and 74 place limitations upon the actions of public employees. In general, these provisions set out specific standards of conduct, restrict certain business and professional activities, and apply while in governmental employment and, in some instances, after leaving governmental employment. Within the procurement context, one issue that arises is whether an employee's actions constitute a conflict of interest. For example, if an employee provides a vendor with "inside" information regarding an AFIS procurement, such an action could violate the ethics requirements. Some ethics requirements broadly obligate employees to avoid even the appearance of impropriety. The employees conducting the procurement must be aware of these requirements and develop procurement processes that ameliorate the possibility of inappropriate actions.

In addition to ethical obligations established by statute and regulation, requirements may also be established by executive order or agency policy. For example, in New York State, an executive order was issued in 2003 responding to public concern about the need to know the people who contact the government, such as lobbyists and vendors, in an effort to influence a procurement decision, and standardizing the collection of such information. These kinds of requirements must be identified and factored into the resulting RFP.

Employees should be provided with up-to-date information and training, in addition to access to legal advice, regarding these ethical obligations. The solicitation should give vendors notice of these requirements, through incorporation of the clauses requiring the vendor to acknowledge and agree to comply with such ethical requirements.

9.4 TYPES OF PUBLIC PROCUREMENT

Public procurement can be broadly divided into two categories: competitive and non-competitive. Depending on the factual circumstances, either type may be appropriate for an AFIS procurement. The decision of whether to proceed with a competitive or non-competitive procurement should be made after a thorough examination of all the issues and consultation with the appropriate executive, financial, legal, and control agencies. While there are generally statutory preferences for competitive procurements, there is limited recognition that a competitive procurement does not always best suit the public needs. For example, in New York State, Article 11 of the State Finance Law indicates a preference for competition, but acknowledges several types of non-competitive procurements. Federal procurement statutes and regulations also permit non-competitive procurements under certain circumstances. [See Federal Acquisition Regulations (FAR) set forth at 48 CFR (Code of Federal Regulations) Part 1. Information regarding non-competitive procurements is set forth in Subpart 6.3.]

While a procurement may result from a competitive process, subsequent action may be undertaken as a non-competitive process. This possibility is a natural extension of the proprietary nature of AFIS technology and the huge investment required to establish the database and acquire the technology. Additional importance is placed on initially conducting a thorough competitive procurement and retaining the appropriate records supporting it. For example, suppose that Agency A engages in a competitive procurement to obtain an AFIS for criminal justice purposes with Vendor B. A contract is negotiated and approved for a 10-year term and includes hardware, software, services, and maintenance. Prior to the end of the 10-year term, a decision is made to enter into a new contract with Vendor B, via a non-competitive process, to continue the availability of the hardware, software, services, and maintenance. The decision is justified on the basis of the huge expenses that would be incurred to change to another vendor's proprietary AFIS, ranging from record conversion costs, hardware and software replacement, development of new interfaces with other technology systems, new system training, etc.

9.4.1 COMPETITIVE PROCUREMENT

A competitive procurement is one in which the government develops a specific, detailed set of requirements for goods and services and solicits competitive responses from qualified vendors. Depending on the nature of the procurement, different competitive models can be used. For example, to acquire office chairs, a government would probably use a competitive procurement model that defines the specifications for the office chairs and the terms and conditions for the sale (such as delivery and payment terms). If a proposed office chair satisfies the specifications and the vendor agrees to the terms and conditions, the government's decision is then based on lowest price. Oftentimes referred to as an invitation for bid (IFB) or a request for quotation (RFQ), this competitive bidding model is premised on the use of yes/no decisions; there is no (or only minimal) qualitative judgment involved. It is largely used only in those procurements for which the decisions and the needs can be boiled down to very concrete requirements. In light of the inherent complexities of AFIS technology, it is highly unlikely that this type of competitive procurement would ever be employed for an AFIS procurement. Instead, a competitive procurement for an AFIS would most likely use a request for proposal (RFP), or similar model, that permits the evaluation and relative weighing of qualitative factors. It is awarded on the basis of something other than lowest price, sometimes referred to as best value.

In contrast to the IFB or RFQ, the RFP model employs qualitative judgment in the evaluation process. While the RFP model incorporates defined specifications (e.g., the proposed AFIS must be certified as compliant with specified technology standards), those kinds of specifications are typically only a part of the evaluation. It is common for a RFP to establish a multi-tiered evaluation process, in which the yes/no decisions disqualify unsuitable products or vendors from further consideration and the later evaluation tiers, such as product demonstrations and functionality testing. A weighted scoring methodology is often employed that reflects the relative importance of the various factors to the government's procurement decision.

In general, there is a direct relationship between the complexity of the commodities and services sought and the means by which the procurement is conducted. That is to say, the more complicated the AFIS procurement, the more complicated the RFP and evaluation process.

The RFP model encompasses two distinct steps: development and conduct of the RFP and negotiation and approval of the resulting contract. In contrast, under the IFB and RFQ models, the vendor ordinarily agrees to the terms and conditions set forth in the solicitation and may even submit a contract signature page with the response. Few, if any, terms and conditions are subject to negotiation.

9.4.2 NON-COMPETITIVE PROCUREMENT

There are two main models for the non-competitive procurement: the sole source justification and the single source justification. The sole source model is based on the government's determination on the record that only one vendor can provide the needed commodity or service. The single source model is predicated on the governmental decision that while more than one vendor can provide the requisite commodities or services, for stated business reasons the government has determined it is best to contract with a specific vendor. A non-competitive procurement obligates the government to state on the record why a certain vendor was selected and justify its selection. This type of procurement may open the government's decision making to second-guessing or criticism.

9.4.3 THINGS TO CONSIDER WHEN EVALUATING THE COMPETITIVE VERSUS NON-COMPETITIVE MODELS

While a non-competitive procurement dispenses with the need to develop and conduct a RFP and only requires the negotiation and approval of a contract, much of the effort put into the development of a RFP is not eliminated but instead is only deferred. Developing a RFP forces a governmental agency to examine and articulate its business needs and to assess the relative importance of various factors. It is a very useful, but difficult, component of implementing a complex system like an AFIS. A RFP provides a roadmap for developing the resulting contract, and the vendor proposal may indicate agreement with certain terms and conditions, reducing the scope of negotiations. In a non-competitive procurement, the definition of business needs and implementation must be part of the contract negotiations or conducted simultaneously. Arguably, the time commitment for contracts negotiation in the non-competitive procurement is greater because there has not been the same, intense definition of requirements (especially functional and performance requirements). While the government may have defined its business needs for an AFIS as part of the effort to secure funding, it is unlikely that such a definition would have explored topics such as acceptance testing, protection of the government's business environment, and damages for late or defective performance. As indicated in Table 9.1, there are advantages and disadvantages associated with each procurement model that must be assessed.

Non-competitive procurement negotiations are conducted in an environment that may have resulted in the shifting of relative negotiation positions. In

Table 9.1

Competitive versus Non-competitive Process

	Competitive Procurement Process	Non-competitive Procurement Process
Request for proposals (RFP)	Necessitates development of detailed RFP to document business need and methodology for receiving and evaluating proposals.	While no RFP is required, government must still engage in due diligence and document the decision-making process.
Reasonableness of price	Established through the competitive process.	Must be separately researched and analyzed by government. May be difficult to identify benchmarks to establish reasonableness.
Justification for selection	Based on application of evaluation criteria set forth in RFP. The competitive process tests appropriateness of evaluation criteria as do the questions and answers provided during the competitive process.	Must be separately established by government. May be subject to greater scrutiny by control agencies and allegations of favoritism.
Contract negotiations	RFP may be used to narrow the range of negotiated items, thereby decreasing the time required at this stage. May also be used as means to collect counter proposals. Government is arguably in a more favorable negotiation position, as both parties are invested in the procurement.	No formal mechanism to narrow range of negotiated items or decrease time commitment for negotiations. May need to re-analyze and rearticulate business needs. Government is arguably in a less favorable negotiating position, as it has made the representation that the vendor is either the only one that can provide the AFIS or the preferred provider of the AFIS for stated reasons.
Workload implications	Substantial investment of effort in development of RFP and evaluation methodology. Provides a formal and quantifiable testing methodology to determine that the vendor's AFIS meets needs.	While RFP is not prepared, government must still invest effort to determine its business needs and that the vendor's AFIS meets those needs. While multiple vendors' products may be reviewed, not all are subject to an in-depth review.
Evaluation	Conduct pursuant to the RFP. Use of tiered evaluation process may disqualify unsuitable products or vendors early in the process, decreasing the evaluation time required. Provides greater certainty that the vendor's product meets business needs.	While no formal process, government still must substantiate its business needs and articulate how the vendor's AFIS meets these needs. Provides lesser certainty that the vendor's product meets business needs than competitive process and is a less public process with fewer established controls.

a competitive procurement, the government states its needs and expectations and evaluates the proposals submitted. There is an inherent message that the vendor, who has invested a great deal of time and effort to get to the point of contract negotiation, is not the only game in town. The governmental entity has a motivated vendor who is looking to recoup actual expenses and may bring a more amendable tone to the negotiations. Further, as a result of the RFP process, key issues and potential solutions have already been vetted. From the vendor's perspective, the government is a motivated buyer.

In a non-competitive procurement, the government is sending a different message—either the vendor is the only one who satisfies the government's needs (i.e., sole source) or while others can satisfy the government's needs, the vendor is the "chosen" one (i.e., single source). This message shifts the relative negotiation positions and places each party in a different position. Consideration must be given to how to balance the message sent to the vendor through a sole or single source justification to achieve a mutually acceptable contract.

In addition, under a non-competitive procurement the governmental entity must not only justify its choice of vendor, but also articulate how it determined the vendor's prices were reasonable. In a properly conducted competitive procurement, the competitive process establishes the reasonableness of price and is often reinforced through the inclusion of a contractual requirement stating that the vendor guarantees to provide the same or better pricing for all similar procurements. Such clauses are referred to as price protection or most favored nation clauses. A non-competitive procurement, however, often does not have such controls built into it. While the need to establish the reasonableness of a vendor's price can be employed as a tool to negotiate favorable pricing (and perhaps inclusion of a price protection clause), the governmental entity must be prepared to invest additional resources to confirm the pricing information provided by the vendor and to defend the costs to any control agency or public inquiry.

Additional efforts must be undertaken to address any concerns raised about the ethical considerations of the non-competitive procurement. While use of a competitive bid does not guarantee there will be no allegations of improprieties in the procurement process, the public nature of the transaction and the multi-level review process serve as controls and should decrease the possibility. A non-competitive procurement, on the other hand, does not benefit from these controls and may necessitate additional internal reviews and controls to ensure that the ethical requirements are met.

9.4.4 AFIS PROCUREMENT FLOWCHART

As illustrated in Figure 9.1, many of the same decisions are made during competitive and non-competitive acquisitions of an AFIS. The specifics of the AFIS acquisition and the statutory environment will govern which process is the most appropriate. Each procurement model commences with a business needs analysis and the identification of funding, which are critical steps. Each model requires that the appropriate control agency approvals be obtained. While the

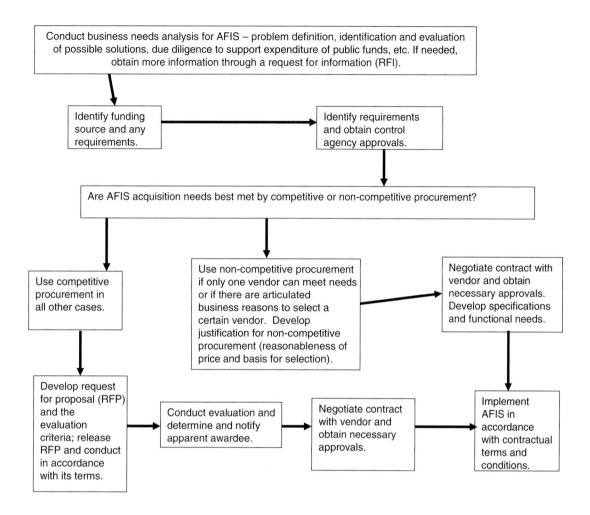

Conduct business needs analysis for AFIS – problem definition, identification and evaluation of possible solutions, due diligence to support expenditure of public funds, etc. If needed, obtain more information through a request for information (RFI).

Identify funding source and any requirements.

Identify requirements and obtain control agency approvals.

Are AFIS acquisition needs best met by competitive or non-competitive procurement?

Use competitive procurement in all other cases.

Use non-competitive procurement if only one vendor can meet needs or if there are articulated business reasons to select a certain vendor. Develop justification for non-competitive procurement (reasonableness of price and basis for selection).

Negotiate contract with vendor and obtain necessary approvals. Develop specifications and functional needs.

Develop request for proposal (RFP) and the evaluation criteria; release RFP and conduct in accordance with its terms.

Conduct evaluation and determine and notify apparent awardee.

Negotiate contract with vendor and obtain necessary approvals.

Implement AFIS in accordance with contractual terms and conditions.

two processes differ regarding how the vendor is advised of the government's AFIS needs and how the contractual relationship is defined, each culminates in the development of written specifications and functionality and a contract to govern implementation and ongoing operation.

Figure 9.1

Contractual Decision Flow

9.5 STATUTORY AND REGULATORY REQUIREMENTS

9.5.1 PUBLIC PROCUREMENTS IN GENERAL

In addition to the general requirements placed on all governmental actions, there are additional requirements imposed on procurements. Complex requirements have developed governing the public procurement process. Governmental procurement has long been recognized as a tool supporting various socio-economic policies, such as minority and women business participation goals or small business purchasing. Thus, a critical early step is an examination of the legal requirements imposed and the guidance available for implementing the requirements. For example, an entire body of law has developed to govern the federal procurement process, covering almost every possible permeation of the procurement process. (See in general FAR set forth at 48 CFR Part 1.) Other statutes provide more generalized parameters for conducting public procurement.

This examination identifies elements that must be incorporated into the procurement. Requirements may include vendor certification that the pricing was independently obtained without collusion with other vendors, vendor certification regarding business operations in Northern Ireland (often referred to as MacBride Fair Employment Principles), and identification of subcontracting and a commitment to use best efforts to engage certified minority- and women-owned businesses. The jurisdiction may also prohibit contracting with certain vendors based on the location of the vendor's business (often referred to as "discriminatory jurisdictions") or on past actions of the vendor (such as presence on disbarment lists or other concepts that speak to the vendor's responsibility). There may also be limits placed on travel reimbursement payable to the vendor that must be incorporated.

Another element to examine is what other governmental bodies must be involved in the procurement process, particularly those with an oversight or approval role. For the purposes of this discussion, these groups are generically referred to as "control agencies." While their roles can differ tremendously, it is important to understand the roles, build the review or evaluation time into the plans, and obtain the necessary input. To the extent possible, it is best to solicit input early in the development process. For example, in some municipal governments, it is necessary that the governing body pass a resolution for an agency to enter into a contractual agreement. In New York State, the Office of the State Comptroller has a statutorily created role in the approval of contracts (see New York State Finance Law Section 112).

9.5.2 TECHNOLOGY PROCUREMENTS IN PARTICULAR

Governments recognize that information technology represents a significant resource and constitutes a large expenditure of funds. The past practice of "every governmental entity for itself" resulted in an inefficient use of resources and a growing incompatibility between systems. Increasingly, governments seek to coordinate technology purchases, develop standards to govern the acquisition of new technology, and promote strategic plans with an eye toward standardization and compatibility. Imposition of technology standards or identification of a specific control agency to pre-approve technology purchases is increasingly used. In New York State, this oversight role is performed by its

Office for Technology (OFT). (See http://www.oft.state.ny.us/ for more information.) A state agency is obligated to undergo a review by and obtain permission from OFT before engaging in most technology-related procurements. Thus, in addition to financial control agencies, an AFIS acquisition may be subject to approvals by a technology-based group.

Depending on the AFIS desired, additional approvals may be required by the control agency obligated to ensure the integrity of electronically transmitted information. For example, if fingerprints will be obtained in remote locations and electronically submitted to a central site through livescan technology, information security requirements must be addressed. Inquiry must be made as to whether there are established minimum requirements, ethics, responsibilities, and accepted behaviors required to establish and maintain a secure environment and achieve the government's information security objectives. If so, those requirements must be incorporated into the acquisition. In New York State, the Office for Cyber Security and Critical Infrastructure Coordination sets the direction, gives broad guidance, and defines requirements for information security-related processes and actions across state entities. (See http://www.cscic.state.ny.us/ for more information.)

9.5.3 ADDITIONAL REQUIREMENTS BASED ON THE INTENDED USE OF THE TECHNOLOGY

While there are certain commonalities in how governmental entities treat data, each state has unique requirements and concerns, especially in relation to criminal history records. If the AFIS will interface with criminal history data, the requirements must be incorporated onto the RFP. For example, in the criminal context, the RFP must identify whether special requirements apply to the sealing of data, levels of access, treatment of selected records, and whether there are statutes, court decisions, or practices governing the return of the information. A governmental agency needs to provide this information in the solicitation and ensure incorporation in the System specifications and evaluation requirements, as appropriate.

9.6 IDENTIFICATION OF FUNDING SOURCES

As part of the planning process, funding sources for the AFIS procurement must be identified. Due to the nuances and specific nature of the public funding process, it is critical that the appropriate staff be involved and fully understand the purpose and goals of the procurement. In addition to program staff, other staff involved in the RFP development and approval should include representatives of the finance or budget office, grants office, and legal office.

Identification of funding sources depends on cooperation and communication to ensure the availability of needed information to evaluate requirements imposed by the funding sources.

9.6.1 LOCATION AND IDENTIFICATION OF THE FUNDING SOURCE

As discussed earlier, public procurements are most often governed by statutory ethical considerations. One of those requirements is to act in good faith toward the vending community and to provide all eligible vendors with a fair and equal opportunity to compete for the work. Responding to a competitive solicitation can be a tremendous amount of work, requiring the investment of substantial vendor resources. In keeping with the concept of fair and open competition and government acting in an appropriate fashion, it is this author's belief that a governmental entity should only request that investment of effort if it has identified the funds to proceed with the procurement. It can be argued the identification of funds constitutes the government's good faith in the procurement. However, it should be noted that the identification of funds and the release of a solicitation do not require the government to make a procurement. As a general rule, the entity releasing a solicitation reserves the right to not award a contract for various reasons. It is strongly recommended, however, that a solicitation not be released without an identified funding stream supporting it.

A very different situation is presented if a procurement is established as a centralized contract or an "indefinite quantity" contract. Unlike the situation in which a government agency seeks to obtain an AFIS to resolve a specific issue, an indefinite quantity contract is generally used for commodities (not services) and is clearly advertised as one for which there is no guarantee of purchase. The government seeks to establish the contract so that the vehicle is available for a larger group of authorized purchasers. A single state agency may be responsible for establishing contracts for statewide purchase and would have no reason to identify the funding source since there is no guarantee of purchase.

Reasonable minds differ about whether the amount of available funding should be released in the RFP. One concern is that the release of the funding amount will result in cost proposals equal to that amount less one dollar. While it is a decision that differs by jurisdiction, it should be noted that oftentimes other publicly available documents detail the funding available. For example, a governmental agency's annual budget request may detail how much of its appropriation will be expended on an AFIS procurement. Similarly, a grant application and award will identify the funds and available resources committed to the AFIS project.

The lack of an identified funding source does not preclude the government from taking action, but suggests a different course. A tool that is widely used to request ideas or proposals from industry is often referred to as the request for information (RFI). Basically, the RFI identifies the government's problem or business need and asks the industry for ideas or information on how to solve it. The key difference from a competitive solicitation is that there is a clear statement and disclosure that no acquisition will result from the RFI. Specific financial information is not collected at this juncture since it is not relevant. If desired, "ballpark" estimates or a copy of a publicly available price list may be requested to provide some guidance about the costs associated with various solutions. However, the RFI is intended as a tool to define the nature of the procurement and can be useful in the development of funding requests.

9.6.2 DETERMINATION IF THE FUNDING SOURCE IMPOSES ADDITIONAL OBLIGATIONS

A practical reason for identifying the funding source is to determine if it imposes any additional requirements for the procurement. These additional requirements take four key forms: (1) additional approvals required by the funding source (which impact the time lines for conducting the procurement), (2) the time frame in which the funds are available for expenditure (impacts the scope of the procurement and the proposed payment schedules), (3) restrictions/limitations on the permissible scope of expenditures, and (4) affirmative requirements imposed by the funding source. While the additional restrictions are commonly associated with grant funds, state laws can illustrate other areas where the restrictions can be found. For example, it is highly possible that an AFIS procurement may involve federal grant funds, as almost all states have received National Criminal History Improvement Program funds in support of AFIS acquisitions.

9.6.2.1 Additional Approvals Required by the Funding Source

Funding sources can require additional approvals before legal obligations can be met. Allowances need to be made for the effort and time required to obtain these approvals. For example, federal funds oftentimes impose additional approval requirements for certain expenditures, such as criminal justice information and communication systems and consultant services. While approval can be obtained through the application process, when a description of the proposed expenditure is detailed in the budget narrative, often an entity will not possess sufficient detailed information at the application stage to explain the request. In that situation, the grantee must submit a separate written request to the contracting authority for approval of the proposed expenditure.

An additional approval may also be required if federal grant funds are used toward a sole source procurement. The governmental agency must comply with the specific grant terms and conditions, but in general it must justify its proposed course of action based on the expertise, management, and responsiveness of the vendor and knowledge of the engagement, experience, and uniqueness of the vendor. The federal grant funds may also cap the daily amount payable to a vendor without prior written approval from the federal agency.

9.6.2.2 Time Frame in Which the Funds Are Available for Expenditure

Without addressing the technical aspects of governmental budgeting, it can be stated that funds are not available for indefinite periods of time and affirmative action may be necessary to make the funds available. Grant funds are generally only available for a specific period of time, and if not spent before the end of that period, the funds are returned to the granting agency. While it may be possible to extend the period in which the grant funds can be spent, it cannot be assumed that an extension will be granted. A few years ago, for example, many governmental agencies were caught off guard when the federal government declined to extend the availability of grant funds distributed under the Local Law Enforcement Block Grant Program.

The planning stages should include discussions with the financial and grants offices to ensure understanding of the actions required to obligate grant funds and the time period to actually spend the funds. For example, issuance of a purchase order obligates the funds, but the product or services need to be both received and accepted before the end of the liquidation period. (A more detailed discussion on obligating and expending the funds can be found in the U.S. Department of Justice Office of Justice Assistance Financial Guidelines, available at http://www.ojp.usdoj.gov/FinGuide/part3-ch2.htm.)

The availability of funds is relevant to the time period for System delivery and implementation and heavily factors into development of the payment structure and consideration of the ramifications of schedule slip or difficulties encountered in the acceptance testing process. For example, an agency needs to consider what will transpire if the commodity or service is not accepted before the end of the liquidation period.

9.6.2.3 Restrictions/Limitations on Permissible Scope of Expenditures

When a governmental agency applies for and receives a grant, it is usually for a specific purpose or project, which necessarily limits the permissible scope of expenditures. However, many grants contain additional spending restrictions that are not as readily identifiable, but that could greatly impact an AFIS procurement. For example, as part of the federal grant application process, an applicant is required to agree to a series of terms and conditions. (See http://www.ojp.usdoj.gov/Forms/assur.pdf for more information.) While referred to as "assurances," these clauses place binding restrictions on the expenditure of funds. Further, many of these clauses must expressly be passed on to the contractor. For example, clause 6 of the federal certified assurances requires compliance with all the requirements of the federal sponsoring agency, including special requirements of law, program requirements, and administrative requirements, and includes a commitment that the contractor must comply with a listing of non-discrimination statutes.

The key funding restriction derived from federal funding is probably the non-supplantation requirement. For example, the federal Edward Byrne Memorial State and Local Law Enforcement Assistance Program, administered by the U.S. Department of Justice (DOJ) Office of Justice Program, is used to support state and local law enforcement efforts. (See http://www.ojp.usdoj.gov/BJA/grant/byrneguide_03/b_strategy.html for more information.) The recipient must agree that these federal funds will not be used to supplant state or local funds, but will be used to increase the amount of such funds that would, in the absence of federal funds, be made available for law enforcement activities. (See http://www.ojp.usdoj.gov/BJA/grant/byrneguide_03/b_budget.html.)   What this requirement means is that the recipient must not have already budgeted funds to perform the work and then substituted the budgeted funds with the grant funds. Again, this is an issue that should be discussed with the finance or grants office.

Another requirement that can be difficult to comply with in an AFIS procurement that is also derived from DOJ funds is when a single state agency is responsible for receiving a grant and then distributing the funds to other eligible recipients. For example, as part of its standard terms and conditions, the state of New York, through its state agency the Division of Criminal Justice Services (DCJS), passes forward the federal requirement that "if the grant support provided by DCJS is federally sponsored, the federal awarding agency also reserves a royalty-free, nonexclusive, and irrevocable license to reproduce, publish or otherwise use, and to authorize others to use: (a) the copyright in any work developed under a grant, subgrant or contract under a grant or subgrant; and (b) any rights of copyright to which a Grantee, Subgrantee, or a Contractor purchases ownership with such grant support." (See http://criminaljustice.state.ny.us/ofpa/appendixa1.htm for more information on this clause.) As a practical matter, the most efficient way to comply with this requirement is for the governmental agency to take an ownership interest in the resulting intellectual property. If this is a requirement of the funding source, it must be built into the solicitation so that the vendor fully understands the expectations regarding the ownership of customized work products.

9.6.2.4 *Affirmative Requirements Imposed by the Funding Source*

Governments may engage in alternative forms of procurement funding. Lease purchasing arrangements are one such funding source that could impose additional requirements. In this instance, if a governmental agency determines that a procurement will be funded through a lease purchase arrangement, the specific requirements must be incorporated into the solicitation. For example, in New York State, lease purchasing is permitted under express circumstances and requires the inclusion of contract language addressing the ownership of customized products. (See http://www.budget.state.ny.us/bprm/bulletins/h-1026.html for more information.) It imposes minimum expenditure requirements and precludes financing of maintenance and training costs. The vendor must also be obligated to execute such documents as required by the government under these financing arrangements.

9.7 LEGAL CONSIDERATIONS WHEN DEVELOPING THE PUBLIC PROCUREMENT SOLICITATION

At this junction, the governmental entity would have completed an analysis of its business needs, identifying the problem it seeks to solve and means for a resolution. It would have acquired the necessary approvals to obtain an AFIS, including any approvals associated with the funding, and is ready to develop the solicitation document. What follows is a discussion about specific issues to consider when developing the solicitation.

In general, the RFP or solicitation answers the questions of who, what, where, how, and when associated with a public procurement, but not necessarily in that order. Recall that an underlying requirement of public procurement is a fair and open process, and a critical part of providing a fair and open process is that everyone gets the same information in the same manner at the same time. The RFP is the key instrument used to convey all relevant information to vendors. It provides the framework for the vendors' submissions of proposals and establishes the basis for evaluating proposals. Further, it identifies many of the terms and conditions that will be included in the resulting contract. A well-thought-out and thorough RFP is critical to the successful implementation of an AFIS.

Statutory provisions often govern how the RFP or solicitation is provided to the vendor community. Generally, specific public notification is required of the procurement opportunity. A copy or notice of the RFP may also be sent to the known vendors in the field, advising of the opportunity. For example, in New York State, a law requires notification of procurement opportunities over $15,000 in value in a specific publication, entitled the *New York State Contract Reporter*. (See New York State Economic Development Law Article 4-C.)

It is recommended that the governmental entity establish a multi-discipline team to develop the RFP. The team should at a minimum include representatives of information technology, the end users of the technology (typically a business unit), and the finance, business, grants, and legal units. For a highly complicated and multi-site AFIS, consideration should also be given to including representatives from other agencies that may use the AFIS. This team approach helps ensure that all relevant information is addressed and is provided to all parties.

Development of a RFP for AFIS technology can be very time consuming and involved; however, it is a necessary investment. Installation and implementation of an AFIS tends to be just the beginning of a long-term relationship with a vendor. AFIS technology is based on proprietary systems for image capture, transmission, processing, searching, storage, and decision. Systems use different algorithms for the classification and searching of the databases. There is very little, if any, interoperability between the various vendors' technologies. There can also be a significant investment in the conversion of existing records. Change of vendors may cause these conversion costs to be incurred again. Thus, absent substantial issues, it is unlikely that an agency would change vendors. Or to state it another way, every effort is warranted to help ensure that the right choice is initially made.

Care should be taken to ensure that the RFP requests only information relevant to the procurement and taken into consideration as part of the evaluation. It is very time consuming and expensive for a vendor to respond to a RFP. Requests for extensive or non-material information may have a chilling impact on vendor participation—just the opposite of what is desired.

While practices differ, a RFP is normally broken into the following topical areas:

1. Introduction and background
2. General information and response format
3. AFIS specifications and scope of work requirements
4. Evaluation criteria and relative weights of the criteria
5. Contractual terms and conditions

Issues for consideration are presented in each area, with detailed discussions reserved for the key topics. Keep in mind that the RFP forms the basis for the submitted proposals and the resulting contract. Moreover, the RFP provides a measure for gauging the government's actions. The government must be prepared to accept the logical consequences of each and every requirement or term placed in a RFP. If an element is set forth as a mandatory requirement, the failure of a vendor to meet that requirement results in its disqualification.

The government must follow the requirements it sets forth, and cannot elect to disregard requirements, for whatever reasons. A requirement should not be set forth as mandatory unless it really is. Similarly, a RFP should request only the information that will be used. If the RFP requests work and personal references for key vendor employees, the government needs to be prepared to use and evaluate that information.

Some jurisdictions permit releasing a draft RFP or holding a pre-RFP meeting with vendors to solicit input and answer questions about the technology. The key consideration is that the government agency acts in a fair manner. If there are 30 known vendors, each vendor should be solicited for input or invited to the pre-RFP meeting. A fair evaluation should be undertaken of the comments received. And the government agency should make changes based on its judgment of what will best aid a successful procurement.

9.7.1 INTRODUCTION AND BACKGROUND

As a general principal, the introduction and background segment of a RFP informs the reader about the governmental agency making the procurement, the problem and how it was defined, its vision of how the procurement will solve the problem, and an overview of how the procurement will be conducted. A government agency may already have an overview document that can be used for this segment. The prior analysis on the problem identification and the business needs also provides valuable source material for this section.

9.7.2 GENERAL INFORMATION AND RESPONSE FORMAT

This segment of the RFP sets out the rules for the procurement. It identifies the time frame for conducting the RFP and the various steps involved in the RFP. Generally speaking, once the RFP is written and necessary reviews and approvals are obtained, the process is commenced through public advertising and release of the RFP to vendors who are believed to provide the technology and to those who request the RFP. A period is provided for the submission of questions and provision of responses. Consideration should be given to how the government wishes to handle questions of a proprietary nature. It is common for a RFP to specify that proprietary references will be removed from the questions and answers circulated. Such a practice provides a means of addressing possible vendor concerns associated with the question-and-answer period. It is strongly recommended that the RFP permit only written questions and responses and that it designate a single point of contact. Such requirements help protect employees from allegations of favoritism or providing different information to different vendors. In keeping with the concept of fairness and ensuring everyone is provided the same information at the same time, the written questions and responses should be provided to all vendors that received the RFP. Use of a single point of contact helps to ensure that consistent information is provided and to minimize possible omissions in circulating information.

Depending on the nature of the AFIS procurement and the complexity of the request, the RFP may include a pre-bidders conference. This is a recognized forum for vendors to verbally pose questions and seek clarifications about a solicitation. In keeping with the concept of fairness, these conferences are usually audio- or videotaped or transcribed with the questions and answers provided to all vendors. As a result of the question-and-answer or pre-bidders conference, the government agency may decide to amend the RFP. This section normally addresses how an addendum would be issued.

It is fairly common for a RFP to require vendor registration to indicate interest in the solicitation. While the registration does not compel the vendor to submit a proposal, it often is set up so that only registered vendors receive the questions and answers, RFP addendums, etc. It may also be set up as a precondition to submitting a proposal. Registration can reduce the number of vendors that must be sent ongoing materials (and arguably can reduce costs associated with the procurement) and give the government a working estimate of how many vendors are interested in the solicitation. On the downside, missing the registration date can have massive ramifications for a vendor, especially if registration is established as a condition to submit a bid.

This section also addresses the manner in which the proposal must be submitted. It details who is authorized to receive the proposals, the format of the proposal, the number of copies required, and, most importantly, when the proposals must be submitted and the consequences of late submission. Generally speaking, for large, complicated procurements like an AFIS, the RFP provides detailed instructions and perhaps even forms for submitting information. A key issue to be aware of is whether the cost proposal must be submitted separately from the remainder of the proposal. In some jurisdictions, separate sealed submission of cost information may be statutorily required. Many evaluation schemes are established as multi-tiered reviews, and cost may become a review factor only if the proposal passes earlier evaluations with sufficient points (or whatever criteria is established). The thought seems to be that cost should not be reviewed earlier so it does not influence the evaluation process. Additionally, a separate team may be established to review the cost proposal, as it requires a very different skill set from a review of functional and technical specifications. As a result, many RFPs require the separate, sealed submission of the vendor's cost proposal.

This section may also set forth the government's general reservation of rights, including the right to not award any contract under the RFP. Public access requirements (such as the freedom of information law or sunshine laws) to the procurement process and the steps for a vendor to request restricted public access would be outlined here. General expectations or assumptions are also detailed, for example, the vendor bears all costs associated with submitting a proposal and assuring timely submission of its proposal.

9.7.3 AFIS SPECIFICATIONS AND SCOPE OF WORK REQUIREMENTS

In this section of the RFP, the government details what it wants to obtain. For example, it will specify if the AFIS must handle latent print searches. Factors to consider when evaluating the functionality needed for the AFIS are set forth in Chapter 7. Evaluation of the strengths and weaknesses of different AFIS functionality is a critical component of the specification process. These decisions necessarily form the basis of the evaluation. The information conveyed in the RFP reflects conclusions reached during the business needs assessment process. It is strongly recommended that the RFP consider both the short-term and the long-term AFIS needs. As previously discussed, most probably, once a jurisdiction selects an AFIS vendor, it is unlikely to change vendors.

The RFP should be developed in such a way that it not only addresses the immediate need, but also obtains the information needed for development of a contract vehicle that can "grow" with the AFIS application, including the introduction of new technology and features. It should be a proactive mechanism, not just a reactive mechanism intended to address the currently identified need. For example, while the government recognizes the need to train current employees and requests pricing for six training programs, consideration should be given to building in a mechanism for training future employees or providing a refresher program. One solution is to obtain hourly pricing as part of the RFP for subsequent training programs, with a clause to permit increases to the hourly fee based on a known index, such as the Consumer Price Index. Or if the AFIS will be used to conduct employment background checks based on statutory authorization, consideration should be given to developing the RFP to readily permit the governmental response to a legislative increase in the number of background checks. That goal could be accomplished by obtaining (and incorporating into the contract) the entire product line offered by the vendor as part of the response.

It is important to clearly distinguish between the elements the government requires in the resulting contract (this specific AFIS) and those it wants to have "on option." Furthermore, it should be understood that even though the final contract may provide the authority to acquire these "optional" services and goods, additional approvals might be required. For example, it may be necessary to develop a mechanism for the control agencies to approve a work order for additional software customization. Inclusion of these options in the contract eliminates the time involved in developing a new contract (either through competitive or non-competitive means) or amending the existing AFIS contract to address the new needs. It should be used as a planning tool.

In a procurement for which the vendor will operate the AFIS, this section would address the need or expectations for backup power systems, such as uninterruptible power supplies and data backups. It would address hours and days of availability, location of services, and other related topics.

Stated broadly, an AFIS acquisition and related scope of services addresses six main items: (1) hardware, (2) software, (3) training, (4) consulting (or extra) services, (5) conversion services, and (6) maintenance (of hardware and software). While maintenance is sometimes negotiated as a separate contract using a non-competitive procurement, in order to obtain an accurate reflection of the total costs associated with the acquisition, it is strongly recommended that maintenance pricing be obtained in the same procurement. Otherwise, a governmental agency may find itself in the difficult position of obtaining an AFIS with unexpectedly high annual maintenance costs.

9.7.3.1 Hardware

Without belaboring the obvious, the nature of machines and equipment such as central processing units, disks, tapes, modem, cables, etc., raises issues different from services or software. The kinds and types of hardware obtained are dependent upon the specific nature of the AFIS and how it will be deployed. These concepts, however, should be addressed in the RFP regardless of the nature of the AFIS. While numerous other concepts must be addressed (e.g., shipping and delivery, installation of the AFIS), these issues are not uniquely handled in an AFIS procurement.

• *Purchase Transaction:* In most governmental transactions, the government will take ownership of the hardware through a straight purchase. After installation and successful completion of acceptance testing, the government pays for the hardware and becomes the owner. However, this is not always the case. Depending on the requirements of the jurisdiction and the funding source identified, other financial options could be considered. If an alternative to a straight purchase is contemplated, it should be clearly stated in the RFP. Possible alternatives include a straight lease (the government pays for use of the hardware but does not acquire ownership), a lease with option to purchase (the government pays for use of the hardware, but reserves the right to exercise an option to purchase the hardware), and a lease to ownership (the government pays for use of the hardware and at the end of term owns the hardware).

Consideration might be given to whether it is best to obtain all the hardware through the AFIS vendor. Centralized governmental contracts may provide some of the hardware and operating software at a competitive price, perhaps better than the AFIS vendor's pricing. The downside of separate hardware procurement is the warranty and maintenance issues. If the AFIS software does not operate properly, the two vendors may engage in finger pointing rather than problem solving. A separate hardware acquisition could also complicate provision of maintenance, as the government may assume responsibility for coordinating maintenance rather than the AFIS vendor. It would also impact the installation, acceptance testing, and deployment processes. If it is determined that the non-proprietary hardware will be obtained through a separate acquisition, such information should be clearly conveyed in the RFP and details provided. A clause should also be included obligating the AFIS vendor to work cooperatively with any third party vendors identified by the government. If hardware is separately acquired, it may be beneficial to incorporate cross-references or acknowledgements in the two contracts.

• *Acceptance Testing:* It is somewhat artificial to discuss hardware acceptance testing separate from software acceptance testing. An AFIS is composed of both hardware and software components, and testing must incorporate the entire AFIS to be meaningful. However, if the governmental entity decides to obtain the non-proprietary hardware and operating software from a third party vendor, it must conceptualize how best to minimize or address potential conflict resulting from the separate acquisition. For example, suppose that in an AFIS deployment requiring extensive storage capacity, it is decided that the storage hardware and its operating software will be obtained directly from the manufacturer through an existing centralized contract. The government must minimize potential conflicts in the acceptance testing process that the AFIS vendor could attribute to the storage hardware. The government may wish to consider including a mechanism that would allow the AFIS vendor to "certify" that the storage hardware meets its requirements. The government would have (probably) already accepted the storage hardware in accordance with the centralized contract, but this mechanism may help to mitigate some of the risk associated with a separate hardware acquisition.

• *Warranty Issues:* A warranty is basically a guarantee of what the hardware is supposed to do and how long the vendor guarantees performance without a problem. Warranties can be applied by operation of law, such as the implied warranty of merchantability provided under Uniform Commercial Code Section 2-314, or by the agreement of the parties. Legal counsel should be consulted for specifics on warranties, and appropriate clauses should be incorporated into the RFP. There are several practical issues that will be covered in the RFP. The RFP and resulting contract need to be clear as to when the warranty period commences and when the maintenance period commences. Generally speaking, the warranty period would not commence until after successful completion of acceptance testing. However, whether acceptance must be of the entire System or some phased approach is dependent upon the nature of the acquisition. From the government's perspective, it can be argued that it contracted for a System and the System does not have value until it is tested and accepted. From the vendor's perspective, it can be argued that it is fundamentally unfair to require full system acceptance, especially in a large AFIS. Acceptance is very important to the vendor, as it generally triggers the government's obligation to make payment and establishes when the government assumes its responsibilities for the operation of the AFIS. Further, in the hardware environment, the maintenance period normally does not commence until the end of the warranty period. Hardware maintenance payments would not start until that time, so the longer the warranty period, the longer the maintenance expenditures are deferred.

- *Test Bed System:* Depending on the nature of the AFIS, it may be beneficial for the RFP to request information and pricing on the availability of used hardware or hardware dedicated to a test bed system. This concept is most relevant when the AFIS environment must have extremely high availability, such as a criminal application that runs 24 hours a day, 7 days a week, 365 days a year. The used equipment could be configured into a test bed system so that interfaces, patches, new releases, upgrades, etc., can be tested in an environment that does not impact the production system. While some would argue that this testing is an obligation of the vendor and should be conducted on the vendor's equipment, such an argument disregards the fact that many AFIS are just one component of a larger system. In a criminal justice context, the AFIS processes the fingerprint images and identifies likely candidates. The identifying information on the candidates, however, is maintained in a separate database, often referred to as computerized criminal history (CCH) records. The government separately maintains the CCH and may establish separate access to the CCH, such as for law enforcement and judicial purposes. There are numerous interactions and relationships between the two systems that must be maintained and tested. Different vendor systems may be used for the capture of fingerprint information and the associated identifying information, which must be segregated between the AFIS and the CCH. There are numerous scenarios in which a test bed would be of extreme value to a governmental agency.

While incorporation of a test bed system necessarily adds to the overall costs because of increased hardware, software, and maintenance needs, in certain circumstances it may be the most effective way to balance the competing needs. If a test bed system is a part of the acquisition, the vendor should also be asked to provide separate pricing for the software licenses and the maintenance. The RFP should provide details about the anticipated vendor usage of the test bed system so that appropriate costing models can be developed.

9.7.3.2 Software

The government's expectations regarding the software are set forth in this section. It details the specifications and functionality of the application software and defines the mandatory technical requirements, such as data standards, interfaces, or connections needed to other databases. It may set forth the government's expectations regarding its rights to operate the software and how it proposes to determine if the software performs in the manner specified (often referred to as acceptance testing).

Generally speaking, there are two types of software involved: operating or system software, which manages the hardware, and application software, which processes the data for the user. In an AFIS procurement, the application software is the critical component. Extensive effort will be expended defining and redefining the functionality and the technical requirements of an AFIS acquisition. It is established on a case-by-case basis, is technical in nature, and is not addressed here. Rather, selected non-technical concepts are presented for consideration in the RFP process.

- *Rights to the Software:* In most instances, the government will seek a license to the application software. Application software is a form of intellectual property, proprietary in nature, owned by the vendor and distributed in accordance with specified terms and conditions. Funding source requirements may dictate what rights are sought. As previously discussed, some funding sources require the reservation of an unrestricted right of distribution of products developed with the federal funds. Other funding sources may require that the vendor agree to the transfer or assignment of license rights under certain conditions.

Software licenses address various rights between the parties, such as the ability to transfer the license to another governmental body. Common licenses arrangements include a perpetual, non-exclusive license to use the software, a license for an express term (such as a period of years), and a license for an express location (site). A license details the permissions or the authorized uses of the software. One issue for advance consideration is whether the vendor may assert contractual rights to terminate the software licenses (in contrast to commencing litigation for breach of contract actions). The concept should be carefully reviewed with legal counsel. This review should factor in the government's interest in the AFIS and (depending on the nature of the AFIS) the impact such termination would have on the health, welfare, and safety of the citizenry.

A related concept is whether it is permissible for the vendor to incorporate hardstop or other coding that permits the vendor to "turn off" or disable the software under specified conditions. Such a clause is extremely disruptive and can constitute a major breach of security. In general, the vendor will have numerous other ways to protect its intellectual property rights, due in part to its maintenance responsibilities requiring constant contact with the System, and such severe remedies are not warranted. Again, legal counsel can provide assistance in this issue.

The software license also clarifies whether the government can transfer the license and the permissible circumstances for the transfer. The government needs to consider if it might need the ability to transfer or co-locate the software on a consolidated data system.

When seeking the pricing for the software license, if a test bed system will be acquired, the vendor should provide different pricing for this license. Arguably, since the test bed system is not a production system and serves to benefit the operations of the System, there should be favorable pricing for such licenses.

- *Verifying Functionality:* At the RFP stage, the means for verifying the functionality of the software will be stated in very general terms, if at all. Language may indicate that there will be acceptance testing and that such acceptance testing is subject to the mutual agreement of the parties. It may even broadly outline time frames for the development of acceptance test procedures and plans. Rarely does the RFP detail the process, the expectations, or the consequences of not passing the acceptance test; such language is reserved for the contract negotiation stage. Given the critical importance of acceptance testing from both the government's perspective (to ensure that it obtains the System it needs) and the vendor's perspective (since successful completion of acceptance testing usually triggers payments and commences the software maintenance period and associated fees), acceptance testing issues should be considered early in the process. The government should ensure that anything relied on during the evaluation is part of the acceptance test. For example, suppose that during the RFP process or the contract negotiation process, the vendor provides product literature with various representations. If that product literature or the representations are not part of the contractual requirements, arguably they should not be part of the acceptance testing and are not a requirement of the software. While there are different ways to address this issue, it is something to be aware of and incorporate into the planning process.

9.7.3.3 Training

Training is another area in which the initial needs may be readily identifiable, but the RFP should be structured to allow contract development providing for future training needs. Obtaining specific prices for the known training needs in conjunction with hourly rates for subsequent training needs (subject to an agreed-upon price increase index) should provide sufficient flexibility in the long run.

With respect to the initial training needs, while it may be acceptable for the RFP to state that certain details are subject to the mutual agreement of the parties, elements that have a fiscal impact should be detailed in order to permit the vendor to develop pricing and to minimize possible misunderstandings. The RFP should clarify which party is responsible for the administrative aspects of the training, e.g., whether the vendor or the government will organize the training, arrange or contract for the site, provide the video recording of the training, notify participants, etc. Another important consideration is the location of the training, as location may impact the cost of travel and the time commitment required. This aspect, however, may be addressed through the inclusion of caps on travel reimbursement for a vendor (it is a mandatory requirement in some jurisdictions).

The kind of training can also impact the pricing. If a lecture format is specified, many people can attend, and the number of attendees has minimal impact on the vendor (with the exceptions of when the vendor is responsible for the reproduction of handout materials or the administrative aspects). If hands-on training is required, the possible number of attendees is reduced, and someone must provide the necessary hardware and software and ensure that the equipment is properly configured. For example, it is not uncommon to specify a maximum of five trainees for hands-on training, as opposed to 25 for a lecture. The RFP should address whether the vendor will be responsible for conducting a pre- and post-test of the trainees or otherwise evaluate them. While these are all solvable issues, lack of specificity can readily lead to misunderstandings.

The RFP should also address the government's expectations with regard to ownership of any training materials or alternatively provide for licensure to use, reproduce, or modify the training materials. Textual materials, such as training materials, are forms of intellectual property that are subject to the protection of copyright laws. While as a general proposition, it may be sufficient for the government to obtain a license from the vendor to use, reproduce, and, perhaps, modify the training materials (especially if a train-the-trainer format is desired), consideration should be given to whether the government wishes to take ownership rights over custom-developed materials. As noted in the section on funding sources, there may be situations in which the government must take ownership to comply with the funding requirements. (Note: while beyond the scope of this chapter, the government could mitigate the costs of taking ownership by licensing the vendor to use the materials and make derivative works.)

9.7.3.4 Consulting/Customization Services

This section addresses the anticipated modifications to the software and obtains information for future changes. As part of the business needs assessment, the governmental agency may have identified non-standardized codes needed to achieve its purposes. For example, in the criminal justice context, the RFP may specify that the vendor must successfully develop an interface to accept electronic data from another vendor's livescan system. Data exchange specifications would be provided along with any other specifics that are available.

A mechanism to obtain future customization or consulting services from the vendor should be addressed in the RFP. The idea is to obtain sufficient information from the RFP process to develop a formalized contractual means for the government to present the vendor with a problem and for the vendor to present a proposal (and price) for solving the problem within the framework of the existing contract. Both the mechanism and the pricing (such as maximum hourly prices by category of work) would be established in the contract; however, only the pricing must be obtained in response to the RFP. The RFP should also address the expectations about which entity takes ownership rights over the custom work product and whether the work product is subject to the escrow requirements. The mechanism should also specify whether such customized work products are subject to the acceptance testing procedures in the resulting contract.

Consideration must be given as to whether control agency approvals are needed before the commitment to any future work. For example, in New York State, the AFIS contract for the criminal justice system includes a similar mechanism and further specifies that prior to committing to a customer enhancement request exceeding $15,000, prior written approval must be obtained from the Office of the State Comptroller. The needed flexibility was acquired to permit additional customization without development of a new contract vehicle or formal amendment, while still satisfying the control agency.

9.7.3.5 Conversion Services

Depending on the AFIS application, it may be necessary to obtain services to incorporate pre-existing fingerprint images into the AFIS database. These fingerprint images may exist as hardcopy ink-and-rolled prints or could exist in a different digitized format. Even if the AFIS application is intended to consist of newly enrolled prints (such as from those enrolled in a public benefits eligibility program), there may be valid reasons for including conversion services within the scope of the RFP—namely, program expansion/modification and technological advances. It is not difficult to envision the possibility of program expansion or merger of two separate programs into one. Similarly, it is not difficult to envision the introduction of technological advances requiring a different digitized format for a fingerprint image. Conversion of the existing image may be the only practical way to continue its inclusion in the database. For example, in the criminal justice context, it may be difficult to obtain new fingerprint images.

If there is a known need for conversion services, the RFP should address such requirements as where the conversion is conducted and how long the conversion will take. The degree of importance placed on these factors depends upon the AFIS application and whether it is a new AFIS or an upgrade running in parallel to an existing AFIS. Thought should be given to how the government will verify that the conversion was properly conducted. Consideration should also be given to how the government requests conversion pricing. It may be possible to request the pricing based on volume. For example, pricing could be requested for up to a certain number of cards converted in a given time span, with a separate pricing proposed based on additional volume increments.

Consideration should also be given to incorporating the means to "reconvert" the records at some point in the future. As technology advances, more information can be extracted from previously converted records.

9.7.3.6 Maintenance

An AFIS solicitation should be structured to obtain maintenance; however, there are appropriate circumstances where maintenance may be separately obtained. Generally speaking, maintenance is a large, ongoing expense associated with an AFIS that must be identified if a total cost of ownership evaluation is undertaken. The RFP should collect information to permit the maintenance services, and pricing, to grow with the System. It should have the ability to roll hardware and software on and off from coverage. Generally, the RFP will identify the key elements of necessary maintenance. Defining the key elements, however, is dependent on the type of AFIS. Accordingly, what follows is a broad discussion on maintenance issues for consideration. The RFP might pose a series of "explain how" questions for vendor response based on this information. For example, one question might ask the vendor to explain how its proposal will escalate AFIS maintenance problems within its organization. The RFP may inquire whether the vendor's practices comport with various independent standards, such as ISO-9000.

There are two different types of maintenance that need to be considered. The first is the easier to articulate: preventative maintenance, or the routine testing and cleaning of the hardware and upgrades to the software. The RFP, and resulting contract, will determine the periods when the vendor can conduct this routine work, perhaps defining a maximum amount of allowable "downtime" for this function.

The second kind of maintenance, which tends to be more difficult to define and reach agreement upon, is remedial maintenance, or maintenance in response to a problem. How much downtime or unavailability is acceptable to the government depends on the use of the AFIS. In a 24/7/365 operation used to support criminal justice efforts, various court orders may permit very little downtime. In contrast, an AFIS used on a business hour and day basis may provide large blocks of time for maintenance. The AFIS use will also impact whether the government must require a vendor representative to be on the premises during core hours to address urgent issues.

It can be beneficial to identify whether different maintenance requirements and response times are acceptable for different types of problems or components of the AFIS. It may be possible to define the types of problems and associate each problem with a relative degree of importance, perhaps on a three-tiered scale. The contractual response time is based on the degree of importance associated with each tier. If a triaging mechanism is employed, it is important to carefully analyze the government's needs and ensure that the government has a role in defining the degree of importance assigned to a problem. Consideration should also be given to permitting the government to escalate the problem under certain circumstances.

Similarly, if an AFIS is comprised of multiple sites, such as a central site and numerous regional sites, the government may want to differentiate maintenance response times based on location or component. The highest level of service would most likely be reserved for the central site. Also, with certain exceptions, there is probably greater flexibility and less demand for the test bed system, and so a less intensive maintenance response may be acceptable. Consideration should be given to requiring a different maintenance response, however, when the test bed system is used for critical testing purposes.

The parties' expectations about communication of information during problem resolution and problem escalation must also be expressed in the maintenance plan. This is critically important in the criminal justice context, since the liberty of individuals can be affected by System downtime and it tends to be very high profile. The documents should define how and when information must be communicated (e.g., for the most severe type of problem, the vendor's designated contact will speak to the government's designated contact every hour with a progress update) and how the reported problem will be escalated within each organization (e.g., the most severe type of problem, if not resolved within 4 hours, will be escalated to the next level of each party's management).

These kinds of communication mechanisms acknowledge the importance of the application and the long-term nature of the parties' relationship and articulate the expectations of the parties.

The maintenance plan should also address how and where information about problem resolution will be retained. While it is an acceptable practice for the vendor to program a workaround or develop a patch, a repository is needed for information about how problems were solved. This information is valuable and may be needed to test the impact on interrelated systems or deposit into the escrow.

In addition, the parties need to express how they will determine if the maintenance requirements are met and what the ramifications will be if the maintenance requirements are not met. Oftentimes, a required period of availability and level of performance is contractually defined. It is beyond the scope of this chapter to discuss the various ways of defining periods of availability and performance metrics used in AFIS technology. While relatively easy to state, the devil is in the details. Substantial effort and time must be invested in developing a methodology acceptable to both parties in terms of costs to implement and results. If maintenance or performance requirements are not met, the resulting contract will often provide a financial consequence, such as a credit or refund. Care must be taken to ensure that the resulting clause meets the legal requirements as a disincentive, and is not construed as an unenforceable penalty. Legal counsel can provide assistance in this area.

Another topic to consider is how the credit or refund is given or expended. If the period of availability and level of performance are not met, the vendor may agree to provide the government with a credit reflective of the lost System value or the value not received under maintenance, or some other agreed-upon figure. The vendor may have legitimate concerns regarding cash flow and how different transactions are recorded. Similarly, the government may have requirements imposed on the receipt of funds that should be considered when shaping the agreement. For example, there may be a requirement that any cash refunds received by a state governmental agency must be deposited for the benefit of the state, and not made directly available for expenditure by that specific agency. It is highly likely the specific agency would want to structure any credit or refund so it gains the benefit. This is another topic for which advice must be sought from the finance or business office.

With respect to software maintenance, it is important to specify and understand what is and is not included within the scope of the maintenance. While software maintenance generally includes bug fixes and software upgrades, it generally does not include new releases or versions. The RFP may also distinguish between types of software upgrades, establishing different requirements depending on the complexity of the upgrade. For complex upgrades, it may be important to have additional vendor staff on the premises, or at least available to assist with the upgrade and any required troubleshooting. This is especially important in those AFIS applications that can tolerate only minimal downtimes.

Thought should also be given to whether it is acceptable to lose functionality with an upgrade. It is not unheard of for a software upgrade to eliminate or significantly modify prior functionality. In a highly interrelated AFIS application, a loss of functionality could be very problematic. Consideration should be given to how the government might best address these concerns. One way is to require the vendor to identify any functionality to be lost and give the government an "approval" right to determine if such loss is acceptable. If the loss is not acceptable, this requirement should be coupled with a vendor commitment to restore such functionality, at no cost to the government.

Consideration should be given to whether the government wishes to acquire other kinds of maintenance services. Depending on the AFIS, it may be beneficial to obtain pricing or develop a mechanism (such as the consulting services option discussed above) to obtain disk or file maintenance. Equipment relocation is another kind of maintenance or extra service that may be desirable.

9.7.4 EVALUATION CRITERIA AND RELATIVE WEIGHTS OF THE CRITERIA

In theory, the concept of evaluation criteria and their relative weights is simple. The evaluation criteria represent factors reviewed to determine how closely a vendor's proposal matches what the government seeks and how important each factor is relative to the others. Commonly included in the evaluation criteria are administrative requirements (e.g., was the bid submitted on time and complete?), technical requirements, functional requirements, and costs. Identifying the elements for inclusion is fairly straightforward. The challenge lies in quantifying each factor's importance. It is extremely difficult to do and difficult to test, since the government cannot know how a vendor bids until the proposals are opened, and the evaluation methodology must be completed prior to that time.

Development of the evaluation criteria and the relative weights is done on a case-by-case basis because the elements that go into each criterion can differ, as can the relative weight. For example, suppose that the government entity seeks an AFIS to determine eligibility for certain public benefits and requests pricing to operate the entire AFIS from enrollment through eligibility determination. In this instance, the technical requirements may have a lesser degree of importance while cost has a greater degree of importance. So while there may be a definable range of possible evaluation criteria, the components making up each criterion and the relative weights are not so limited and are highly subject to variation.

From a legal perspective, it is critically important that the vendor be provided with sufficient information to determine how the proposal will be evaluated, but there is generally no obligation to provide the vendor with the fine details of the evaluation. Jurisdictional requirements must be researched on this point. Development of evaluation criteria has two major components. The first is the public component, the information presented to the vendors identifying the topics to be evaluated and the relative weights of importance. The second component is the specific detailed elements used by the government in evaluating the proposals, which are kept confidential before the opening date for the proposals. In keeping with the concept of fairness, these elements must be finalized prior to the opening.

Careful consideration and thought must be given to the evaluation criteria, because once established, they must be used. Criteria cannot be discarded, disregarded, or substituted without amending the RFP, and that step cannot occur after the proposals have been submitted. Similarly, relative weights cannot be changed without amending the RFP. Depending on the jurisdiction, there may be a limited ability to waive a requirement that no vendor can satisfy. As indicated below, each tier in the evaluation tends to become more complex and time consuming. Consideration should be given to establishing thresholds that a proposal must pass to be considered for the subsequent evaluation tier. That way, the governmental entity is not investing substantial effort evaluating the technical requirements of a proposal that fails to meet the mandatory requirements. However, it should also be recognized that disqualifying a proposal from full consideration is a severe step. The RFP must clearly identify these consequences and expectations so a vendor has a full understanding and can assess the risks associated with submitting a proposal.

Whatever criteria are established, it is strongly recommended that a standardized method for collecting and evaluating the responses be incorporated into the RFP. For example, if a vendor's proposal is presented as free form narrative text, the government will need to locate the relevant information. That is not only a time-consuming exercise, but also one with a high potential for errors. It would be better, to the extent possible, to develop forms to collect the information. The obligation is then placed on the vendor to provide the information. Depending on the requirement, the questions could be presented with yes/no responses, with the vendor able to incorporate supplemental materials if desired.

Evaluation criteria for an AFIS procurement will often be multi-tiered. Generally, there is no requirement that each tier be evaluated the same. A tier can be set up as "pass/fail," a weighted point system, or the top three scores, among other options. The obligation is to clearly articulate how the evaluation will be conducted and to follow the established procedures. The tiers must be developed with a logical sequence, generally holding the most complex analysis until the end. For example, a RFP could set forth a series of mandatory data standards for the AFIS and provide that if a vendor's product does not satisfy all such standards it "fails," or is disqualified at that tier so the proposal goes no further. If the proposal satisfies those mandatory standards, it proceeds to the next level of evaluation, which is a weighted evaluation.

9.7.4.1 *Administrative Review*
Commonly, an early review tier asks whether the proposal meets the administrative requirements of the RFP. The vendor is advised that the administrative review considers whether the RFP was submitted on time, whether all the requested elements and necessary certifications have been included, whether the proposal is responsive to the request (e.g., if the government sought apples, did the vendor propose apples or apple juice), etc. This tier is generally a yes/no evaluation, with a single "no" response disqualifying the proposal from further consideration. The government generally uses a standardized document to record the evaluation results. It could be a form requiring the reviewer to indicate yes or no with inclusion of data to support the conclusion. For example, the form could inquire if the proposal was received on time, with a yes/no response required, supported by the details about when it was received. Inclusion of simple cross-references helps to mitigate risks associated with human errors in the review process. Due to the severe consequence if the vendor does not satisfy the administrative requirements, the government must carefully consider what elements are included and set up an evaluation process minimizing the possibility of error.

9.7.4.2 *Mandatory Technical and Functional Requirements*
The next common tier sets forth the mandatory technical and functional requirements. This section identifies those AFIS requirements the government determined it absolutely must have for the System to meet its needs. This evaluation is usually set up as a yes/no evaluation, with a single "no" response disqualifying the proposal from further consideration. This section considers whether the proposed AFIS meets the data standards or technical requirements, such as FBI certifications or data compression ratios. It may go further and establish certain features or functions as mandatory technical requirements. For example, the RFP may require that the product proposed be tested and found in compliance with the Federal Bureau of Investigation's Integrated Automated Fingerprint Identification System (IAFIS) Image Quality Specifications (IQS). If using standards, the RFP process must ensure vendor accessi-

bility to the information, by providing copies of documents as appendices or references to obtain the documents, such as on the Internet.

As with the administrative review, the tool used by the government to evaluate the vendor's proposal for the mandatory technical and functional requirements probably will be a form with the evaluators recording information and assessing whether the proposal qualifies for continued review.

A word of caution: unlike the initial administrative requirements review, for which the vendor essentially controls whether the proposal meets the requirements (i.e., the vendor assumes the responsibility to ensure timely delivery and a completed proposal), the government's decisions in establishing the mandatory technical and functional requirements could be subject to scrutiny or challenge by a vendor. One possible basis for a challenge is an allegation that a mandatory technical requirement was selected to favor or disqualify a vendor. Defending against these types of challenges ties back to the government's initial analysis of its business needs and substantiating the decisions made early in the development of the procurement.

9.7.4.3 Technical and Functional Evaluation

The next tier in the RFP might be the technical and functional evaluation of the System, which is often given a weighted score. The government has determined that these elements are not mandatory to the AFIS procurement, but are important in differing degrees. There are many different ways to structure this section and to indicate the degree of importance. One common way is to ask a series of questions about the desired functionality, which can be responded to with yes/no answers and supplemented with additional information. The government indicates the relative importance of these factors in the aggregate, e.g., the proposal has 70% of the features inquired about, or individually, e.g., a given feature is stated to be high, medium, or low in importance.

This is a difficult section to prepare. It reflects a series of assumptions about the operating environment and requires a thorough analysis of anticipated needs and how an application will be employed. If the AFIS acquisition is a new type of processing, it may be difficult to assess the relative degree of importance of a feature.

9.7.4.4 Testing

Depending on the nature of the AFIS acquisition, there may also be a testing or benchmarking component built in. From a legal perspective, it is critical that any testing be conducted in a uniform manner for every vendor. Such uniformity helps to instill confidence that the process is fair and no vendor was given an advantage over another. For example, the governmental agency can select a series of fingerprint cards or fingerprint transactions representing real world fingerprints and transactions. Each vendor is given the same set or duplicate master copies and, under the observation of the government agency, is given the same amount of time and same amount of tries to perform the process. There are many acceptable ways to conduct and evaluate testing. The RFP could establish specified performance requirements and if the product fails to meet the requirements, it is considered no further. Alternatively, the RFP could determine that only some specified number of products will advance in the evaluation process, or it could establish a "passing" grade needed to proceed in the evaluation. The RFP should detail the manner and means for testing with the goal of developing and implementing a process that is fair to the various vendors and that provides the government with the information necessary to undertake its evaluation.

9.7.4.5 Review of the Vendor

The evaluation process must also consider the vendor. While the concept may be expressed in different ways, the idea is that there must be a determination as to whether a vendor has the integrity, skills, and ability to perform the required work. In many jurisdictions, this concept is referred to as a responsibility determination (i.e., is the vendor a responsible vendor?) and is derived from an obligation that the government contract only with responsible vendors. Many means can be used to collect information about responsibility. The RFP may require submission of financial statements or audits, financial reviews from independent third parties, work references, or information about prior, similar engagements. Standardized questionnaires can also be used to collect information about previous governmental determinations about the vendor's responsibility or actions, such as if the vendor was fined for failure to pay prevailing wages or comply with environmental laws. Similar to the effort expended to define the nature of the AFIS acquisition, this is the government's due diligence inquiry into the vendor. The government must confirm the information received and determine if other relevant information is available.

Generally, this component does not lend itself to an exclusively paper-based review. The government needs to develop standardized questions for use with the references so that the same specific questions are asked about all vendors. As the information obtained tends to be subjective in nature, the government may consider the use of a sliding scale based on opinion (e.g., strongly agree to strongly disagree) rather than a quantified scale (e.g., 1 to 5). Consideration should be given to discussing with legal counsel the possible open records law implications of these evaluations. Such advice may factor into whether it is in the government's best interest to structure this part of the evaluation as opinion based (which is often not releasable) or as factual, quantifiable information, which may be releasable. While this topic is beyond the scope of this chapter, it is noted that there are due process implications if a vendor is determined to be non-responsible and such non-responsibility determination is the basis for not awarding a contract. A vendor has the right to know the basis for the non-responsibility determination and must be provided an opportunity to be heard. There may be specific jurisdictional requirements governing when and how the responsibility determination is made. For example, the Federal Acquisition Regulations provides fairly detailed requirements on the responsibility determination. (See FAR 48 CFR Part 9.)

This section of the RFP may also collect and evaluate the information submitted about the key vendor employees proposed for the project. A review would be conducted to determine if the identified employees appear to possess the necessary skills and background to complete the work. If desired, the government may request references for these employees. However, if a decision is made to request additional references, the government should plan on making the inquiries. As a general proposition, information should not be requested if it is not relevant or is not going be used as part of the decision-making process.

9.7.4.6 Project Implementation

The RFP may also seek and evaluate a vendor's proposal regarding project implementation. Depending upon the nature of the procurement, the vendor may be required to detail its concept of how the project would be implemented. The government may request specific information, such as the vendor's quality assurance process and identification of employees authorized to generate new releases and patches. The government has a significant interest in preventing malicious or faulty code from entering the System, and this is one means of control. Such information would be evaluated in terms of the vendor's understanding of the government's needs, reasonableness of the proposed time frames, and conformance with industry standards.

9.7.4.7 Cost Evaluation

The final evaluation undertaken will probably be the cost or financial evaluation. Oftentimes the RFP will require the separate sealed submission of the cost information. A cost evaluation is often broken down into several weighed components. As with other parts of the evaluation process, it is recommended that the RFP include forms to capture the cost information. The forms will ease the evaluation process and help ensure that costs are analyzed in the same manner. Pricing should be broken out to specify the acquisition being made immediately, the maintenance costs for that acquisition, costs if additional hardware and software is obtained, costs for consulting/customization work, training, etc. This document may also capture the vendor's proposal for price increases over the life of the contract. Price increases are often stated as set percentages or calculated on the basis of a known index, such as the Consumer Price Index (CPI) or Core CPI.

Generally speaking, the government requests that costs be stated in one of two ways: as a fixed price contract or as a cost reimbursement contract. While there are many other variations, these are the two methods most typically used. Each has its benefits and drawbacks. The key difference between the cost models is which party assumes more risk. The type of costing methodology used depends on the jurisdiction and agency practice.

With the fixed price contract, the vendor assumes the risk of contract performance and its performance determines its profit. The vendor would seek to tightly define the scope of work to be performed and seek establishment of a mechanism to obtain reimbursement for additional work performed. The benefit of the fixed price contract is the certainty provided to the government over how much funding is needed. The opposing view is that vendor may resist efforts perceived as expanding the scope, may have based the proposal on a set of assumptions that were not well understood by the government, or may have bid higher than expected in order to compensate for the additional risk. Thus, in order to mitigate the risk with the fixed price contract, there needs to be a clear definition of the deliverables and incorporation of a change order process.

Under a cost reimbursement contract, the government reimburses the vendor for its work and assumes the risk of contract performance. The vendor provides an estimate of how much effort is needed and provides an hourly rate for different categories of services. However, the vendor is not bound by the estimate of effort. The cost reimbursement model requires the government to make diligent inquiries to ensure the vendor has the necessary knowledge and skills to perform the work so it does not pay for the vendor's learning curve. The vendor has less incentive to control costs, so the government must be prepared to closely monitor the vendor's performance and billings, resulting in increased administrative costs for the government. It does not provide a firm figure to use for funding purposes.

Consideration should be given to how the cost evaluation model treats cost proposals that exceed the available funding. As the cost factor decreases in relative weight, this concept could become increasingly important to the AFIS acquisition.

9.7.4.8 Determination of Apparent Awardee

The RFP establishes the steps followed to determine the apparent awardee of the AFIS acquisition. One common process is that a committee obtains all the results from the various evaluation stages and applies the weighting factors to the scores. From those results, a recommendation is made to an executive level committee or other individual authorized to commit the government to a contract. If everything satisfies the executive review and authorization is received to proceed, a letter to the selected vendor is prepared advising that it is the apparent awardee. Receipt of the contract, however, is contingent upon the successful negotiation of a contract. Contract negotiations would then commence. If the negotiations are unsuccessful, if the governmental agency so provided in its RFP, it could discontinue negotiations and instead award to the next highest evaluated vendor, with the award process starting anew.

Some jurisdictions permit "best and final" offer negotiations. Under this process, a previously defined subset of vendors is invited to submit their best and final offers. These offers would be evaluated against a pre-defined set of criteria and a decision would be made. The apparent winner would be notified and the contract negotiations commenced.

Depending on the process set forth in the RFP, the non-winning vendors are notified of the evaluation results and are provided with an opportunity to be debriefed. Generally speaking, a debriefing that reviews only a vendor's proposal can occur before the completion of the contract negotiation and approval process. While the rules vary, generally if the briefing will be comparative in nature (comparing one proposal to another), it would not occur until after the resulting contract was negotiated and fully approved. Jurisdiction practices differ and inquiry is warranted.

9.7.5 CONTRACTUAL TERMS AND CONDITIONS

In addition to the information presented as part of the evaluation criterion, vendors should be placed on notice regarding the nature and types of terms that will be included in the resulting contract. Frequently there are costs or risks associated with contract terms and conditions that a vendor must factor into the proposal. Governmental contractual terms and conditions fall into three general categories: mandatory terms and conditions that cannot be negotiated, sometimes referred to as boilerplate clauses; agency-specific preferred terms and conditions that could be negotiated; and terms that as a matter of practice tend to be negotiated. Consideration should be given to clearly identifying, to the extent possible, the categories of terms and conditions.

Mandatory terms and conditions are just that: mandatory. The governmental agency has no authority to vary the wording or omit the inclusion. The terms and conditions could result from statutory requirements or the requirement of control agencies. For example, in the state of New York, there are a series of statutory provisions that must be included in any contract exceeding $15,000.

Referred to as Appendix A, this document reflects both statutory requirements and control agency mandates. A New York State governmental agency issuing a RFP has no authority to amend these terms. It is in everyone's best interest that the vendor clearly understands that these terms exist and assesses the risk and costs the terms place on the procurement.

The second category can be referred to as agency-specific clauses. These terms result from the governmental agency's efforts to standardize terms and conditions for its contracts. While not required in statute or regulation, these terms and conditions represent preferred (or internally mandated) practices. However, consideration should be given to whether these standardized terms and conditions are appropriate for an AFIS procurement. One way to test the appropriateness of these terms is to permit vendors to take written exceptions as part of the proposal. This approach has the benefit of continuing standard- ized terms and conditions (and facilitating the governmental agency's ultimate implementation of the contract), but still providing the flexibility to permit changes to reflect the unique circumstances. If this approach is selected, however, the government is obligated to determine how such exceptions will be evaluated.

The third category includes those terms that the government acknowledges will be subject to negotiation. The RFP could include proposed contractual lan- guage with an express acknowledgement that the government reserves the right to negotiate the terms and conditions. Alternatively, the government could include the proposed language with the reservation of rights and require the vendor to provide counter language. In the former option, the proposed lan- guage puts the vendor on notice and permits the vendor to take the concepts into consideration when costing out the proposal. The latter course of action moves contract negotiations forward by identifying areas of agreement and pos- sible resolution.

This "subject to negotiation" category identifies those clauses typically result- ing in negotiation or that the government intends to negotiate, such as payment schedules, escrow requirements, indemnification, and consequences for the failure to perform. This recognition should facilitate negotiations and permit identification of different solutions employed to address common contractual matters.

9.7.6 OTHER SUGGESTED CONTRACTUAL ISSUES TO ADDRESS IN THE RFP

As noted initially, this chapter does not address all the elements that must be included in a RFP. The following sections describe topics that may require special consideration within an AFIS procurement. The contractual language is highly dependent upon the nature of the AFIS being acquired, so what follows is stated in general terms.

9.7.6.1 Term of Contract

This clause defines how long the parties intend to be committed to the contractual requirements. It sets forth the starting point of the contract, which may be defined by law (i.e., not until after certain approvals are received), and the ending point. The duration of the contract should not only reflect the likelihood that it is the beginning of a long relationship, but also provide the government with the ability to discontinue the relationship without invoking the termination clause. One way to achieve these goals is through a term composed of a fixed number of years followed by a series of options to renew upon the mutual agreement of the parties. If a party elects not to renew, notice would need to be provided in advance.

9.7.6.2 How the AFIS Will Be Implemented and Deployed

Treatment of this concept depends on the nature of the acquisition. The implementation of a single location AFIS to operate on a 5-day, business hour availability is very different than a multi-site, criminal AFIS with latent searching capabilities, operating on 24/7/365 availability. For the more complex systems, consideration should be given to a phased approach. If a phased approach is used, it should be supported by payment schedules tied to the various phases, acceptance methodologies that permit acceptance of the phase without acceptance of the entire system, and termination rights for each phase in the event of significant schedule slips or if acceptance tests cannot be satisfied.

If the solicitation seeks proposals from the vendors on build schedules, in order to address delays in contract award or negotiations, it is recommended that such proposals be submitted in terms of the amount of time to build or a 0 plus amount of time. For example, proposals should be phrased in terms of 45 days to accomplish a milestone, and not that the milestone will be reached by June 1.

9.7.6.3 Payment Structure

The payment structure is integrally related to the implementation and deployment schedules negotiated. Accordingly, the RFP will probably only cover general information, such as when the obligation to make payments occurs, when payments must be made, and how payments can be made (e.g., via electronic transfers of funds). Many governmental entities have statutory requirements governing the determination of when late payments accrue.

One other topic to address is the government's expectations regarding payment holdbacks. This concept recognizes that while value may be received from delivery of a phase, the real value is received only when the entire System is accepted. Holding back an agreed-upon amount or otherwise deferring a portion of the payment provides an incentive for the vendor to deliver both the individual phases and the total System. Statutes may dictate the amount that may be held back. Otherwise, it will be the topic of negotiation with the winning vendor.

9.7.6.4 Technology Substitution or Refreshment (or Updated Price Lists)

Consistent with developing a contract with flexibility to address future growth or technological advances, contractual language could be included describing a process for adding new or updated technology or prices to the contract.

9.7.6.5 Price Adjustments During the Term of the Contract

If the cost evaluation does not request a proposal from the vendor about price increases, language could be included to address the matter. For example, it could be proposed that price increases for the hardware and software will be keyed to the vendor's public price list (with a percentage discount), and increases to the hourly rates for training and consulting services will be keyed to the Consumer Price Index. The language should set both a floor and a ceiling for the price increases. Also, it should be as specific as possible regarding which Consumer Price Index or other index is used and how increases are calculated. Inclusion of contractual terms addressing price increases should decease the number of amendments and increase the flexibility of the contract to serve long-term needs.

9.7.6.6 Guarantees for Performance

A guarantee for performance can be compared to an insurance policy the government would access to ensure it obtains the needed AFIS. There needs to be a mechanism to protect the government's interests in case the vendor does not fulfill its contractual obligations. A number of means are available, such as requiring the winning vendor to supply a letter of credit or performance bond. The value of the guarantee should be keyed to the payment stream. For example, if the payment stream anticipates that funds will be paid before full system acceptance, these payments need to be protected. It is not difficult to imagine a situation in which the parties have agreed to payments upon completion of milestones, but the entire System never satisfies the performance requirements, or a situation in which the System provides a higher level of performance than required in one area, but a lower level of performance than required in another area. Various possibilities must be considered and addressed in the contract.

Payment holdbacks may also be used as a means for guaranteeing performance or at least keeping the vendor focused on the later stages of deployment. Consideration can also be given to obligating the vendor to repay all moneys in the event the entire System does not satisfy the contractual performance requirements. While not traditional guarantees, these clauses help mitigate the risk associated with the procurement. This is an area in which legal counsel will provide valuable assistance.

9.7.6.7 Warranty

As noted previously, the warranty expresses the vendor's promise of how the hardware and software will perform and for how long it will perform without problems. Requirements differ by jurisdiction; however, consideration should be given to any warranty exclusions. Warranty language should be read in concert with the acceptance testing requirements and the maintenance provisions. In this section, the government may wish to propose a period for the warranty to run and define when the warranty commences.

9.7.6.8 Damages Clauses

The damages clauses address the "what ifs" of an AFIS implementation and deployment, such as what if the vendor does not deliver on time, what if the vendor fails to meet acceptance testing, what if the vendor fails to meet the maintenance standards or the availability requirements, or any of the other critical contractual requirements. These clauses are commonly subject to negotiation because of the multitude of possible ways to address them. For example, in a damages clause addressing late delivery, a critical component will be the process for determining which party is responsible for the slip in schedule. It would be unfair to hold the vendor to a delivery schedule if inaction or actions of the government delayed the process, for example, if the government agreed to provide specific environmental conditions for the hardware and failed to do so on schedule.

The vendor may also seek to limit or cap its total liability under the contract. It may wish to cap to the amounts paid under the contract or to a specific dollar amount. Often such clauses seek to cover most every aspect of the contractual relationship. Careful consideration must be given to such clauses, based on an examination of the possible risks and nature of the procurement.

9.7.6.9 Indemnification Clause

Similar to warranty provisions, an indemnification clause is a vendor's promise that it will stand behind the actions of its employees and the operation of the

System. The government seeks the broadest promise possible, while the vendor seeks to limit its promise (or at least the fiscal consequences of its promise). In general, the indemnification clause provides that the vendor will cover the government's liability or expenses due to claims of personal injury or property damage arising from the contractual commodities or services or from the fault or negligence of the vendor. The clause will include specific notification requirements (such as immediate notification or notification within a certain time period as a condition of indemnification) and identify the roles of the parties with respect to the litigation.

In light of the government's business needs to continue using the intellectual property in the System, additional clauses may be needed in the contract. An intellectual property indemnification clause protects the government from claims based on allegations that the software or other System components infringe a patent, copyright, trade secret, or other property rights. Such allegations often seek to prevent further use by the government. Depending on the nature of the AFIS application, continued use could be critical. In order to mitigate this potential risk, the government should seek to contractually obligate the vendor to secure the rights for continued use of the allegedly infringing property or to provide acceptable replacements. In AFIS applications with significant numbers of interfaces, consideration should also be given to protecting the government's investment in the interfaces in the event that the underlying intellectual property rights are challenged.

Identification of who owns intellectual property employed in the System may be beneficial in certain circumstances. While not a step undertaken during the RFP, it may be valuable during the contract negotiations stage. It may identify possible problematic areas and will provide additional information to use when developing the listing of materials to be included in an escrow or that must be addressed outside the escrow (such as third party software that the vendor will not be able to include in its escrow).

9.7.6.10 Termination Clauses

Statutory requirements, control agency requirements, and advice of legal counsel will generally determine the contractual bases for terminating the contract between the parties. In an AFIS acquisition, the government may also wish to incorporate the ability to terminate a specific phase of the project (but not the entire contract) or the entire project if acceptance testing cannot be met within a defined period or number of tries.

9.7.6.11 Contractual Means for Keeping Issues in Front of the Vendor

Vendors often create and host user groups for their product lines. There are benefits on both sides. User groups allow the vendor to obtain customer input about current and future products. From the government's perspective, participation provides access to other governmental users, who may have common issues and experiences. It also provides a means of keeping its specific issues before the vendor and advocating for resolution.

Very often, the ability to actively participate in a user group is affected by the financial fluctuations experienced by governments. A government may impose restrictions on travel, both within and outside of the state. While this must be researched and approved first by the entity responsible for compliance with the government's ethics rules, it may be possible to include as a cost of the contract that the vendor pay for the travel, lodging, and meals for a select number of persons from the government to participate in the user group. This kind of clause would be especially valuable in those instances where the user group is composed of international representatives. The governmental entity would still be responsible for paying the attendee's salary, but a term and condition of the contract would be the vendor's payment of those out-of-pocket expenses. Such a clause may address the constraints periodically arising when governmental travel is curtailed.

9.7.6.12 Security Issues

Large-scale systems, like an AFIS, that connect to other large-scale systems retaining personally identifying information present a certain appeal for attack, theft, compromise, and malicious or fraudulent use. While the AFIS may not contain readily identifiable personal information, it is connected to a database containing such information. Further, an AFIS application that transmits data over a telecommunication line must thoroughly consider security requirements. Such a clause would also incorporate requirements established by the governmental agency charged with information security.

9.7.6.13 Disaster Recovery

While it is beyond the scope of this chapter to discuss disaster recovery, governmental entities need to fully consider the concept of disaster recovery during the planning stages. If it is intended that the vendor will provide all or some of these services, it must be addressed in the solicitation. Disaster recovery can be very expensive. If a redundant system is considered as a possible solution, it would be beneficial to include different licenses for the redundant system, or perhaps permitting purchase of used equipment.

The concept of disaster recovery runs both ways. The solicitation needs to make provisions for a disaster occurring at the vendor's site. Again, the nature of what must be considered is highly dependent upon the specifics of the AFIS. At a minimum, this concept is generally covered as part of the escrow and how the government's business needs will be protected.

9.7.6.14 Escrow Requirements

Escrow requirements can be hotly negotiated clauses for valid reasons. In general, under an escrow arrangement, a neutral third party holds property that belongs to one entity with permission to release such property to another entity under express circumstances. The government's purpose in seeking an escrow arrangement is to ensure its ability to continue operations and protect its business environment, in the event of certain negative occurrences, by ensuring it can obtain the software source code and other information relevant to the AFIS. The vendor's purpose is to protect its investment in its proprietary software and to limit access to its source code. There is a natural conflict between the two goals. Very often the solution lies with the establishment of an escrow arrangement, with a neutral third party permitting the government access to materials under very limited circumstances. The RFP clauses should outline the features the government seeks in the escrow arrangement.

For the escrow clause to have meaning, the escrow account must hold everything necessary to understand and operate the System. Deposit of the source code is not enough. The clause should require deposit of release notes, installation guides and tools, source release guides, patches and bug fixes, equipment configurations, and so on. The deposit requirements are unique to the AFIS application, but must be comprehensive enough to permit continued operation of the System. The parties must develop an understanding regarding any third party intellectual property used in the System and how the vendor proposes to protect the government's business needs with respect to such property.

The escrow deposits must be kept up to date. In addition to including an annual verification process in the escrow agreement, it may be beneficial to require updated escrow deposits before the government is obligated to pay for customizations or enhancements performed after the initial escrow deposits. This arrangement works most effectively if the escrow agreement obligates the third party provider to send written notification when additional materials are submitted for deposit. It also serves as a further control that the necessary deposits are made and up to date.

9.8 WHAT CAN GO WRONG IN THE PROCESS

Despite the substantial planning, effort, and training that goes into a solicitation, things can and do go wrong. But not everything that goes wrong is fatal to the procurement effort. Oftentimes the general reservation of rights language provides the ability to correct honest mistakes or omissions (case law usually will define what constitutes an honest mistake or omission). So if a vendor's proposal presents cost figures with an obviously misplaced decimal point, it is probably a correctable matter. Other mistakes, however, are not correctable. For example, the RFP will usually set an absolute date and time by which the proposal must be received. If the vendor entrusts delivery of the proposal to a third party service and the proposal is delivered late, the proposal is disqualified and the vendor's remedies are probably limited to obtaining a refund from the third party service.

It is more problematic if the governmental entity is the party making the mistake. Assuming the RFP so provides, mistakes and errors can be corrected by issuing an amendment or addendum. However, if the mistake is discovered at the last minute, providing additional time to respond to the RFP may be warranted. A vendor could challenge a last-minute modification, especially one that could be perceived as placing the vendor at a disadvantage.

If the proposals are already submitted, the government is without power to correct the mistake, but other limited remedies may be available. For example, if the government erroneously describes what it wishes to procure and none of the bids are responsive, assuming it has included language reserving the right to not award a contract, the government can withdraw or cancel its solicitation. While that procurement effort may be terminated, it is free to proceed with a new procurement that properly describes the scope of the solicitation. Similarly, if the government determines that a mandatory requirement criterion is wrong, once the proposals have been submitted, correction is not possible. The downside, however, is that the vendor has already invested significant resources in responding to the RFP and may not wish to invest more effort responding to the new solicitation. In some jurisdictions, however, the solicitation may permit the waiver of a mandatory requirement that no one can meet. Such a remedy, however, is available only if no one satisfies such a requirement. If one vendor can satisfy the "wrong" mandatory criterion, it cannot be waived.

Problems can also arise if there is a perception that the solicitation was drafted to favor one vendor over another. As noted before, an underlying concept of the competitive bid process is fairness. If a governmental entity decides to make certain requirements that could be perceived as favoring one vendor over another, it is imperative that there be a record of the decision-making process. At a minimum, there needs to be a valid business reason for the decision. For example, suppose that Agency A operates on hardware platform B supported by a specific telecommunications protocol. It makes a determination that the livescan submissions to its new AFIS must comply with its already existing specific telecommunications protocol. Even if this may be perceived as favoring one vendor over another, it does not appear to be a violation of the fairness requirements. Instead, the requirement is supported by a valid business reason and should be defendable if challenged.

A belief that insufficient information was provided as part of the RFP can also form the basis for complaints about the procurement. This can be especially true regarding the evaluation criteria and the relative weight of each factor. As stated before, it is imperative that the RFP clearly communicate the expectations and requirements for the acquisition.

The government's failure to follow the procedures and requirements set forth in the RFP is another area of vulnerability. Following the procedures and requirements is critical to the underlying concept of fairness. The complaint can take different forms but ultimately comes back to disparate treatment of the vendors, either through omissions or malfeasance.

One of the most important things a government can do in support of its procurement effort is to document its decisions and its processes. Documentation existing prior to the issuance of the complaint can establish the government's good faith decision making and demonstrate that there was no intent to harm a vendor and that its decision comports with legal requirements.

9.9 HOW PROBLEMS AND COMPLAINTS ARE MADE KNOWN

A vendor can complain about the solicitation process in a number of forums. Depending on the governmental entity issuing the procurement, the vendor may complain to the executive branch, the legislative representatives, or the control agencies. This process tends to be an informal, but effective, mechanism. Action regarding the complaint takes different forms depending on the jurisdiction.

Many entities have established informal or formal administrative processes to address bid problems, often referred to as bid protests or dispute resolution procedures. Bid protests can be set forth as a part of the RFP or as a separate regulation generally applicable to procurement that is referenced in the RFP. The RFP should identify the information, including all the relevant factual and legal documentation that must be submitted as part of the protest. The procedure can establish time frames for instituting the protest.

Bid protests present an economical way to protect the rights of bidders and ensure the integrity of the procurement process. While there are many possible reasons for submitting a bid protest, generally the protest needs to establish a relationship between the action complained of and some impact on the vendor. For example, the federal government has a very formalized and defined procedure for handling bid protests as part of the Federal Acquisition Regulations. (See FAR set forth at 48 CFR Subpart 33.) Bid protests can be submitted to the procuring agency or to the federal General Accounting Office. While the use of the informal complaint process or the filing of a bid protest does not necessarily negate the procurement, it can result in delays to the contract award or the refusal of a control agency to approve a contract.

A vendor can also institute litigation to challenge procurement-related decisions. Generally speaking, once there is a final decision by a governmental official, litigation can be brought to challenge the basis of the decision on the grounds that it was wrong, unreasonable, or arbitrary and capricious. For example, in New York State, Civil Practice Law and Rules Article 78 governs litigation challenging the government's procurement decision. Litigation often is accompanied by an order from the court prohibiting the government agency from continuing with the procurement. Litigation may delay the contract award for an extended period, rendering the pricing and the technology obsolete.

9.10 CONCLUSION

An AFIS procurement is incremental in nature. Each analysis and decision builds on prior ones, providing the foundation for the procurement and project implementation. A well-thought-out and researched RFP, reflecting both the short-term and the long-term AFIS needs, provides the necessary framework for a successful acquisition. Statutory and regulatory requirements and the control environment guide the acquisition process, necessitating early identification and consideration. Selected funding streams may impose additional requirements. The business needs analysis identifies the AFIS specifications, functionality, and scope of work requirements. Business needs analysis further defines the evaluation criteria and the relative weight assigned to each component. The contractual terms and conditions support and implement the business needs analysis, while satisfying the statutory, regulatory, and control requirements.

While it can be time consuming and labor intensive to develop an AFIS RFP, such effort is warranted not only due to the sophistication of the technology, but also because of the public funds expenditure and the direct impact AFIS can have on people's lives. Government has an obligation to engage in due diligence before acquiring and implementing an AFIS. This due diligence obligation can be satisfied with a thorough and well-thought-out RFP.

REFERENCES

Biometrics; Identity Verification in a Networked World, A Wiley Tech Brief, by Samir Nanavati, Michael Thieme, and Raj Nanavati, John Wiley & Sons, 2002.
Computer Contracts Negotiating and Drafting, Esther C. Roditti and Matthew Bender, 1998.

Computer Law: Drafting and Negotiating Forms and Agreements, Richard Raysman and Peter Brown, Law Journal Press, 2003.

Contracts between New York State Division of Criminal Justices Services and SAGEM MORPHO, reference number C002047 (maintenance) and reference number C002060 (copies on file with author).

Executive Order Number 127 issued by New York Governor George Pataki on June 16, 2003.

Federal Acquisition Regulations, 48 Code of Federal Regulations Part 1 et al.

Getting Started in Federal Contracting: A Guide Through the Federal Procurement Maze, 3rd ed., Barry L. McVay, 1995. Panoptic Enterprises.

Law Enforcement Tech Guide: How to Plan, Purchase and Manage Technology (Successfully!). A Guide for Executives, Managers and Technologists, Kelly J. Harris and William H. Romesburg, Washington, DC: U.S. Department of Justice, Office of Community Oriented Policing Services, 2002.

New York State Finance Law Article 11.

New York State Public Officers Law.

CHAPTER 10

CASE STUDY—DIAMONDS IN THE ROUGH: INCREASING THE NUMBER OF LATENT PRINT IDENTIFICATIONS

10.1 INTRODUCTION

The following was presented by the author at the 2002 International Association for Identification (IAI) Educational Conference. This chapter describes how the New York State Division of Criminal Justice Services (DCJS) doubled the number of latent print identifications through a combination of technical improvements and human intervention. Better matchers, coders, and databases contributed to this success, but the greatest single cause was the management decision to make it happen.

The New York State DCJS initiated a Statewide Automated Fingerprint Identification System (SAFIS) in 1989. DCJS is the state identification agency and houses all the records for anyone fingerprinted under New York State law. This encompasses all municipal governments, including the city of New York. DCJS completes over 1 million transactions per year, and all SAFIS transactions interface with a Computerized Criminal History (CCH) file. The sheer volume of transactions requires speed, reliability, and accuracy in responses. Most criminal inquiries can be answered in approximately 30 minutes.

There are approximately 5.5 million records in the SAFIS tenprint (two index finger) database, which is used for criminal and applicant identifications. The 11 million image records (5.5 million records × two fingers) are a mix of inked tenprint impressions and livescan records. The percentage of tenprint records on the database that are from inked impressions is diminishing as livescan is becoming the predominant method for image capture and transmission. Nearly all of the images from New York City are taken via livescan.

A latent cognizant subset of this database, used to search latent prints, contains all ten images of approximately 2.5 million records, or 25 million images. A latent print can be searched with parameters such as geographic area or crime type that can narrow the area or the database that is searched. Latent print examiners can also search the entire database in a "cold search," in which no parameter is selected.

Since SAFIS serves the entire state, latent print examiners can search this database whether they are in the Latent Print Section of the New York City Police Department, the Suffolk County Police Department, the Latent Print Unit at DCJS, or any other location within the state. This provides a more complete database than any single city or county might have and also allows the SAFIS to be administered by one central agency.

Except for the latent print staff at DCJS, all other latent print staff at the regional sites are employed by the local law enforcement agency. To access the latent print services of DCJS, the law enforcement agency must complete a use and dissemination agreement and other agreements that specify the proper handling of the equipment. In most instances, the equipment is owned and maintained by DCJS.

When the inked tenprint records were converted to digital images starting in 1988, the minutiae and other image characteristics were extracted using then state-of-the-art coder software. Likewise, the matchers that compared the images from the submitted records to the image characteristics in the SAFIS database were also state-of-the-art at the time of their introduction.

10.2 PLAN FOR INCREASED LATENT PRINT IDENTIFICATIONS

To maintain continuity and provide the best opportunity to make as many latent print identifications as possible, DCJS embarked on a plan to increase the number of latent print identifications using SAFIS. Elements of this plan included the following:

1. Continual training of latent print examiners on the use of the SAFIS equipment.
2. Meeting with latent print managers to stress the value of SAFIS.
3. Exploiting system opportunities to use SAFIS to make more identifications.

To meet the first objective, a plan was developed for SAFIS system managers to meet with latent print examiners at their offices twice a year. These face-to-face meetings provided an opportunity to respond to any questions about the functionality of SAFIS and to suggest improvements to make more identifications. A recommendation, for example, might be to allow the coder to find the minutiae on a latent print image to provide consistency with the way that the coder will place the minutiae on enrolled images on the SAFIS database. As a follow-up, the examiner might then replicate the image and select minutiae and other characteristics. Latent print examiners might also suggest improvement to the system, such as easier access rights so that managers could assign examiners to cases created by examiners who were no longer immediately available to check their cases. Another suggestion might be to improve the screen flow to make the transition from one screen entry field to another easier.

To meet the second objective, two meetings were held each year for managers and supervisors at DCJS offices in Albany, New York. At these meetings, senior DCJS staff under the direction of Deputy Commissioner Clyde DeWeese provided background on recent changes to the identification technology and responded to questions regarding the use of SAFIS from a manager's perspective. These meetings provided a forum for latent print managers from different agencies to discuss areas of mutual concern, as well as to consider alternative methods of managing caseloads. For example, one manager might assign a case to only one latent print examiner, while another might send the case to a second latent print examiner if the first did not make the identification. Different latent print examiners use different techniques to search SAFIS. As they were often told, the best method to search SAFIS was the method they felt most comfortable with. But there may be other techniques to consider, such as sending fewer cases to the unsolved latent file.

The third objective was to look for ways in which the enormous capabilities of SAFIS could be used to make more identifications, for example, annually providing a list of cases that would be removed from the unsolved latent file following the statute of limitations, relaunching a case from the unsolved latent file months or years after the first search, and using other search engines such as the FBI Remote Fingerprint Editing Software (RFES) to search the IAFIS with the same image used to search SAFIS. With the ability of SAFIS to search the 25 million image records in minutes, the skill of the latent print examiner could be concentrated on examining the candidates, not the mechanics of the search.

10.3 REVIEW OF UL FILE PROCEDURES

The unsolved latent file became recognized as a valuable resource for making identifications. Identifications from the unsolved latent file accounted for between 15 and 20% of the approximately 1,000 latent print identifications made annually across the state by latent print examiners using SAFIS. Reporting of latent print identifications was standardized to assure uniformity and consistency throughout the agencies using SAFIS.

Although the unsolved latent file offers enormous opportunities for identifications, it can also drain personnel resources. During training, examiners were encouraged to enter into the UL file only those cases for which there might be a reasonable chance of making an identification or cases that were high profile. Since every latent print image characteristic is searched by every new latent cog record entered into the database, it would be possible for a poor-quality image with only a few minutiae points to spawn hundreds of false candidates, particularly if it was saved as a "cold" case. At times, the sheer volume of tenprint to unsolved candidates awaiting verification could be daunting. Examiners had to ask whether the time spent in reviewing hundreds of TP/UL candidates produced more identifications than reviewing only a few TP/UL candidates by making the search more restrictive and using the remaining time for latent to tenprint (LT/TP) searches. This was an individual as well as a management decision.

10.4 SYSTEM-WIDE UPGRADE

In 1998, DCJS embarked on another bold plan to improve SAFIS through a system-wide upgrade. The multi-year program, under the direction of Deputy Commissioner Dan Foro and Chief of Biometric Identification Jack Meagher, had several enormous tasks, such as the following:

1. Recode the entire tenprint database.
2. Recode the latent cog database.
3. Install and test new operating and application software.
3. Install new coders.
4. Install new matchers.
5. Install new workstation terminals.

In the 10 years since the original conversion of the DCJS database, digital coding algorithms had greatly improved, as had the matching algorithms. The operating system software was faster and more reliable. Critical operating software and hardware components were available as commercial-off-the-shelf (COTS) items. There was less equipment required for faster processing.

To accomplish these objectives, while the day-to-day work at DCJS continued, copies of the tenprint and latent cog image databases were sent to Sagem for recoding. Samples of the recoded images were checked for accuracy and reliability. The improved coders found minutiae where the older coders did not, and more reliably distinguished between clear and marginal minutiae. A new random array of independent drives (RAID) storage system was introduced, which provided images faster and more reliably than in the past. New tenprint and latent print workstations that had the newer coders were installed. As of July 1999, all new tenprint images were coded using the new coders. Likewise, latent print examiners also had the benefit of new coders on their workstations to more clearly identify minutiae and other image characteristics. By the end of 1999, the new SAFIS was fully in place. Accuracy tests of both the tenprint and latent cog databases, conducted by the Manager of Tenprint Operations, Michael Tymeson, showed improvements in accuracy and performance. The investment in funding and personnel resources was reaping huge benefits. Managers began to ask if other opportunities for improvements existed.

10.5 OPPORTUNITIES FOR INCREASING UL FILE IDENTIFICATIONS

Since the inception of SAFIS operation in 1989, latent print examiners had been saving their unsolved cases to the UL file. A field in the case file, the UL retention year, allowed the examiner to have the case automatically removed after a certain date. For example, if a burglary occurred in 1991, the statute of limitations was normally 7 years, i.e., 1998. In 1999, the case would be administratively removed from the UL file if the examiner so desired. This process allowed the examiner to spend time only on cases of value and eliminated unnecessary time commitment for cases that might never be prosecuted. Some cases, such as homicides, have no statute of limitations and would be retained in the UL file in perpetuity.

The introduction of new coders, new matchers, and a recoded latent cog database demonstrated immediate improvements in the number of latent print identifications that were made. The new imaging technology could mask backgrounds, the coders could identify minutiae more exactly, and the matchers searching the recoded database presented better candidates with higher matching scores. The improvements in latent to tenprint (LT/TPlc) searches led to the question, "Could more cases on the unsolved latent file be solved?"

The DCJS management team recognized that the unsolved latent file contained three groups of records: (1) those that had been created using the original coders and matchers, (2) those created during a transition when new matchers and coders were in place, but the database was primarily composed of originally coded records, and (3) those that had been created since July of 1999, when the new coders and matchers were introduced. These older cases searched on a database whose minutiae features were extracted with an earlier version of coder technology. Now the entire database had been reconverted, and more and/or better minutiae were available. Table 10.1 shows these combinations as the system transitioned from the "original" SAFIS platform to the new SAFIS platform.

With approximately 100,000 latent print images on the UL file, the opportunity for making identifications on older cases was obvious. DCJS staff, with the assistance of Sagem Morpho staff, searched the UL file for cases entered by the latent print examiners, and created two lists for each examiner that included each case number, the date of entry, the original crime (e.g.,

Table 10.1
Unsolved Latent File
Matrix

Workstation Coder	SAFIS Matcher	TPlc Database
Original	Original	Original coder conversion
New	New	Original coder conversion
New	New	New coder conversion

burglary), and a priority. The first of the two lists contained the cases that had been entered when the new coders and matchers were installed, but when the search was against the database coded with the earlier version of coders. This was akin to the best-quality latent having been searched against a less than state-of-the-art database at the time of the original latent print search on SAFIS. The second list contained the cases entered using the original coders, matchers, and converted TPlc database. Re-searching these cases from the UL file (referred to as reactivation) would require slightly more effort.

A series of training sessions was conducted at each latent print site in the state that used SAFIS. The systemic upgrade of SAFIS was explained, as was the immediate and potential benefits of the improved coders, matchers, and re-coded database. The preparation and use of each list was reviewed, and the potential for making more identifications through relaunching existing cases on the UL file was highlighted. Since the lists provided the crime type for each case on the UL file, examiners could quickly identify high-profile cases, such as homicides, and search those first.

The latent print examiners were encouraged to relaunch the cases on the first list and search them against the improved database, a relatively simple process. Since these old cases were now being searched against a better database with better placed minutiae, the examiners were able to make identifications. Many of these identifications were from records that existed in the database at the time of the original search, but that, due to the limited technology at the time, did not receive a score high enough to appear on the candidate list.

The results of this effort can be seen in Table 10.2: the number of annual latent print identifications doubled over the time period from 1998 to 2001. The benefits of this overall system upgrade, combined with the management decision to exploit these opportunities, produced amazing results. These two elements provided the tools for the latent print examiners to do what they do best: examine candidate, make comparisons, and ultimately make identifications.

These improvements were carried out over several years. The introduction of new workstations in the fall of 1998 was followed by the introduction of new

Year	Number of Identifications
1995	1,011
1996	1,033
1997	971
1998	1,015
1999	1,292
2000	1,549
2001	2,004

Table 10.2

Annual Latent Print Identifications

matchers and coders in the spring of 1999. By the fall of 1999, the entire latent cog (TPlc) database had been reconverted. Within 1 month of the installation of this new database, the first of the two lists of cases on the UL file was prepared and distributed. Meetings with latent print examiners were held across the state to explain the process and opportunities. Note that in Table 10.2 there is a nearly 30% improvement in the number of latent print identifications from 1999 to 2000.

By the spring of 2000, the second list of cases on the unsolved latent file had been prepared and distributed. As with the distribution of the first list, face-to-face meetings of latent print examiners and supervisors were held to explain the process and answer questions. For the year 2000, latent print examiners using SAFIS made over 2,000 latent print identifications!

10.6 SUMMARY

The reasons for the improvements can be summarized in a statement made by Richard Higgins, former Chief of Criminal Identification for the New York State Division of Criminal Justice Services, "The name of the game is idents, idents, idents." By embracing this philosophy, DCJS managers sought to provide not just an adequate Statewide Automated Fingerprint Identification System, but the best Statewide Automated Fingerprint Identification System. The improvements did not end with upgrading the technology. Managers also examined methods of harnessing the power of SAFIS to make faster identifications, to better interface with the CCH file, and to pass along this information on submitting agencies. Managers also worked closely with latent print examiners and supervisors to provide them with the tools and knowledge to use SAFIS to produce more identifications.

The identification process is a people process (see Table 10.3). A booking officer captures an inked impression on a tenprint card or rolls the subject's fingers across a glass platen. Evidence technicians search crime scenes for latent

Table 10.3

The Human Element in AFIS

1. Accuracy depends on a good database
2. Good investigative work finds latent prints
3. AFIS system are only tools in the latent print identification process
4. Latent print examiners, not AFIS, make identifications
5. The process begins and ends with people

prints. AFIS computers, which are designed, maintained, and improved by people, search databases and produce candidates. For latent print examiners, these candidate lists act as the starting point for identifications by presenting them with candidates that have varying probabilities of matching the latent print. Ultimately, it is the latent print examiner, who, with training, experience, and skill, determines if there is an identification. The best matchers and coders cannot improve on a finger image carelessly taken by a booking officer. Once operational, systems have to be maintained and re-calibrated by people.

AFIS are tools; remarkable tools, but tools nonetheless. Their success will always be dependent on the political will to keep them state of the art and the people who use them to ensure justice is done.

GLOSSARY

The following glossary was developed from many sources. To support the standardization of use, wherever possible the acronyms and abbreviations and their definitions were extracted from industry-recognized sources such as the *Integrated Automated Fingerprint Identification System (IAFIS) Program Office Glossary.*[1]

ACCEPTANCE TESTING—Thorough test of an AFIS prior to taking ownership and making payment.

ACCESS RIGHTS—Options for an AFIS user that enable specific AFIS functions. For example, tenprint staff cannot access latent print functions unless granted access rights to those functions.

ACCURACY—A software quality metric that provides those characteristics for required precision in calculations and outputs.

ACE-V—Scientific procedure for identifying latent fingerprints that involves analysis, comparison, evaluation, and verification. Analysis is the qualitative and quantitative assessment of level 1, level 2, and level 3 details to determine proportion, interrelationship, and value for individualization. During comparison, the latent print examiner looks at the attributes noted during analysis for differences and agreement between the latent print and the candidate. Evaluation involves making a determination if two impressions are from the same source, are not from the same source, or are inconclusive. Verification is an independent analysis, comparison, and evaluation by a second qualified examiner.

AFIS—Automated Fingerprint Identification System. An automated minutia-based identification system. May consist of two or more distinct databases composed of two finger identification records and ten finger latent cognizant records (records of individuals more likely to be found at crime scenes, e.g., burglars).

---

[1] That document is intended to standardize the use of terms and establish a common language reference base for government support personnel, contractors, engineers, customers, and others associated with the IAFIS.

AFIS/FBI—The Automated Fingerprint Identification System segment of IAFIS for the Federal Bureau of Investigation. AFIS/FBI is a system that provides (1) repository maintenance services, such as receipt, storage, and retrieval; (2) powerful search functions that attempt to match submitted fingerprints with fingerprints in the repository; and (3) fingerprint characteristic processing capability to derive unique aspects of fingerprints for storage and matching.

ALGORITHM—Mathematical routine used in computer processing. In AFIS processing, the matcher algorithm searches for relationships between search print and tenprint print.

ALPHANUMERIC—Non-image information related to a person, tenprint card, or latent case. May also be referred to as demographic data.

AMERICAN CLASSIFICATION—The system of fingerprint classification developed by Captain James Parke with values derived from the sequence of fingers in the right then left hand, patterns, and ridges. Consists of primary and secondary classifications.

ANSI—American National Standards Institute. Founded in 1918, it administers U.S. voluntary standardization and conformity assessment.

ANSI/NIST STANDARD—Standard proposed by NIST and adopted by ANSI.

ANTHROPOMETRIC CARD—Bertillon card used to record physical measurements such as head width, head length, and trunk.

APPENDIX F—Image Quality Specifications (IQS) of the electronic fingerprint transmission specification (EFTS) for printers, monitors, and scanners.

APPENDIX G—Interim Image Quality Specification for scanners until IAFIS became operational.

AUTHENTICATION—Process to determine whether a digital image has been altered in any way or a process used to determine whether an electronic file has the correct association, as with unique identifier, name, images, and criminal history record.

AXIS—One of two intersecting lines superimposed on a displayed fingerprint image. Used as a reference point to indicate orientation in a side-by-side comparison.

BENCHMARK—A standardized task given to versions of the same device to evaluate their performances against a standard.

BENCHMARK TESTING—Standardized testing of a device or software to evaluate performance against a standard.

BERTILLON CARD—Devised by Alphonse Bertillon to record physical measurements such as head width, head length, trunk, and arm length.

BIFURCATION—A point on a finger image where the friction ridge divides into two ridges.

CANDIDATE—A master file record selected as a possible match to a current minutiae record, which results from either an automated name search or an automated technical (AFIS) search.

CANDIDATE LIST—The list of potential mates listed in descending order of their matching scores as determined by the matching process within the fingerprint minutiae matcher. A candidate list can also be produced by Interstate Identification Index (III) automated subject search.

CARD SCAN—An electronic scanning method of transmitting inked fingerprint impressions that meets local standards and the FBI's image quality specifications. Card scan images are suitable for store and forward processing. May also be referred to as a flat-bed scan. For transmission to the FBI, such scanners must have FBI certification with at least Appendix G.

CCD—Charged-coupled device. An electronic chip capture device used in optical recording devices to convert light into electrical current. AFIS applications include digital camera, card scan, livescan, and other imaging equipment that captures fingerprint images on a chip.

CCH—Computerized Case History or Computerized Criminal History. Online case history information management system that lists all the criminal and non-criminal events that the identification agency is authorized to release to an inquiring agency. It is also referred to as the rap sheet.

CJIS—Criminal Justice Information Services Division of the Federal Bureau of Investigation.

CLPE—Certified latent print examiner. A latent print examiner certified by the Latent Print Certification Board of the International Associate for Identification. Qualifications include education and experience, endorsement, and passing an examination. The examination consists of a written test, pattern recognition, comparison of latent prints to inked prints, and either an oral board testing or presentation of a case for review.

CODER—Term for hardware, software, or both used to detect minutiae in a finger image.

CODIS—Combined DNA Index System. Consists of three hierarchical tiers of the DNA Index System: local (LDIS), state (SDIS), and national (NDIS). The FBI serves as the connection for NDIS and links participating agencies.

COMPARISON—The process of evaluating fingerprint images to be classified and/or identified for proper identification per user request.

COMPRESSION, LOSSLESS—Compression in which no image data is lost and the image can be restored to its original form.

COMPRESSION, LOSSY—Compression in which image data is lost and the image cannot be restored to its original form.

COMPRESSION RATIO—Ratio of original file size as compared to the compressed file size. For AFIS, a 15:1 ratio is most often used.

CONSOLIDATION—The merger of two or more records that are filed under more than one FBI number when it is determined that all pertain to one subject.

CORE—Usually a well-defined center or focal point of a finger image.

CTA—Control Terminal Agency. A state or territorial criminal justice agency on the NCIC system that provides statewide or equivalent service to its criminal justice users regarding NCIC data. There is only one CTA per state or territory. Operates under the supervision of a Terminal Agency Coordinator (TAC).

DATABASE—A collection of data, of a particular type, organized for efficient storage and retrieval (e.g., fingerprint minutiae data, fingerprint image data, and mug shot image data).

DELTA—That point on a ridge of a fingerprint image at or nearest to the point of divergence of two type lines, and located at or directly in front of the point of divergence.

DIRS—Digital Image Retrieval System. An AFIS subsystem that contains the electronic fingerprint images.

DMS—Data Management System.

DNA—Deoxyribonucleic acid.

DOWN SAMPLING—Process of representing an image with a smaller number of samples. May also be referred to as subsampling.

ELECTRONIC FINGERPRINT TRANSMISSION SPECIFICATION (EFTS)—An FBI-published standard for electronically encoding and transmitting fingerprint images and identification and arrest data between federal, state, local users, and the FBI that specifies file, record content, format, and data codes.

ELECTRONIC TENPRINT SUBMISSION—An electronic submission that originates at a livescan booking terminal or card scanner at the federal, state, or local level and transmitted via the Criminal Justice Information Services (CJIS) wide area network (WAN) to IAFIS for processing. This type of electronic transaction contains fingerprint images and personal descriptor data. Processing of the transaction, including image comparison and effecting the ident/non-ident decision, is performed by FBI personnel.

ELIMINATION FINGERPRINTS—Fingerprint images taken from persons with legitimate access to evidence under examination for latent fingerprints.

ENCODING—AFIS process used to record minutiae.

EURODAC—AFIS formed by the European Union to track asylum seekers who applied for benefits.

EXPUNGEMENT—The process of either fully or partially purging data from a subject's record in the subject criminal history file. It results in the removal of all charges associated with the arrest covered by expungement while retaining the date of arrest (DOA) and submitting originating agency identifier (ORI). Expungement requests are submitted by arrest or judicial agencies when an individual has been exonerated after initial arrest or released without charge and recorded as "detention only," or as ordered by a court of appropriate jurisdiction.

FALSE CANDIDATE—A candidate selected by an AFIS search as a possible match that is subsequently determined not identical.

FBI NUMBER (FNU)—A unique identifying number assigned by the FBI to a subject of a fingerprint record of arrest who has not been identified as a previous offender in a search of the files. Thereafter, the FNU is used as a unique identifier for the subject, and any subsequent arrests are added into the records associated with that FNU.

FEATURES EXTRACTION—The system's capability to identify, from a scanned fingerprint digital image, separately definable attributes, which may be discretely stored and used to classify and uniquely identify that fingerprint. The AFIS/FBI design shall provide a means of automated features extraction.

FFT—Fast Fourier transfer algorithm. Used in digital image processing to decompose and compose a signal.

FINGERPRINT CHARACTERISTICS—The word "characteristics," used in conjunction with fingerprint processing, indicates any aspects of fingerprints that can uniquely identify them.

FINGERPRINT CLASSIFICATION—A method for describing the common pattern characteristics of fingerprints (e.g., pattern types, ridge counts) for the purpose of subdividing a fingerprint file into "classes" or groups having the same general characteristics so as to reduce the amount of the file needed to be searched to locate the mate. In IAFIS, the term fingerprint classification may involve either Henry Classification or pattern-level classification.

FINGERPRINT FEATURES—Unique physical characteristics of a fingerprint that are used to perform automated fingerprint searches.

FINGERPRINT FEATURES MASTER FILE—The set of all records on which fingerprint feature data exists.

FINGERPRINT IMAGE—A representative two-dimensional reproduction of the ridge detail of a finger acquired by an electronic scanning device or ink and roll.

FINGERPRINT MATCHER SCORE—A numerical score that indicates the degree of similarity between search fingerprint features and a repository of fingerprint features.

FINGERPRINT MINUTIAE—Unique identifying characteristics of fingerprints (e.g., beginning and ending points of ridges).

FINGERPRINT MINUTIAE MATCHER—The matching subsystem equipment that compares the minutiae data-based features of a search print with file prints and selects the file print that comes closest to matching the search print. It will also perform a minutia verification match.

FINGERPRINT MINUTIAE MATCHER ACCURACY—(a) A measure of the matcher subsystem's ability to identify the correct candidate as a result of the matching process or to select no candidate if the mate is not in the file print database being searched. (b) The closeness of agreement between the matcher subsystem's generated representation of a fingerprint compared with the fingerprint it represents.

FINGERPRINT MINUTIAE MATCHER RELIABILITY—(a) The probability that the mating fingerprint will be selected as the primary candidate by the matcher subsystem if that mate is in the file prints being searched, or that no candidate will be selected if the mate is not in the file prints being searched. (b) The probability that an entity will perform its intended functions for a specified interval under stated conditions.

FINGERPRINT MINUTIAE MATCHER SELECTIVITY—The function of selecting the candidate, both correct and incorrect, and its relationship to other close candidates based upon minutiae scoring algorithms within the matcher subsystem.

FINGERPRINT PLAIN IMPRESSIONS—Fingerprint impressions taken by simultaneously capturing all of the fingers of each hand and then the thumbs without rolling, using a pressed or flat-impression.

FINGERPRINT REPOSITORY—A term for the AFIS/FBI capability to store fingerprint characteristics data and perform database-like functions, such as storage retrieval, search, and update. The AFIS/FBI segment has at least three subcategories of repository. (1) The FBI criminal repository contains one entry for each subject meeting retention criteria. The data included are extracted from criminal tenprint submissions. At a minimum, the FBI criminal repository contains fingerprint characteristics for all ten fingers. (2) The unsolved latent repository contains single latent fingerprints not identified to any subject in the criminal fingerprint repository. It is used to provide leads for unsolved criminal cases. (3) The special repositories have separately defined uses and data. Each has its own sponsor who controls its use. The data in each repository may be used for either tenprint and latent fingerprint searching, or for specially defined fingerprint searching.

FINGERPRINT ROLLED IMPRESSIONS—The impressions created by individually rolling each inked finger from side to side in order to obtain all available ridge detail.

FLATS—Fingerprint plain impressions.

FRICTION RIDGE—The ridge-shaped skin on a finger or palm surface that makes contact with an object.

GRAYSCALE IMAGE—An image using more than two radiometric values, i.e., 256 shades of gray in an eight-bit image. Not a strictly black and white image.

GROUP IV FAX—A facsimile-transmitted fingerprint card suitable for identification processing.

HENRY CLASSIFICATION—The system of classification developed by Sir Edward Henry that uses values derived from the odd/even finger numbers, patterns, and ridges. Consists of primary and secondary classifications.

HIT RESPONSE OR HIT ON FINGERPRINT SEARCH—An identification of minutiae-based data of a fingerprint image with minutiae-based data from another fingerprint image as being a mate for the finger of the same person.

IAFIS—Integrated Automated Fingerprint Identification System of the FBI. Has a 46 million record criminal record database. As of February 2004, 47 states, the District of Columbia, and four territories are participating in IAFIS.

IAI—International Association for Identification. Professional association whose members are engaged in forensic identification, investigation, and scientific examination of physical evidence.

IDAS—Identification Automated Services of the FBI. Data warehouse predecessor to IAFIS.

IDENT—An IAFIS term that means a positive fingerprint identification.

IDENTIFICATION—The positive match of a current tenprint or latent fingerprint card to a prior fingerprint card stored in the fingerprint files. The match is made on a comparison of one set of fingerprints to another.

IISS—Identification and Investigative Services Section of CJIS.

IMAGE—Processed or stored fingerprint image from a tenprint card or latent lift.

INKED ROLLED PRINT—An inked fingerprint impression taken by physically rotating the inked finger from side to side (nail to nail) on the fingerprint card stock.

INTEROPERABILITY—Seamless communication of AFIS with the same or different operating systems.

INTERPOL—Originally the International Police Commission, established in 1923 with the first headquarters in Vienna. General Secretariat now in Lyon, France, Interpol focuses on the international crimes of terrorism, criminal organization, drug-related crimes, financial and high-tech crimes, trafficking in human beings, fugitive investigative support, and other crimes that threaten public safety.

INTERSTATE IDENTIFICATION INDEX (III)—A national network for the exchange of criminal history records. It includes elements of participating state systems, the NCIC system, IDAS, the NLETS, and the U.S. Postal Service, among other systems. There are 47 states participating as of February 2004.

IQS—Image Quality Specification of the EFTS. Specification that has two components, Appendix F and Appendix G.

JFI—*Journal of Forensic Identification*. A publication of the International Association for Identification.

JPEG—Joint photographic experts group. A compression file format with the ".jpg" file extension. Most JPEG images use lossy compression.

LATENT COGNIZANT DATABASE—Fingerprint features records of all ten fingers of a subset of criminals in the tenprint database. Used for matching latent fingerprint submissions, which may be partial fingerprints.

LATENT FINGERPRINT—A fingerprint impression left at a crime scene by touching, holding, or moving an object that has a firm surface. Typically, several latent fingerprints are overlaid and/or only portions of the print are available.

LATENT FINGERPRINT SUBMISSION—A submission to the FBI or other agency that contains a latent fingerprint search request accompanied by the latent fingerprint information, which can be a piece of evidence or a high-quality photograph of the latent print. This type of submission can be electronic or hard copy.

LATENT LIFT—A reproduction of the friction ridge detail of a latent print.

LATENT SEARCH—A comparison of the fingerprint features extracted from a latent fingerprint with the fingerprint features contained in a fingerprint features file to determine whether a latent fingerprint has a potential mate on file within the AFIS repository. This may involve searching a latent cognizant repository, which contains prints of known subjects. It may also involve searching an unsolved latent repository, which contains fingerprint images of unknown subjects collected from evidence.

LATENT SPECIALIST—An FBI or other law enforcement agency employee who performs latent processing.

LATENT SUBMISSION—Normally, one image and associated descriptor data received by latent processing services; may be part of a case.

LEO—Law Enforcement Online. National interactive communications system maintained by the FBI exclusively for law enforcement.

LIGHTS OUT—AFIS searches without any human intervention at verification.

LIVESCAN—An electronic method of taking and transmitting fingerprints without using ink that produces fingerprint impressions of high quality to perform identification processing.

LIVESCANNER—An electro-optical scanning device used to capture a live fingerprint ridge detail by converting it to a digital representation for the detection of minutiae-based data and other usages such as producing an image.

LIVESCAN PRINT—A fingerprint image that is produced by scanning a live finger and printing out an image of the friction ridges.

LOCAL MODE—Process by which a workstation can perform some function independent of AFIS. Function may be limited to acquisition of new records.

LT/LT SEARCH—A search of a latent print against other latent prints, which are usually stored in the unsolved latent (UL) file. Has potential to link crimes committed by the same person, even though that person is as yet unidentified. Also referred to as a LT/UL search.

LT/TPid SEARCH—A search of a latent print against the tenprint identification database.

LT/TPlc SEARCH—A search of a latent print against the tenprint latent cognizant (ten finger) database.

LT/UL SEARCH—See LT/LT search.

MASTER NAME INDEX—A subject identification index maintained by criminal history record repositories that includes the name and other identifiers for each person with a record on the database.

MATCH—Condition of retrieving a file subject that, because of matcher score, falls within selection criteria for the probability of a mate to a search suspect.

MATCHER—An AFIS component that compares the minutiae database features of a search print with file prints and selects the file print that comes closes to matching the search print.

MATCHER ACCURACY—A measure of the matcher subsystem's ability to place the correct mates as the selected candidate as a result of the matcher process. Also a measure of the matcher subsystem's ability to select no candidate if the mate is not in the database.

MATCHER QUALITY INDEX (MQI)—Value representing the sum of the "equivalent number of minutiae" for fingers 2 and 7 (generally the search fingers). The index is a complex metric that weights the actual minutia count using local image quality and the number of neighbors in computation. On the average fingerprint, AFIS/FBI produces about 88 minutiae, and the average value for the equivalent number of minutia is about 56. Images with higher values for MQI are more likely to be successfully matched by IAFIS.

MATCHER RELIABILITY—Probability that the mate fingerprint will be selected as the primary candidate by the matcher if the mate is in the file being searched or that no candidate will be selected if the mate is not in the file being searched. Also the probability that the matcher will function as intended for a specified interval under specific conditions.

MATCHING SCORE—The numerical result of comparing the minutiae data of two fingerprint digital representations.

MATE—A fingerprint that matches another impression from the same finger.

MINUTIAE—Friction ridge characteristics, which are used to individualize that print. Minutiae occur at points where a single friction ridge deviates from an uninterrupted flow. Deviation may take the form of ending, dividing into two or more ridges, or immediate origination and termination.

MINUTIAE DATA—The data representing the relative position and orientation, and in some cases, the relationship and/or types of the minutiae in a fingerprint image.

MINUTIAE SEARCHING—The process of comparing the search print against the file prints by scoring the match of minutiae data in the prints and ranking the scores to produce one candidate with the highest score that is the potentially identical mate for the same finger or to produce no candidate when the potentially identical print does not exist within the file print database.

MINUTIAE VERIFICATION MATCH—The process of comparing minutiae data from a subject's previously entered single file print with minutiae data from a single incoming search print and, thereafter, comparing the resultant match score with a threshold to determine if the prints are potential mates.

NAIL-TO-NAIL ROLL—See rolled impression.

NAME SEARCH—A database program/file that is routinely searched that can yield the SID number of individuals in the database if they have used the same descriptive information for a prior event.

NATIONAL INSTITUTE OF STANDARDS AND TECHNOLOGY (NIST)—Formerly known as the National Bureau of Standards. This division of the U.S. Department of Commerce ensures standardization in non-defense government agencies.

NCIC—National Crime Information Center. Established in 1967 to provide criminal record history, fugitives, missing persons, and stolen property information to local, state, and federal agencies. Succeeded by NCIC 2000.

NCIC 2000—National Crime Information Center 2000. Successor to NCIC that provides information to local, state, and federal criminal justice agencies through computer terminals as well as mobile applications. Categories of information include the following: enhanced name search based on New York State Identification and Intelligence System (NYSIIS) to provide phonetically similar names:
- Fingerprint searches of the right index finger of records on file
- Probation/parole subjects
- Online manuals for download applications through state Control Terminal Agency
- Improved data quality with point-of-entry checks
- information linking that connects two or more records
- Mug shots may be entered along within a signature and ten other SMTP images
- Other images such as boat
- Convicted Sex Offender Registry of individuals convicted of sex offenses or violent sexual predators
- SENTRY file of individual incarcerated in federal prison system.

NFF—National Fingerprint File. Intended as a component of the Interstate Identification Index, NFF would decentralize interstate exchange of criminal history records. NFF would contain fingerprints from all federal offenders and only one set of fingerprints from select state offenders. Only the first arrest fingerprints would be sent along with other biometric data. The state would maintain criminal history.

NIBRS—National Incident-Based Reporting System. An outgrowth of the uniform crime report (UCR), NIBRS information is a byproduct of the state and local Incident-Based Reporting (IBR) Systems. The NIBRS collects specific crime information on 22 offense categories consisting of 46 specific crimes collectively called group A offenses. Crimes in this group are reported as complete incidents including data on victims, offenders, and circumstances. There is also a secondary list, referred to as group B, which consists of 11 offense categories for which only arrest information is captured. Group A reported categories include the following: arson; assault offenses—aggravated assault, simple assault, intimidation; bribery; burglary, breaking and entering; counterfeit/forgery; destruction/damage/vandalism of property; drug/narcotic offenses—drug/narcotic violations, drug equipment violations; embezzlement; extortion/blackmail; fraud offenses—false pretenses/swindle/confidence game, credit card/ATM fraud, impersonation, welfare fraud, wire fraud; gambling offenses—betting/wagering, operating/promoting/assisting gambling, gambling equipment violations, sport tampering; homicide offenses—murder and non-negligent manslaughter, negligent manslaughter, justifiable homicide; kidnapping/abduction; larceny/theft offenses—pocket-picking, purse-snatching, shoplifting, theft from building, theft from coin-operated machine or device, theft from motor vehicle, theft of motor vehicle parts or accessories, other larceny; motor vehicle theft; pornography/obscene material; prostitution offenses—prostitution, assisting or promoting prostitution; robbery; sex offenses, forcible—forcible rape, forcible sodomy, sexual assault with an object, forcible fondling; sex offenses, non-forcible—incest, statutory rape; stolen property offenses (receiving, etc.); weapon law violation. Group B offenses for which only arrest data are reported are the following: bad checks; curfew/loitering/vagrancy violation; disorderly conduct; driving under the influence; drunkenness; family offenses, nonviolent; liquor law violations; peeping tom; runaway; trespass of real property; all other offenses.

NICS—National Instant Criminal Background Check. Check on presale stage of firearms purchase. Federal firearms licensees obtain descriptive information on alcohol, tobacco, and firearms (ATF) form 4473 and call or access NICS through the Internet. This is not a fingerprint-based search.

NLETS—National Law Enforcement Telecommunications Network. Outgrowth of Law Enforcement Teletype System (LETS), NLETS was incorporated in

1970 as a not-for-profit. NLETS provides an international, computer-based message switching system that links local, state, and federal criminal justice agencies for information exchange. Also provides information services support for justice-related applications by supporting data communications links to state networks using commercial relay services.

NON-IDENT—Jargon term for "non-identification." A determination that two fingerprints do not belong to a particular person; or when no mate is found as the result of a fingerprint comparison by a human.

NON-IDENT FINGERPRINTS—Current fingerprint images that have been searched against the IAFIS's criminal master file without identification.

NON-IDENTIFICATION—The result of a search when the fingerprint information provided does not match any record in the FBI's files based on comparison of images by a human.

NSOR—National Sex Offender Registry.

ORIGINATING AGENCY IDENTIFIER (ORI)—An identification number assigned by the NCIC or IAFIS to each agency that may submit information into, or receive information from, either system. The format of this number varies from agency to agency, except that the first two characters always designate the state, territory, province, or country of the contributor.

PALM PRINT—An inked and rolled print or livescan of the palms of both hands. May also include the side of the hand, referred to as the writer's palm.

PATTERN CLASSIFICATION—Characterizing a fingerprint as containing one of seven fingerprint patterns: arch, tented arch, right-slant loop, left-slant loop, whorl, amputation, and scar. IAFIS provides for both pattern-level and Henry (NCIC) Classifications.

PCN—Process control number. Used as a temporary identifier for a tenprint record until a matching SID is found or a new SID is assigned. If there is a match, the SID number would be added to the inquiry record. If there is no match, i.e., the subject has no record on the AFIS and CCH, a new SID number is added.

PEAK MINUTE—A minute during which the system must process a statistically significant greater number of user support functions than it is required to process during an average minute.

PIXEL—Picture element.

PLAIN, TOUCH, OR FLAT IMPRESSION—The impression of the ridge detail taken by a livescanner or inked impressions taken without rolling the live finger to convert it to a digital representation for the detection of minutiae-based data and other usages such as producing an image.

PPI—Pixels per inch.

PROTOTYPE—A simulation of a program, report, menu, or system.

QC—Quality control. Editing of fingerprint minutiae to improve accuracy for identification. The quality of tenprint images is automatically determined, and poor quality images are sent to QC for editing.

RADIOMETRIC RESOLUTION—Number of intensity levels, e.g., shades of gray or color values in a digital image.

RELAUNCH—Searching a latent print case after the initial LT/TPlc search using different search parameters while maintaining the same case identifiers and images.

RELIABILITY—The probability that the mating fingerprint will be hit if the mate is in the file being searched.

REMOTE TENPRINT FINGERPRINT FEATURE SEARCH (NATIVE MODE)— A search request transmitted to the FBI originating outside the identification, tasking, and networking (ITN) workstations. The fingerprint features submitted for the search were derived by an AFIS in a similar manner to those derived by AFIS/FBI. The transmission includes fingerprint features along with the necessary fingerprint classifications and other data. The search request is performed automatically by AFIS/FBI without human involvement.

RFES—Remote fingerprint editing software. Software package from the FBI used to perform remote searches on IAFIS. Supports remote IAFIS transactions, including image- and features-based searches for latent and tenprint applications.

ROLLED IMPRESSION—Fingerprint impressions created by individually rolling each finger from side to side (nail to nail) to obtain all available friction ridge detail. The images appear in the individual print boxes on the tenprint card.

SCANNER—Capture device to create digital image. Must meet at least Appendix G standards for AFIS applications that connect to the FBI.

SEARCH SELECTIVITY—The total number of incorrect candidates divided by the total number of searches conducted during the time period. That is, the number of incorrect candidates, averaged over time periods, produced for comparison per search at the operating point at which search reliability is measured.

SEARCH, THE NATIONAL CONSORTIUM FOR JUSTICE INFORMATION AND STATISTICS—A nonprofit membership organization dedicated to better criminal justice information management, effective identification technology, and responsible law and policy.

SEGMENT—One of the constituent parts into which an automated system may be logically divided. IAFIS consists of the segments of ITN, AFIS, and III.

SERVICE PROVIDER—A member of the FBI staff who supports or provides FBI identification services to the criminal justice community (federal, state, and local users) and other authorized users. Service providers perform activities that include data entry, fingerprint classification, fingerprint image comparison and verification, document processing, and latent fingerprint processing.

SID NUMBER—The state identification number assigned to each individual on a state file.

SMT—Scars, marks, and tattoos.

SMTP—Simple Mail Transfer Protocol transfers mail across networks.

SOW—Statement of work. Describes the tasks and responsibilities for a project.

SPATIAL RESOLUTION—Relationship of the individual pixels to the size of the actual area represented.

SPECTRAL RESOLUTION—Color bands of light detected during image acquisition.

STATE-OF-THE-ART TECHNOLOGY—The highest level of development of a device or technique achieved at any particular time.

STORE AND FORWARD—A system capable of electronically receiving and processing fingerprint cards at the state and then sending the fingerprints electronically into AFIS and to the FBI.

SUBJECT MATTER EXPERT (SME)—Person who exhibits the highest level of expertise in performing a specialized job, task, or skill.

SUBJECT SEARCH—A search, using biographical and/or physical data, to identify a list of candidates having records that match the descriptors specified. Subject search can be based upon name, gender, DOB, FBI number, state identification number, Social Security number, and other biographical or physical data (height, weight, age) or combinations of these characteristics.

SWGFAST—Scientific Working Group on Friction Ridge Analysis, Study and Technology. Consists of 30 to 40 local, state, and federal law enforcement officials and members of the community who will establish guidelines for the development and enhancement of friction ridge examiners' knowledge, skills, and abilities and methods and protocols; establish guidelines for quality assurance; and cooperate with national and international standards organizations to disseminate the findings of SWGFAST.

TAC—Individual in the Control Terminal Agency (CTA) responsible for monitoring system use, enforcing system discipline, and assuring that the National Crime Information Center (NCIC) operating procedures are followed.

TECHNICAL SEARCH—Using AFIS, a minutia-based fingerprint search of the index fingers of the tenprint record. Some systems use thumbs or other finger combinations.

TENPRINT[2]—A fingerprint card (or fingerprint card equivalent) containing rolled and plain impressions from the ten fingers of an individual. The stan-

[2] Tenprint Fingerprint Certification Program of the IAI uses "Tenprint" as one word. Henceforth all IAI publications will reflect that spelling.

dard format contains 14 impressions: ten "rolled" fingerprint impressions of each finger and four "plain" fingerprint impressions; one of the right thumb, one of the left thumb, one with the four fingers of the right hand taken simultaneously, and one with the four fingers of the left hand taken simultaneously.

TENPRINT CARD SUBMISSION—A fingerprint card submitted to the FBI by mail or as a facsimile or other electronic image for the purpose of identification and possible incorporation into the FBI's fingerprint repository.

TENPRINT IMAGE SEARCH—An electronic transaction submitted to the FBI, which contains fingerprint images, classification information as required by the AFIS/FBI, or remotely extracted fingerprint characteristics. The subsequent FBI search will be conducted automatically with no additional manual editing or processing. If candidates are identified, the candidates' FBI numbers are returned to the transmitting agency along with fingerprint images from the highest scoring candidates. The search request is performed automatically by AFIS/FBI without human involvement.

TIFF—Tagged image file format. An image file format with the ".tif" file extension. TIFF images can be either lossless or lossy.

TP—Tenprint record.

TPid—Tenprint identification database consisting of two finger images, usually the index fingers, sometimes the thumbs.

TPlc—Tenprint identification database consisting of all ten finger images. May be a subset of the TPid database. Used in latent to tenprint (LT/TPlc) searches.

TP/TPid—Search of a tenprint record against the records in the tenprint database.

TP/UL—Tenprint to unsolved latent search. New tenprint records are searched against the records in the unsolved latent file. The expectation is that the owner of the latent print did not have a record in the tenprint database at the time of the LT/TP search. The TP/UL search ensures that the complete database has been searched, including new and updated records.

TRANSPOSITION—Incorrect position of hands on tenprint card, e.g., images of the right hand appear in boxes for the left hand. In the past, identification staff would visually inspect the rolled impressions against the plain impressions for consistency. Livescan software and extraction and comparison reduce this on digitally retrieved images.

TWAIN—Technology without an important name. Image acquisition and output protocol commonly used between computers and printers and image capture devices.

UCR—Uniform crime report. Voluntary reporting to the FBI CJIS Division. Reportable crimes include murder and non-negligent manslaughter, forcible rape, robbery, aggravated assault, burglary, larceny-theft, motor vehicle theft, and arson.

UL/UL—Unsolved latent to unsolved latent search. A search of the unsolved latent print file using another unsolved latent print. The goal is to determine if latent images from the same subject are on file even if the subject remains unknown. May be used to determine serial offenders and to share information with another agency.

ULW—Universal Latent Workstation Software Program of the FBI CJIS Division. When installed on a COTS computer, this allows the operator to create a native feature set for Printrak, Cogent, Sagem Morpho, NEC, and IAFIS. Currently databases in Anaheim (Printrak), Ontario Police Department (Cogent), Pierce County Sheriff's Department (Sagem Morpho), and the IAFIS can receive and search an ANSI/NSIT-formatted record.

UPGRADE—Introduction of new software and/or hardware into an existing system. The upgrade may fix problems unique to one AFIS customer; fix problems applicable to all customers; improve the AFIS in a way not related to a problem, or move customers to a new platform, such as from a Windows-based system to Linux, or from Windows 98 to Windows XP. The upgrade may require extensive on-site testing prior to installation on the live system.

VALIDATION—Process of comparing data or images against a previously verified set of data; a double check of the verification.

VERIFICATION—Process of visually comparing as search fingerprint with a candidate fingerprint to determine if there is a match.

WIDE AREA NETWORK—A network that interconnects geographical entities such as cities and states, generally covering a distance of 50 miles or greater.

WIN—Western Identification Network.

WSQ—Wavelet Scalar Quantization. A lossy compression algorithm used to reduce finger or palm print images size.

ACRONYMS LIST

AFIS—Automated Fingerprint Identification System

AMN—Amnesia Victim

APB—Advisory Policy Board

ARG—Attributed Relational Graph

ATB—AFIS Test Bed

BCI&I—Bureau of Criminal Identification and Investigation

BDM—Basic Demonstration Model

CAN—Criminal Tenprint Submission (No Answer Necessary)

CAR—Criminal Tenprint Submission (Answer Required)

CARC—Criminal Tenprint CSS Submission (Answer Required)

CAXI—Core and Axis Independent

CJIS—Criminal Justice Information Services

CMF—Criminal Master File

CNAC—Criminal Tenprint CSS Submission (No Answer Necessary)

CONOPS—Concept of Operations

CSS—Card Scanning Service

DCJS—NYS Division of Criminal Justice Services

DEU—Unknown Deceased

DPS—Department of Public Safety

EFCON—Electronic Fingerprint Converter

EFTS—Electronic Fingerprint Transmission Specification

FANC—Federal Applicant—No Charge Federal Agency Name Check

FAR—False Acceptance Rate

FAUF—Federal Applicant User Fee

FBI—Federal Bureau of Investigation

FIC—Fingerprint Image Comparison

FIMF—Fingerprint Image Master File

FNCC—Federal Applicant CSS Submission (No Charge)

FPF—Focal Point Filtering

FpVTE—Fingerprint Vendor Technology Evaluation

FUFC—Federal Applicant CSS Submission (User Fee)

IAFIS—Integrated Automated Fingerprint Identification System

III—Interstate Identification Index

IMAP—Internal Miscellaneous Applicant Civil

IRC—Indeterminate Ridge Count

ITN—Identification Tasking and Networking

LEIF—Law Enforcement Interconnecting Facilities

LMC—Lockheed Martin Corporation

LT—Latent

LT-ARG—Latent-Attributed Relational Graph

MAP—Miscellaneous Applicant Civil

MAPC—Miscellaneous Applicant CSS Submission (No Charge)

MCAXI—Modular Core and Axis Independent

MCS—Minutia Comparison Standard

MPR—Missing Person

MQI—Matcher Quality Index

NCIC—National Crime Information Center

N-FACS—National Fingerprint-Based Applicant Check Study

NFFC—Non-Federal Applicant CSS Submission (User Fee)

NFUF—Non-Federal Applicant User Fee

NICS—National Instant Criminal Background Check System

NIST—National Institute of Standards and Technology
NLETS—National Law Enforcement Telecommunication System
NOE—Non-Operational Environment
ODRC—Ohio Department of Rehabilitation and Correction
OE—Operational Environment
ORI—Originating Agency Identifier
PC/RC—Pattern Class/Ridge Count
PSS—Public Safety Strategy
RFI—Request for Information
RRI—Repository Retrieval Index
SID—State Identification Number
SoS—System-of-Systems
SP/CR—System Problem/Change Report
SSN—Social Security Number
TAR—True Acceptance Rate
TBD—To Be Determined
TOT—Type of Transaction
TP_CMF_CAXI—Tenprint Criminal Master File Core and Axis Independent
TP-ARG—Tenprint-Attributed Relational Graph
TP—Tenprint
TPIS—Tenprint Image Search
USSS—United States Secret Service
WAN—Wide Area Network
WDS—Workflow Distribution Server

INTERNATIONAL ASSOCIATION FOR IDENTIFICATION—1998 IAI AFIS COMMITTEE REPORT ON CROSS-JURISDICTIONAL USE OF AFIS SYSTEMS

Prepared by

Peter T. Higgins
Chair, IAI AFIS Committee

and

Cynthia L. Way
IAI Member

Higgins & Associates, International
3116 Woodley Road, NW
Washington, DC 20008
202-625-7780 Voice
202-625-7781 FAX
PeterHAI@aol.com
Cynthiaxyz@aol.com

Version 1.0   7/7/98

TABLE OF CONTENTS

EXECUTIVE SUMMARY

The International Association for Identification (IAI) Automated Fingerprint Identification System (AFIS) Committee has demonstrated a method of conducting remote fingerprint searches across jurisdictional and fingerprint equipment vendor boundaries. Using AFIS systems at operational sites, vendors conducted remote searches of tenprint and latent images over the National Law Enforcement Transmission System (NLETS) frame relay network using ANSI-NIST and FBI approved standards. NLETS is a private network designed for the Criminal Justice community.

The AFIS Committee consists of leaders in fingerprinting from state and local law enforcement, the FBI, the National Institute of Standards and Technology (NIST) and private industry. Participating in the demonstrations were three major AFIS vendors—Cogent Systems, Printrak International and Sagem Morpho, along with Aware, who used their commercially available Electronic Fingerprint Transmission Specification (EFTS) Software, and the National Law Enforcement Transmission System (NLETS) who provided access to their frame relay network.

In 1997, testing was conducted to and from vendor facilities using the Internet as the transmission medium. Although the Internet is not a transmission medium of choice for regular law enforcement use due to security implications, the Internet allowed us to prove the feasibility of transmission using the Simple Management Transfer Protocol (SMTP) and Multipurpose Internet Mail Extensions (MIME), required for the FBI's Criminal Justice Information System (CJIS) Wide Area Network (WAN) and for potential application outside the criminal justice area.

This year, after regression testing on the Internet, we moved the tests from a simulation of vendor sites over the Internet to operational customer sites over the NLETS frame relay network. Sites that were not already directly connected to the NLETS network were given dial-up access to the central NLETS site.

Testing was successful and further proved the AFIS Committee's theory that today searches can be run across jurisdictional and AFIS vendor boundaries. It was also shown that simply because a vendor is FBI certified for certain areas and considered standards-compliant doesn't necessarily guarantee interoperability with other vendors. The FBI's Electronic Fingerprint Transmission Specification (EFTS) document was crucial to interoperability for it defined a common implementation of the ANSI-NIST standard within which vendors could communicate, but we also needed to modify certain aspects of the transactions to make it applicable to cross-jurisdictional use (see Appendix C).

This testing has not been funded by the IAI or any outside source. All who participate do so at their own expense of staff time, equipment, travel and other expenses. The Committee Chair extends many thanks to the three AFIS vendors who contributed significant resource investments: Cogent Systems, Printrak International and Sagem Morpho. Thanks to Aware who did the same. Thanks to NLETS who accommodated our testing during a period of their own upgrade testing and contributed the extra equipment we needed at no cost to us. And special thanks to the three operational sites that graciously supported the live testing.

This project, conceived 2 years ago at the IAI 81st Annual Educational Seminar, will be discussed by a Panel at this year's IAI 83rd Annual Educational Seminar in July at Little Rock, Arkansas. For more information, see the IAI-AFIS Committee home page at http://www.iaibbs.org/afis.htm or contact Peter Higgins or Cynthia Way at 202-625-7780.

1. INTRODUCTION/BACKGROUND

At the 1996 IAI Annual Training Conference, the AFIS Committee sponsored a Panel designed to provide an educational experience for the IAI members in the audience and to explore the possibility of establishing links between the various state and regional AFIS systems, regardless of the hardware and software vendor used to capture, store and compare the fingerprints.

Working with the major vendors of AFIS and scan equipment, the AFIS Committee, FBI, NIST and other law enforcement agencies, we developed a *Concept of Operations* that outlined how remote searches might be performed. The *Concept of Operations* explains the relevant U.S. standards and how they could be implemented to support cross-jurisdictional, multi-vendor AFIS searches. This document was also a basis for a series of cross-jurisdictional AFIS search demonstrations.

Next, a *Demonstration Test Plan* was written for the 1997 tests that specified a series of demonstrations to prove interoperability of AFIS systems and scanners. These demonstrations employed the transmission, reception and processing of image-based Types of Transactions (TOTs). Communication was via the Internet using Simple Mail Transfer Protocol (SMTP) and Multi-purpose Internet Mail Extensions (MIME).

Sagem Morpho, Inc. documented the agreed upon test message specifications for the 1998 testing in *Inter-AFIS Message Specifications/NIST Record Layouts/IAI Inter-AFIS Demonstration Project.*

2. DEMONSTRATION PARTICIPANTS

All AFIS vendors were invited to participate in 1996. The following list reflects the three AFIS vendors that participated in both last year's and this year's testing, the operational customer sites and other involved parties.

AFIS Vendors:

Cogent Systems	Alhambra, CA Vendor Facility
	Ontario, CA Police Department (PD)
Printrak International	Anaheim, CA Vendor Facility
	NC Bureau of Investigation, Raleigh, NC
Sagem Morpho	Tacoma, WA Vendor Facility
	Arizona Dept. of Public Safety

Electronic Fingerprint Transmission Specification (EFTS) Software:

Aware, Inc.	Bedford, MA Vendor Facility

Criminal Justice Communication Network

NLETS	Phoenix, AZ

3. TEST APPROACH

3.1. STANDARDS-BASED

To communicate across jurisdictional and vendor boundaries, standards are essential. In developing our tests, we adhered to the ANSI-NIST *Data Format for the Interchange of Fingerprint Information*. We used the FBI *Electronic Fingerprint Transmission Specification* as a standard, but found it necessary to make a few modifications based on the specific needs of cross-jurisdictional use. These are outlined in Appendix C. And lastly, we used the FBI's *CJIS Wide Area Network Interface Specification* to specify the mode of transmission, specifically, the use of SMTP with MIME partitioning.

3.2. INTERNET TESTING

Last year, ComnetiX, a software integrator who participated in our testing, sent a suite of test messages to vendors via the Internet using SMTP with MIME partitioning, and vendors sent test messages back. ComnetiX confirmed the vendors were WSQ and ANSI-NIST compliant by nature of the fact they were able to decipher the messages. Higgins & Associates, International, then confirmed the messages were EFTS and ANSI-NIST compliant with help from FBI and NIST personnel. This year, we repeated the Internet testing, adding the latent transactions.

3.3. NLETS TESTING

NLETS is the common name referring to the National Law Enforcement Telecommunications System message switching system created in 1968 for and dedicated to the criminal justice community. NLETS includes a wide area frame relay network (installed in 1997). For the IAI testing, we were concerned only with the frame relay network, not the message-switching computer.

Two of the sites (NC and AZ) connected to the NLETS frame relay network using existing circuitry to access their state's NLETS network at a speed of 56 KBS. The Cogent site in Ontario, CA and Aware in Bedford, MA used a dial-up line running at 14.4 KBS. The dial-up connections required modems and routers in Ontario and Bedford in order to connect to the NLETS Phoenix location.

While 14.4 KBS certainly sufficed for the testing where we compressed latent images using WSQ compression, this speed is rather slow for sending uncompressed images, as is desirable for the transmission of latent prints.

4. DEMONSTRATION TEST MESSAGES

We selected the following series of test messages, called Types of Transactions or TOTs, to include in our demonstrations. Our goal was not to be all encompassing, but to select a sampling that would be easily achievable and relevant to "real life" scenarios. We used Type-1, Type-2 and Type-4 records. A Type-1 record, mandatory for all transactions, provides information describing type and purpose of the transaction. A Type-2 record provides biographic and demographic details about an individual or an error message. Each Type-4 record contains a fingerprint image.

4.1. TOA/ATR

The Type of AFIS transaction (TOA) requests the make and model of the AFIS system, TOTs supported, maximum score obtainable, and response time. The AFIS Type Record (ATR) contains the response to the information requested in the TOA. These are two new messages devised by the AFIS Committee specifically for cross-jurisdictional use.

4.2. TPIS/SRT

The most relevant of the tests, the Tenprint Image Search (TPIS) AFIS transaction allows a PD to remotely search another jurisdiction's AFIS remotely with no manual intervention at the receiving site. The originating PD sends fingerprint images in a TPIS with descriptive data, the remote end automatically searches and responds with a Search Results—Tenprint (SRT) transaction. The SRT includes a candidate list with images of the top candidate.

4.3. IRQ/IRR

The Fingerprint Image Request (IRQ) transaction allows the receiver of the SRT to request fingerprint images for other candidates from the candidate list. The remote site responds with a Fingerprint Image Request Response (IRR) which provides the requested fingerprint images.

4.4. LFIQ/SRL

The Latent Fingerprint Image Request (LFIQ) allows the originator to send a latent image to a destination site. The destination site must edit the minutiae, then submit the request for processing in the destination AFIS. The destination AFIS returns the candidate list along with the image of the top candidate to the originator in a TOT called the SRL, or Search Results—Latent. The originator then must determine if there's a matching candidate.

4.5. ERRT, ERRI, ERRL

We purposely tested Error messages ERRT, ERRI, ERRL, which correspond to TPIS, IRQ and LFIQ respectively.

5. SCHEDULE

	Start	Finish
IAI-AFIS Committee Panel Met	7/96	
Concept of Operations Published	10/96	
Demonstration Test Plan Published	2/97	
Sample Record Specifications Published	11/1/96	2/6/97
AFIS Vendor S/W Tuning & Development	2/7/97	4/4/97
Vendor Testing with ComnetiX	4/7/97	7/11/97
Brief NLETS Annual Conference	7/4/97	
Vendor Testing via Internet	7/14/97	7/25/97
Reconvene IAI Panel	7/27/97	8/2/97
Regression Internet Testing	5/98	5/98
Operational Testing via NLETS	6/1/98	6/4/98

6. ISSUES AND RESOLUTIONS/RECOMMENDATIONS

The following categorized issues were encountered throughout the year.

6.1. LATENT PRINTS

Issue L-1: Although the ANSI-NIST standard defines minutiae extraction standards in the Type-9 record, it is not considered optimal for latent searches due to each AFIS system having proprietary encoding and matching software. Thus, we could not send minutiae extractions, and required remote intervention for completing the minutiae extraction.

   Resolution: The FBI, NIST and vendors continue to work on creating a more satisfactory solution. For purposes of our testing, we developed a variation of the EFTS Latent Fingerprint Image Search (LFIS). The LFIS specifies automatic extraction at the remote site with no human intervention. Instead, the IAI AFIS Committee participants on this effort created a transaction called an LFIQ, Latent Fingerprint Image Query, which specifies that the remote site must intervene to extract minutiae before processing.

Recommendation A: Support the FBI/NIST/Vendor effort.

Recommendation B: Establish the LFIQ as the standard for cross-jurisdictional use in the interim.

6.2. STANDARDS

The FBI-EFTS and ANSI-NIST Standards don't address everything needed for cross-jurisdictional interoperability. We had specific questions arise on the EFTS that we plan to discuss when the IAI-AFIS Committee reconvenes in late July 1998.

Issue S-1: While the EFTS is key to cross-jurisdictional interoperability, there is no governing body that certifies EFTS compliance (other than Appendices F and G, Image Quality Specification).

Recommendation A: The IAI-AFIS Committee considers becoming the governing body, or find an organization that will.

Recommendation B: The EFTS becomes an ANSI-NIST standard and is expanded to accommodate cross-jurisdictional use.

Recommendation C: In order to implement Recommendation B, either NIST, the IAI or FBI hold a series of workshops to review what is needed for cross-jurisdictional use.

Issue S-2: Individual states and localities are implementing their own versions of the standard by defining their own transaction types and Record Type-2 tags (new field designators). This could inhibit future interoperability.

Recommendation: One near-term option is the FBI listing a description of all EFTS Type-2 tags and transactions (including non-Federal) on their home page and/or the IAI-AFIS Committee home page. This will allow local police departments to standardize more easily.

Issue S-3: The EFTS was primarily designed for hierarchical transmission, i.e., transmission to the FBI. Thus, there arose several questions on how to accommodate non-FBI transmissions. Our approach to these is documented in Appendix X. New transactions were devised for this testing.

Recommendation: The IAI-AFIS Committee takes the lead to identify and resolve these issues.

Issue S-4: Most of the issues and questions on the EFTS documented in last year's report have been resolved (see Appendix C). However, a few items are still pending FBI resolution.

> **Recommendation:** The IAI-AFIS Committee works with the FBI and NIST on resolution.

6.3. NLETS

Issue N-1: The NLETS frame relay network is accessed via a State Network. Some states and localities do not support TCP/IP (an Internet protocol), needed for cross-jurisdictional AFIS searches.

> **Resolution:** NLETS offered us the solution of a dial-up line into the central NLETS facility in Arizona.
>
> **Recommendation A:** If law enforcement wants to begin cross-jurisdictional use of AFIS systems, they will have to work with NLETS to set up the transmission for long term use. Note: A dial-up speed of 14.4 KBS is rather slow to transport images.
>
> **Recommendation B:** It would be useful to publish a list of law enforcement ORI and IP addresses on a secure network such as NLETS. This would allow a police department to remotely search another AFIS by merely looking up the address information and submitting a request.

Issue N-2: NLETS Board of Directors expressed an interest in seeing a policy emerge on the use of cross-jurisdictional AFIS searches.

> **Recommendation:** Initiate an IACP/NSA/IAI (International Association of Chiefs of Police/National Sheriff's Association) Policy meeting on the use of this new capability.

7. CONCLUSION

Overall, testing was extremely successful and proved the IAI-AFIS Committee's theory that searches can be run across jurisdictional and AFIS vendor boundaries. It was also shown that simply because a vendor is FBI certified for certain areas and considered standards-compliant doesn't necessarily guarantee interoperability. The FBI's Electronic Fingerprint Transmission Specification (EFTS) document, while crucial to interoperability, will need to be supplemented with standards that are specific to cross-jurisdictional use.

The Internet, a public network, is not a viable transmission medium for most law enforcement agencies at this time due to security restrictions. The Internet, however, may be useful for non-law enforcement use, e.g., interstate welfare enrollment checks. The secure NLETS network is a more appropriate transmission medium for law enforcement.

There seems to be a strong interest at all levels for this effort, from the vendors' users group members, the vendors, and law enforcement. The IAI-AFIS Committee would like to see this effort continue.

Most of all, the IAI wishes to thank all who participated in this volunteer effort–law enforcement, vendors, independent consultants, the FBI, NLETS and NIST, all of who committed valuable resources to an unfunded effort. The IAI-AFIS Committee is especially grateful to the vendors who stayed for the duration and displayed teamwork, dedication to our vision and commitment to support local and state law enforcement.

APPENDIX A—BIBLIOGRAPHY

ANSI/NIST-CSL 1-1993 Data Format for the Interchange of Fingerprint Information, Sponsored by National Institute of Standards and Technology, Published by American National Standards Institute, November 22, 1993.

CJIS Wide Area Network Interface Specification, CJIS-IC-0020, Federal Bureau of Investigation, November 1995.

Criminal Justice Information Services (CJIS) Electronic Fingerprint Transmission Specification (EFTS), CJIS-RS-0010 (V5), Federal Bureau of Investigation, June 1997.

IAFIS Planning Guide Integrated Automated Fingerprint Identification System, FBI/CJIS Advisory Policy Board with Assistance from SEARCH, Revised March 1995.

WSQ Gray-Scale Fingerprint Image Compression Specification, IAFIS-IC-0110V2, Criminal Justice Information Services (CJIS), Federal Bureau of Investigation, February 16, 1993.

IAI Concept of Operations for Cross-Jurisdictional Use of AFIS Systems, V3.0, Higgins & Associates, International, April 16, 1997 (available on the IAI-AFIS Committee Home Page at http://www.onin.com/iaiafis/

Demonstration Test Plan for IAI Cross-Jurisdictional Use of AFIS, V2.0, Higgins & Associates, International, April 16, 1997.

Inter-AFIS Message Specifications/NIST Record Layouts/IAI Inter-AFIS Demonstration Project, Document Number D 349-001A, Sagem Morpho, May 6, 1998.

APPENDIX B—GLOSSARY

AFIS	Automated Fingerprint Identification System
ANSI	American National Standards Institute ANSI Standard—Shorthand for the American National Standard for Information Systems—Data Format for the Standard for the Interchange of Fingerprint Information
ATR	AFIS Type Record (Type of Transaction or TOT)
CJIS	Criminal Justice Information Services Division (of the FBI)
CTA	Control Terminal Agency
DAI	Destination Agency Identifier
EFIPS	Electronic Fingerprint Image Print Server (the system at the FBI which prints out electronically submitted fingerprint cards)
EFTS	Electronic Fingerprint Transmission Specification—the FBI's implementation of the ANSI Standard
IACP	International Association of Chiefs of Police
IAFIS	Integrated Automated Fingerprint Identification System—the FBI's new system for integrating fingerprint comparisons with criminal history record processing
IAI	International Association for Identification
IRQ	Fingerprint Image Request (TOT)
IRR	Fingerprint Image Request Response (TOT)
ISP	Internet Service Provider
LAN	Local Area Network
MIME	Multipurpose Internet Mail Extensions
NIST	National Institute of Standards and Technology
NLETS	National Law Enforcement Telecommunications System
NSA	National Sheriffs Association
ORI	Originating Agency Identifier
SMTP	Simple Mail Transfer Protocol
SRT	Search Results–Tenprint (TOT)
TBD	To Be Determined
TCP/IP	Transmission Control Protocol/Internet Protocol
TOA	Type of AFIS (TOT)
TOT	Type of Transaction
TPIS	Tenprint Fingerprint Image Search (TOT)
WAN	Wide Area Network—a way of connecting computer sites across the country using special telephone lines, satellites, etc.
WSQ	Wavelet Scalar Quantization (the compression method required for submitting fingerprint images to the FBI)

APPENDIX C—EFTS

ISSUES DOCUMENTED IN JULY 1997

Existing Scope of EFTS:

1. **SRT "No Hit" Condition:** There is no specification in the FBI-EFTS document on how to return a No-Hit message in response to a Tenprint Image Search (TPIS). Does one merely include the words "No Hit" in the 2.064 field (the mandatory field normally containing the candidate list)? In our testing, we had pre-sent cards to all vendors, so that a No Hit condition would not occur. **Resolution:** Still pending.

2. **DAI Size Discrepancy:** The EFTS lists contradictory size specifications of the Destination Agency Identifier (DAI) and Originating Agency Identifier (ORI) found in Type-1 records. In the ANSI-NIST standard and the EFTS, it says, "The size and data content of this field shall be defined by the user and be in accordance with the receiving agency." However, the EFTS goes on to say, "This field shall be a ten-byte [or nine-byte respectively] alphanumeric field." So if this in fact is true, and since the DAI is merely the other person's ORI, what constitutes the extra byte? **Resolution:** Still pending.

3. **ORI/DAI Size Conflict with ANSI-NIST:** The EFTS specifies a size for the ORI and DAI, but the ANSI-NIST standard says that "the size and data content of this field shall be defined by the user and be in accordance with the receiving agency." Which is correct? **Resolution:** Still pending.

4. **Candidate Scores:** Do we need another field in Type-2 Record for scores of candidates? Currently, scores are not returned with the candidates. **Resolution:** Still pending.

5. **Score Meaning:** Currently, all vendors have different methods and values for scoring, e.g., a score of 1,000 with Vendor A may not have the same significance as with Vendor B. Also, a score of 1,000 is not necessarily "twice as good" as a score of 500. We need to further explore possible uniformity and understanding of the scoring process. NOTE: This point is of interest only if it's decided to return the scores with the candidate lists. **Resolution:** Still pending.

6. **NTR Update:** Nominal Transmitting Resolution (NTR) needs to be updated. The Native Scanning Resolution (NSR) has a minimum value defined, but there is no upward limit. On the other hand, the NTR is limited to a maximum value of 20.47 pixels per millimeter (p/mm) plus/minus .20 p/mm (520 pixels per inch (p/in) plus/minus 5 p/in) for high resolution grayscale images, e.g., Type-4 records. The typical tenprint scanner scans at 600 p/in. Therefore, we are unable to take advantage of

the finer resolution that is today's commercial standard. **Resolution:** Still pending.

7. **MIR Clarification:** The Multiple Image Request (MIR) transaction does not specify how to ask for multiple requests, nor how the response should look. For example, to request images from the 2nd and 3rd candidates on the SRT candidate list, is it correct to insert two State ID Numbers, e.g., 2.015:MD1002>MD2345*? And is the response to this request separate IRRs for each candidate that reference the same MIR? **Resolution:** Still pending.

8. **EFTS Readability/Sample Messages:** It took hours to decipher the EFTS fields. Sample messages from an older version of EFTS proved quite helpful. It would be useful to re-include them as a permanent part of the EFTS document. **Resolution:** Still pending.

9. **FNR Delimiter Discrepancy:** Fingerprint Number (FNR), Field 2.057 has conflicting descriptions of separators. An RS was used for purposes of our testing, but this needs to be clarified. **Resolution:** Still pending.

10. **TCR as Mandatory Field:** The Transaction Control Reference (TCR), Field 1.10 references the originator's Transaction Control Number (TCN). This is not listed as mandatory for responses, but seems that it should be. **Resolution:** Still pending.

Expanded Scope of EFTS (Cross-Jurisdictional Use):

1. **Candidate Names (SRT & IRR):** Many operational sites do not keep a "Names" database in the AFIS system although the trend is toward integration. The EFTS calls out for mandatory fields with Names. For instance, Field 2.064 in the SRT asks for ID numbers and names. The EFTS would need to allow such an occurrence and describe how it would be handled, i.e., merely skip the R/S separator field and list ID numbers separated by a U/S separator, or use R/S separators with a blank or "No Name" as a place holder. The IRR also calls for a mandatory Name (NAM) field, 2.018. This would need to change to optional. **Resolution:** Still pending.

2. **Local ID Use:** There is no accommodation for a Local Identification number. We used the State ID (SID) field (2.015), but that field is limited to a maximum of 10 characters, while local IDs may be more than 10 characters. We need to either expand the definition of 2.015 to include local IDs or designate a new tag for a local ID. **Resolution:** Still pending.

3. **MIME Messages:** Some vendors preferred to put text messages with their MIME message (a valuable debug tool for programmers), but for other vendors? this created a conflict in their software. The standards don't address this. **Resolution:** Still pending.

4. **New TOTs:** For purposes of this test, we devised two new TOTs: 1) a Type of AFIS request (TOA) and 2) an AFIS Type Response (ATR). This response includes the make and model of the AFIS system, the TOTs supported, the maximum score obtainable, and response time in hours. Various questions came up about the usefulness of this information, as presented below. **Resolution:** Still pending.

- If we are talking about cross-vendor communication, what significance is make/model of the AFIS system? The original intention is that if the AFIS was from the same vendor, they would have the option of communication using proprietary protocols. **Resolution:** Still pending.
- What significance is maximum score obtainable on the ATR when no scores currently come back with the candidate list? **Resolution:** Still pending.
- Should the response time, currently measured in hours, be predetermined, stated in minutes, etc.? **Resolution:** Still pending.
- Expand the TOA/ATR to indicate which fingers a vendor would like supplied for a TPIS search. **Resolution:** Still pending.

APPENDIX D—STANDARDS

This IAI effort was based on the following standards:

ANSI/NIST-CSL 1–1993 Data Format for the Interchange of Fingerprint Information, ANSI, November 22, 1993.

Criminal Justice Information Services (CJIS) Electronic Fingerprint Transmission Specification, IAFIS-IC-0010, Federal Bureau of Investigation, December 1995.

WSQ Gray-Scale Fingerprint Image Compression Specification, IAFIS-IC-0110V2, Criminal Justice Information Services (CJIS), Federal Bureau of Investigation, February 16, 1993.

CJIS Wide Area Network Interface Specification, CJIS-IC-0020, Federal Bureau of Investigation, April 1997.

These standards, the first national and the remaining three FBI, cover:

- the scanning of fingerprints,
- the messages for the transmission of fingerprint transactions to and from the FBI's IAFIS (Integrated AFIS) system,
- the compression of fingerprint images, and

- the wide-band communication methods for the transmission of fingerprint transactions to and from the FBI.

These standards do not cover the following areas:

- the ability of scanners to produce and transmit output records in the Electronic Fingerprint Transmission Specification (EFTS) formats,
- the ability of AFIS systems to read EFTS-formatted records, and
- the ability of AFIS systems to process defined transaction types.

For electronic submissions, the transaction must be fully compliant with the ANSI specification, the EFTS and its Appendices, WSQ and CJIS WAN protocols. For more information, see the SEARCH—FBI/CJIS Advisory Policy Board's IAFIS Planning Guide.

NCHIP FUNDING, 1995–2003

State	1995–1999	2000 Award	2001 Award	2002 Award	2003 Award	1995–2003
Alabama	$3,127,103	$879,447	$521,574	$499,880	$894,998	$5,923,002
Alaska	$3,456,318	$760,000	$585,000	$475,000	$600,000	$5,876,318
American Samoa	$800,000	$300,000	$300,000	$285,000	$300,000	$1,985,000
Arizona	$3,888,988	$980,000	$1,000,000	$750,000	$1,028,573	$7,647,561
Arkansas	$2,976,857	$694,330	$630,000	$475,000	$699,960	$5,476,147
California	$23,095,680	$2,350,000	$2,238,414	$2,200,000	$3,000,000	$32,884,094
Colorado	$3,528,113	$960,000	$507,000	$485,000	$735,000	$6,215,113
Connecticut	$4,117,968	$700,000	$545,000	$518,000	$657,000	$6,537,968
Delaware	$3,130,837	$491,470	$500,000	$475,000	$600,000	$5,197,307
District of Columbia	$1,804,095		$350,000	$329,916		$2,484,011
Florida	$9,373,486	$1,980,000	$1,650,787	$1,369,000	$1,800,000	$16,173,273
Georgia	$6,143,349	$803,768	$498,979	$691,628	$1,045,000	$9,182,724
Guam	$799,796	$300,000	$300,000	$285,000	$400,000	$2,084,796
Hawaii	$2,967,125	$600,000	$500,000	$500,000	$600,000	$5,167,125
Idaho	$1,554,561		$342,873	$170,000	$163,200	$2,230,634
Illinois	$10,372,000	$1,590,000	$1,352,000	$1,284,000	$1,669,000	$16,267,000
Indiana	$5,022,273	$900,000	$964,500	$736,000	$975,000	$8,597,773
Iowa	$2,783,525	$238,537	$208,915	$420,620	$561,437	$4,213,034
Kansas	$2,932,319	$520,000	$540,359	$475,000	$669,000	$5,136,678
Kentucky	$3,984,961	$499,536	$507,000	$482,000	$584,000	$6,057,497
Louisiana	$3,903,751	$739,436	$578,698	$499,000	$650,000	$6,370,885
Maine	$4,131,166	$90,000		$453,000	$525,000	$5,199,166
Maryland	$4,630,000	$922,500	$630,462	$595,117	$627,995	$7,406,074
Massachusetts	$8,275,250	$819,762	$1,028,000	$976,000	$1,268,000	$12,367,012
Michigan	$7,151,290	$1,153,032	$1,200,199	$881,382	$1,038,452	$11,424,355
Minnesota	$4,256,989	$413,454	$984,320	$502,000	$600,000	$6,756,763
Mississippi	$3,748,079	$560,000	$534,717	$500,000	$600,000	$5,942,796
Missouri	$5,172,515	$899,133	$904,000	$652,000	$757,627	$8,385,275
Montana	$2,574,486	$512,389	$546,842	$475,341	$599,771	$4,708,829
Nebraska	$3,037,053	$560,200	$553,237	$616,825	$600,000	$5,367,315
Nevada	$2,500,000	$610,000	$810,000	$513,000	$696,000	$5,129,000
New Hampshire	$3,566,713	$381,073	$407,462	$476,996	$600,000	$5,432,244
New Jersey	$6,700,533	$1,200,000	$892,980	$848,000	$1,195,000	$10,836,513
New Mexico	$4,596,416	$579,942	$686,860	$555,998	$563,622	$6,982,838[a]
New York	$17,472,269	$2,210,000	$2,225,000	$2,112,000	$2,745,000	$26,764,269
North Carolina	$4,807,653	$809,498	$635,000	$603,000	$663,000	$7,518,151
North Dakota	$2,931,218	$562,710	$544,470	$475,824	$600,000	$5,114,222
N. Mariana I		$300,000		$285,000	$400,000	$985,000

State	1995–1999	2000 Award	2001 Award	2002 Award	2003 Award	1995–2003
Ohio	$9,456,526	$1,368,256	$1,320,627	$1,389,214	$1,510,000	$15,044,623
Oklahoma	$2,628,198	$702,681	$549,999	$475,000	$600,000	$4,955,878
Oregon	$3,678,348	$1,000,000	$807,300	$122,861		$5,608,509
Pennsylvania	$11,395,537	$916,600	$1,392,000	$1,322,000	$1,499,195	$16,525,332
Puerto Rico	$812,436				$500,000	$1,312,436[a]
Rhode Island	$2,365,294	$520,000	$500,000	$475,000	$600,000	$4,460,294
South Carolina	$5,266,593	$990,000	$1,195,406	$822,000	$1,000,000	$9,273,999
South Dakota	$2,012,211	$672,693	$452,172	$488,156	$606,895	$4,232,127
Tennessee	$4,166,817	$780,161	$550,000	$531,000	$766,000	$6,793,978
Texas	$17,246,275	$795,000		$2,000,000	$2,900,000	$22,941,275
Utah	$3,073,085	$540,256	$530,000	$475,600	$600,010	$5,218,951
Vermont	$4,514,810	$729,157	$683,459	$609,688	$602,959	$7,140,073
Virgin Islands	$203,157		$300,000		$400,000	$903,157
Virginia	$6,507,577	$1,082,781	$1,035,143	$1,203,182	$1,804,670	$11,633,383
Washington	$5,111,682	$846,000	$674,000	$800,000	$1,194,000	$8,625,682
West Virginia	$3,384,564	$668,422	$500,000	$270,000	$600,000	$5,422,986
Wisconsin	$5,267,700	$760,000	$681,000	$647,000	$679,000	$8,034,700
Wyoming	$1,052,389	$240,104	$529,417	$285,000	$399,028	$2,505,938
Total direct awards to states	$273,457,934	$41,482,328	$38,905,171	$36,842,228	$47,973,392	$438,661,053

[a] To be awarded in FY 2004.

INDEX